NONPROFIT MANAGEMENT:

Everything You Need to Know About Managing Your Organization Explained Simply — With Companion CD-ROM

Nonprofit Management: Everything You Need to Know About Managing Your Organization Explained Simply — With Companion CD-ROM

Library of Congress Cataloging-in-Publication Data

Nonprofit management : everything you need to know about managing your organization explained simply--with companion CD-ROM / by Atlantic Publishing Company.
    p. cm.
Includes bibliographical references and index.
ISBN-13: 978-1-60138-246-7 (alk. paper)
ISBN-10: 1-60138-246-4 (alk. paper)
1. Nonprofit organizations--United States--Management. 2. Nonprofit organizations--Management. I. Atlantic Publishing Co. II. Title.
HD62.6.N6643 2009
658'.048--dc22
                        2008035798

Printed in the United States

PROJECT MANAGER: Amanda Miller • amiller@atlantic-pub.com
ASSISTANT EDITOR: Angela Pham • apham@atlantic-pub.com
INTERIOR DESIGN: James Ryan Hamilton • james@jamesryanhamilton.com
COVER DESIGN: Meg Buchner • meg@megbuchner.com
JACKET DESIGN: Jackie Miller • sullmill@charter.net

Printed on Recycled Paper

We recently lost our beloved pet "Bear," who was not only our best and dearest friend but also the "Vice President of Sunshine" here at Atlantic Publishing. He did not receive a salary but worked tirelessly 24 hours a day to please his parents. Bear was a rescue dog that turned around and showered myself, my wife, Sherri, his grandparents Jean, Bob, and Nancy, and every person and animal he met (maybe not rabbits) with friendship and love. He made a lot of people smile every day.

We wanted you to know that a portion of the profits of this book will be donated to The Humane Society of the United States. *–Douglas & Sherri Brown*

The human-animal bond is as old as human history. We cherish our animal companions for their unconditional affection and acceptance. We feel a thrill when we glimpse wild creatures in their natural habitat or in our own backyard.

Unfortunately, the human-animal bond has at times been weakened. Humans have exploited some animal species to the point of extinction.

The Humane Society of the United States makes a difference in the lives of animals here at home and worldwide. The HSUS is dedicated to creating a world where our relationship with animals is guided by compassion. We seek a truly humane society in which animals are respected for their intrinsic value, and where the human-animal bond is strong.

Want to help animals? We have plenty of suggestions. Adopt a pet from a local shelter, join The Humane Society and be a part of our work to help companion animals and wildlife. You will be funding our educational, legislative, investigative and outreach projects in the U.S. and across the globe.

Or perhaps you'd like to make a memorial donation in honor of a pet, friend or relative? You can through our Kindred Spirits program. And if you'd like to contribute in a more structured way, our Planned Giving Office has suggestions about estate planning, annuities, and even gifts of stock that avoid capital gains taxes.

Maybe you have land that you would like to preserve as a lasting habitat for wildlife. Our Wildlife Land Trust can help you. Perhaps the land you want to share is a backyard— that's enough. Our Urban Wildlife Sanctuary Program will show you how to create a habitat for your wild neighbors.

So you see, it's easy to help animals. And The HSUS is here to help.

THE HUMANE SOCIETY
OF THE UNITED STATES.

2100 L Street NW • Washington, DC 20037 • 202-452-1100
www.hsus.org

DEDICATION

For their insight, experience, wisdom, and peerless examples, I am indebted to the current and former chief executives of a number of nonprofit organizations: David Tabak, of the Guild for the Blind; Michael Nameche, formerly of Rock for KidsSM, currently of the Chicago Coalition for the Homeless®; Stewart Cottman, founder of Project: Philanthropy; Kelly Kaminski, Kevin McConkey, Jeremy Bokor, Virginia Tevere, and Phil Truesdale, who served with me on the board of Project: Philanthropy; Terry Selucky and C. Mitchell Turner, cofounders of Sansculottes Theater Company; Lauri Dahl, Rock Fraire, and Dean Corrin, theater board members par excellence; and the incredibly generous executive directors of the C(3)EO Forum, specifically Lanetta Haynes of CASA Cook County, Sandee Kastrul of i.c.stars, Mary Lou Eubanks of the Pay-It-Forward House, John Noel of the Illinois Technology Development Alliance, Melinda Rueden of the Brother David Darst Center, Mark Rodriguez of Changing Worlds, and Jennifer Hill of the Alliance to End Homelessness in Suburban Cook County.

For his endless patience and support, thanks to Joe.

TABLE OF CONTENTS

Chapter 3: Legal Requirements   63

Chapter 4: Organizational Infrastructure   83

Chapter 5: Your Clients   127

Chapter 6: Reaching Out and Spreading the Word   137

Chapter 7: Public Relations and Marketing   153

Chapter 10: Budgeting and Accounting   245

Chapter 11: Leadership
and Management Strategies   261

Chapter 12: Human Resources   279

Appendix: Resources 365

Glossary 383

Bibliography 401

Index 405

PREFACE

Nonprofit Management: Everything You Need to Know About Managing Your Organization Explained Simply was written to provide thorough, up-to-date information about how to manage today's nonprofit organizations. Information on each topic is clear, credible, and to the point. The sole purpose of this book is to guide the interested audience toward successfully managing a nonprofit organization. Not only will this book teach you how to manage a nonprofit organization, it will also teach you how to overcome challenges and cope with the problems you will face.

The authors have drawn extensively on their own experiences with managing nonprofit organizations. We use personal anecdotes where our experience — including our mistakes — can be instructive. We have also spoken with numerous executive directors, both seasoned and new, about their experiences. Experience is frequently the best teacher, and we encourage you to seek out a mentor in your nonprofit community.

This book is designed to be a broad reference to the many different aspects of running a nonprofit organization. No single book can contain every detail; indeed, each nonprofit is so different that no author would be wise to try. Additionally, many aspects of nonprofit management — such as the federal tax code — change frequently. Always check the Internal Revenue Service (IRS) Web site at **www.irs.gov**, as well as the sites of your state and local departments of revenue, for the most current information.

As much as possible, each chapter is self-contained; that is, you can read the book sequentially, or you can dip into different chapters as needed. Words that are defined or explained in the glossary appear in **bold** on their first usage in the text. We use the term "executive director" (ED) to refer to the chief executive of the nonprofit. Some organizations prefer the term "chief executive officer;" still others have an artistic director or a managing director. The title changes, but many aspects of the job are fundamentally the same.

Good luck!

CHAPTER 1
Why a Nonprofit Organization?

This chapter covers the basics: knowing what you want to accomplish and stating it clearly; why a nonprofit organization might be the right way to accomplish what you want to do; a few things you should know before starting any nonprofit enterprise; and some ways you can find guidance and information.

According to the National Center for Charitable Statistics (NCCS), the United States has more than 1.4 million nonprofit organizations. Nearly 900,000 public charities and 110,000 private foundations are registered with the IRS. While the areas of focus may differ, one truth applies to every organization: the challenges of running it are many and varied.

Before delving into the first steps of founding a nonprofit organization, it is a good idea to look at what makes a nonprofit different from for-profit endeavors and why a nonprofit seems like the right structure for your effort.

CHARACTER-
ISTICS

- A nonprofit organization provides a service to the public.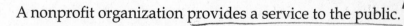
- A nonprofit organization does not exist to generate wealth, unless that wealth is specifically meant for one of the organization's programs, as is the case with, for example, a university's endowment.

- A nonprofit organization may be a <u>way</u> for a community or a group to provide a public service that local government cannot or will not provide — for example, arts funding, disease awareness and treatment, shelter and food for the needy, animal rescue, religious aid, or a myriad of other causes.

- A nonprofit organization is a corporation — a legal entity.

- A nonprofit organization may receive donations from its community.

- A nonprofit organization is <u>not free from all tax obligations.</u> A stringent tax code — designed specifically to prevent abuses — governs the behavior of nonprofits.

Providing Change

Management guru Peter Drucker suggests that, whereas other businesses sell goods and services, a nonprofit provides something less tangible — personal change and growth. This change may be in the form of an improvement in a patient's health. It may be in the form of education. It may be in the form of spiritual growth thanks to a religious experience. It may be in the form of an emotional catharsis brought about by a moving work of art. This change can be difficult to measure or quantify, but that does not mean it is not important.

Remember this idea of change — it will be important when you are thinking about your organization's mission statement.

In this chapter, we will look at things you should know before beginning any nonprofit endeavor.

Nonprofit vs. Not-for-Profit

The title of this book says "Nonprofit Management," but a number of other resources refer to **"not-for-profit organizations."** Is there a difference?

Yes and no. In many cases, the terms can be used interchangeably, and the law treats them as virtually synonymous. Both nonprofits and not-for-profit organizations have 501(c) status. Both are subject to the same state and federal requirements. However, many people in the nonprofit world — or the not-for-profit world — have strong feelings about the nuances attached to each phrase.

Some people believe that *not-for-profit* may describe an activity, whereas *nonprofit* describes an organization that has not been created to generate money. Fundraisers may rely on the phrase *not-for-profit* to reinforce the charitable nature of donors' contributions — although not all nonprofits are charities. In some highly technical spheres, *not-for-profit* designates an organization that is chartered, whereas *nonprofit* refers to non-chartered organizations.

In this book, we use *nonprofit* to refer to both kinds of organizations, unless otherwise specified.

Mission and Mission Statement

Every nonprofit organization has a **mission**, a reason for doing what it does. The **mission statement** describes the essence of the organization's work. It is a promise to the community from the organization.

Crafting a mission statement is harder than it sounds. It may take months before your efforts are focused enough for your mission to be clear. Nonetheless, donors and government bodies will want to see your mission statement early in the life of your organization, and you should be prepared to offer it.

Here are some questions to get you started:

[handwritten margin note: MISSION STMT]

- What is your reason for starting the nonprofit?
- What do you want to accomplish within your community?
- What is your promise to the people you serve?
- What do you want to change?
- What do you want to give to the world?
- What do you want your organization to be known for?

The mission statement should be a constant reminder to you, your staff, and your volunteers of why your organization exists. It can also serve as inspiration. When you are discouraged or desperate, look at the mission statement. Let it serve as a reason to get back to the important work of helping your community.

Once you have a rough draft, evaluate it. Start with this list of criteria. You may want to add a few other criteria based on what you think is important.

- Does the mission statement reflect what you believe in? *[handwritten: VALUES]*
- Does it reflect the input of everyone who should be involved? If you can, try to avoid writing by committee. You *[handwritten margin note: HMM: AVOID WRITING BY COMMITTEE?!]* may get better results if you delegate writing the actual statement to one good writer — such as your grant writer. But it is critical that everyone in the fledgling organization have a chance to offer his or her thoughts about the mission statement. A person who feels slighted or ignored is not going to continue being a productive member of your team.
- Is it simple? A simple mission statement is easier for everyone to remember — which means it is easier for em-

ployees, board members, grant writers, and volunteers to tell others about the organization. When you have a few statements that seem as though they might be right, practice paring them down to the fewest words possible.

FEWEST WORDS POSSIBLE

- Is it specific? Do not fall into the trap of using corporate language just because it sounds impressive. If a mission statement reads, "We provide proactive synergistic solutions," do you have any idea what that organization does? It is better to state exactly what you do and why. Your mission statement introduces your organization to prospective funders, donors, board members, volunteers, and clients. It should be clear and straightforward.

- Does it capture your organization's personality? Your organization might be conservative, faith-based, outraged, or free-spirited, and that should be reflected in your mission statement.

personality

Keep track of your efforts. Think of ten adjectives that accurately describe your organization. Make sure the mission statement seems to speak to all of these qualities. And hang on to that list — you can also use it to build your brand and your graphic identity, as explained in Chapter 4.

10 adjectives

Let us look at an example. Say you have started a nonprofit for aiding abused and neglected dogs. A first draft of your mission statement might look something like this:

Our mission is to take in as many dogs as we can and get them out of bad situations, such as starvation, and never let it happen again, regardless of what we have to do to keep them from starvation. We also provide education and help with food for families having a hard time with their dogs.

OK, not bad. Is this what you believe in? Yes. That is an important start. Have you talked to everyone with a stake in the company's mission? Yes.

So now you know it is time to revise, rather than to throw out this mission statement and try a whole new one. To revise, keep asking questions. Is it as simple as it could be? Probably not. Is starvation the only form of abuse you want to fight? No. So you need to fix that part — it is too specific. You also need to look at that "never let it happen again" phrase. That is a big promise — in fact, an impossible one. And "as many dogs as we can" could be open to a widely divergent number of interpretations.

So you revise, and you get this:

> *Our mission is to rescue dogs from abuse, neglect, and starvation. We take in dogs from abusive situations. We also provide education, food, and other resources to help prevent dog abuse.*

That is a clear mission statement. The main mission is stated in the first sentence — in just 11 words — and it leaves no doubt about the organization's purpose. The next two sentences state exactly how the organization carries out its mission.

Strictly speaking, you could leave out everything but the first sentence. You do not necessarily need to tell the world how you will be executing your mission. But in this case, it could help your efforts. The prevention angle is important. It tells people that your organization is constructive. It does not just wait for emergencies to happen; it tries to keep them from happening. Donors, especially, want to know that their dollars are actually helping prevent problems — not just picking up other people's messes.

But a mission statement is not set in stone. It can be changed as your organization grows.

Anatomy of a Mission Statement

My theater company, Sansculottes, did not have its current mission statement until several months after incorporation —nearly half a year after its first stage production. After trying several different statements that never seemed to feel right, the three company founders met for a long evening of planning. We each wrote our ideal mission statement and five-year plan, then compared notes. By the end of the evening, we had discovered some surprising differences in the ways we approached theater, and we came to a consensus on the mission statement:

> *Sansculottes Theater Company is devoted to producing exclusively original work that surprises and delights its audience, challenges the status quo, and catches the world with its pants down.*

What does that mean? Well, we are a company of writers, and we all believe that new writing is essential to the growth of theater. No matter how much we enjoy Samuel Beckett, we do not want to produce anyone else's work but our own. The clause about "surprising and delighting" is in there because we do not consider ourselves alone in our work. Our audience is the community we serve, and that is how we want to serve them. The bit about challenging the status quo stems from several influences: first, a belief that all good art asks questions about how things are and how things might be; and second, a desire not to let ourselves slip into staleness as artists. We are referring to our own status quo as much as any external status quo. Finally, that little phrase about catching the world with its pants down refers to several things:

- We have a sense of humor as a company. It is one of the most important aspects of our work and our relationship with our community, and we thought it was vital to capture that in the mission statement.

- We all like art that captures unguarded moments. This tends to be the source of both the greatest humor and the most heartbreaking honesty.

- Our name, Sansculottes, is a reference to the peasant rebels in the French Revolution. Literally, it means "without short pants." Short pants were the garb of the aristocracy, so the "pants down" clause refers to the company name. There is nothing aristocratic about this company; we are one of the scrappy, low-budget storefront companies that make Chicago theater so distinctive. I like to think we help people find their inner rebels. If we keep making art that asks questions, sooner or later, our audience will ask questions too.

Five years after that conversation, the company is still going strong — it was recently named one of the "Best of the Fringe" in a *Chicago Tribune* year-end wrap-up — and we have not needed to revise the mission statement. But again, this was the product of months of effort and several hours of focused discussion. It is a considerable amount of work for one sentence.

The Elevator Speech

The elevator speech is a concept borrowed from the film world. Imagine you are a screenwriter and you find yourself in an elevator next to the producer of your dreams. You have less than 30 seconds before the elevator reaches the ground floor — and your opportunity is lost. What do you say? How do you sum up your script?

Everyone in your organization should have an elevator speech prepared. If the speeches are widely divergent, your mission is not visible enough.

ELEVATOR SPEECH

Types of Nonprofit Organizations

- **Health organizations** provide medical care in some form. They may be care providers such as hospitals or clinics for the needy; they may be residential health centers such as nursing homes; they may offer free testing to prevent the spread of disease; they may offer transportation to and from medical facilities; they may simply offer health insurance. The Howard Brown Center, an AIDS clinic, is a medical nonprofit. So is Blue Cross Blue Shield, an insurer. In terms of revenue, health organizations form the largest subgroup of the U.S. nonprofit sector.

- **Religious organizations** include churches, synagogues, and mosques, as well as religion-related charities. While congregations may not receive government funds, no such restriction applies to religious organizations that provide social services. The religious sector is also notable for being the single largest recipient of private charitable gifts in the U.S.

- **Social and legal services** encompass day care, youth programs, residential care, family services, services offering legal advice or assistance, job training programs, and many other such programs designed to help people participate fully in society. These nonprofits tend to depend heavily on government funds.

- **Arts, culture, and humanities** organizations include musical ensembles, dance and theater companies, public radio and TV, some small literary publications, arts festivals, some galleries, and arts education programs.

- **Education and research** organizations provide educational programs and services. This sector includes colleges, universities, libraries, preschools, primary and secondary schools, and independent research groups. This sector includes science-oriented organizations that fund scientists, laboratories, and sponsor research efforts.

- **Environment- and animal-related** organizations work to rescue animals, prevent animal cruelty, prevent or clean up environmental problems, and preserve natural areas.

- **Membership groups** are groups such as alumni clubs, fraternal orders, veterans' groups, labor unions, and business associations. They are typically tax-exempt but not charitable — that is, donations to these groups are not tax-deductible.

- **Social organizations** are groups such as hobbyists' clubs, country clubs, and sports teams. These groups likewise may not accept tax-deductible donations.

- **Foundations** are charitable nonprofits that do not offer services directly to the community but instead channel funds and donations to other nonprofits.

Many people use the terms "charity" and "nonprofit" interchangeably, but not every nonprofit is a charity. Some nonprofits (such as professional or trade associations) are not set up to help people apart from their own members. They receive dues from their members and use the dues to pay for programs for those members. A charity, on the other hand, receives donations of goods, services, or money and uses them to help people outside the organization.

Before You Start

What do you care about passionately? You must have a passion for your nonprofit's cause. Running a nonprofit organization will test you in many ways. Your passion may be the only force that helps you get through these challenges. Seek out other people who feel the same way; recruit and work with them. Working for a cause that you do not truly care about is a recipe for burnout and boredom.

PASSION

If you do not feel passionately about your cause, do not start a nonprofit. That does not mean you cannot still work for the cause. Volunteer at a related nonprofit. Donate. Write letters to the editor. Help raise awareness. If any of these tasks seem like too much effort, it may be a sign that you do not care enough about the cause. Again, that is OK; it is better to figure that out before you have started the organization.

Take a moment to write a few sentences about what you care about and why. As you revise your mission statement, it will come in handy; as you deal with organizational challenges, it will remind you of what you are doing.

Commitment

In starting a nonprofit organization, you are trying in some way to change the way the community works. If your mission succeeds, then you will be changing the behavior of large groups of people. This is not a task that comes easily. You will need to give your organization your full attention and effort. You will need strength to deal with the challenges that arise, courage to believe in what you know is right, and commitment to your principles. It may feel as though nothing but your work matters. Remind yourself to make time for family and friends. Their support will sustain you.

Questions to Ask

The following is a series of questions to consider before you embark on a nonprofit enterprise. Take the time to answer them in writing. Treat this list as a worksheet. In many cases, your answers here will help you with future efforts.

- Do you want to start a business?

- Why do you want to run a nonprofit organization? List every reason, great and trivial.

- Who is going to help you? Who is similarly passionate about your cause? Who has expertise that you need? The answers to these questions can help you form your board and your staff. We will discuss this topic in more detail in Chapter 2.

- What organizational structure do you envision? How will you conduct the day-to-day business that supports your efforts? Where will you do your work? The answers to these questions will help you with Chapter 4.

- At the national, state, and local levels, what efforts are already under way in relation to your cause? Are you up to date on the latest research and methods?

- What similar organizations already exist within your community? Will you be competing for the same donations? Will you serve similar groups? The answers to these questions can help you refine your mission and recognize when a community coalition might be a good idea. Chapter 6 has more information on community coalitions.

- How are you going to fund this organization? The answers to these questions will help you as you consider development and fundraising, which we cover in Chapter 8.

- If you already have funding, what will you do when it runs out?

- If you do not already have funding, how will you pay for the expenses (such as incorporation fees) of getting the organization off the ground?

- How much time can you realistically contribute to this effort?

- What is the worst that could happen?

- What is the best that could happen?

Do Your Research

Starting a nonprofit organization can be a wonderful experience — or a disaster. Your actions will determine your experience.

To accomplish what you set out to do, you will need to enter your endeavors armed with information. Do research about your cause, your field, and nonprofit organizations. Learn as much as you can. Take time and take notes.

One useful step is to talk to other nonprofit executives about their experiences. They may be able to help answer your questions. Many of them can help you avoid common pitfalls. The case studies in this book are a good starting point. Some other options include:

- Explore your community to see if they have discussion forums, networking events, or support groups for not-for-profit founders and staffers. If you cannot find such a group, think about starting one. It can be as simple, and as cheap, as starting an e-mail Listserv® to facilitate online discussions.

- Check to see if you have access to a nonprofit association, such as Chicago's Donors Forum. Joining a nonprofit association may involve an annual fee, but the rich resources, opportunities, and connections are often well worth it.

- Consider asking an executive director (ED) to be your mentor if there is one nonprofit organization you particularly admire. Meet for lunch once a month to discuss your challenges, questions, and triumphs.

- Subscribe to publications such as *The Chronicle for Philanthropy*.

- Read the *Nonprofit Good Practice Guide*, published every year by the Donors Forum and available free online.

- Find online resources, such as **www.Idealist.org.**

Starting a Discussion Group

David Tabak, in his first 501(c)(3) leadership role as executive director of Chicago's Guild for the Blind, wanted to know how other executive directors had dealt with the issues he was facing. With a few colleagues, he started an online discussion group, jokingly named it the C(3)EO Forum, and invited other EDs to join. The format was — and remains — a simple electronic mailing list, a free service of many Internet Service Providers (ISPs) and e-mail providers that allows a user to send an e-mail and reach an entire registered group at once.

Today, the Forum's membership numbers in the hundreds, and the group has sponsored breakfasts and lectures to help EDs deal with specific issues, such as development. On any given day, an ED with a question — such as how to handle a problematic board member or how other organizations with small staffs are coping with soaring health care costs — can send an e-mail to the group in confidence and receive answers within minutes.

David says that, for him, "The Forum has been a great resource to learn of best practices and receive informed opinions on consultants, software, and services to nonprofits. The most valuable lesson I have learned is working effectively with your board of directors. A donor-based nonprofit's board is far different from working with a professional association board. We share a lot of ideas for helping board members remain engaged and aware of the vital role they play."

Joining or forming a discussion group seems like a smart plan for any ED, experienced or not. But David notes, "I was surprised how reluctant some executive directors were to join this group. To me, it seems like a no-brainer. There is no cost, the list is moderated to ensure only non-profit CEOs are allowed to join and post, and it is very easy and convenient to use. Yet some people will not join, preferring their own personal support group."

One reason for that reluctance may be the format of the group: "The greatest strength of the C(3)EO Forum is also its greatest weakness: its use of technology," says David. "Some members are very reluctant to contribute to the online discussion. People are afraid of sharing with people in such a fashion. They are much more comfortable with sharing in person, but not virtually." The lesson? If you want to learn from colleagues who happen to be technophobes, try a combination of e-mail and in-person meetings. Perhaps, eventually, you can be the one who teaches your colleagues about contemporary technology.

The Difference Between Tax-Exempt and Tax-Deductible

Being **tax-exempt** means your organization does not need to pay income taxes. It does not, however, mean you are exempt from *fil-*

ing. You still must file a Form 990 or 990-EZ every year to give the federal government a record of your organization's income.

To be exempt from paying state sales tax, you must register separately with your state as a tax-exempt organization. It is a good idea to do this as soon as you have your nonprofit status. There is no point in using up your budget paying sales tax on purchases. And many funding bodies — especially government funding bodies — may dictate that they will not reimburse you for the cost of sales tax that you could have avoided.

Once you have your status as a 501(c)(3) nonprofit organization, your donors' contributions become **tax-deductible.** That does not affect your taxes — it affects theirs. It means they can take what they have donated to you as an income tax deduction. It is likely not their only incentive for donating, but it can be a big one. Make sure prospective donors know that their donations will be tax-deductible. Make it easy for them; along with your thank-you note, provide a receipt for the donation and a standard form with your organization's Employer Identification Number (EIN). We will explore thank-you notes and donor relations in detail in Chapter 8.

However, being a nonprofit organization does not automatically make you either tax-exempt or tax-deductible. You must register with the IRS.

Preliminary Paperwork

Once you have decided to start a nonprofit organization, review the following steps:

- Register for an Employer Identification Number, a federal tax identification number that the government uses to track business activity. Do not be alarmed by the word "Employer." You need not have employees — or even plan to have them — to have an EIN. Put simply, an EIN is to a corporation what a Social Security number is to an individual.

- Contact your Secretary of State to discover the rules and regulations you must follow when starting a nonprofit organization in your state. For example, you may need to register with the state's Attorney General. Make sure you have a good way of keeping track of these regulations and deadlines, and of monitoring your compliance with them. In some cases, you may incur fees for noncompliance.

- Contact the IRS about federal regulations for nonprofit entities. Most of the information you will need is on the IRS's Web site, at **www.irs.gov/charities.** In particular, look at the remarkably helpful "ABCs for Exempt Organizations." If you are in the habit of viewing the IRS as a scary, monolithic institution, it is time to change that view; the IRS can be a helpful resource, and it presents compliance information clearly and thoroughly.

- Incorporate. You must incorporate before you can receive not-for-profit status. Incorporation will require several documents, including:
  - A list of founding board members
  - A mission statement
  - Articles of incorporation
  - An EIN
  - Other charter documents as required by your state

- Do not worry if these documents are not word-for-word perfect, or if you think you will outgrow your current by-laws. You may revise these documents as necessary after incorporation, though in some states, you must file certain revisions with your Secretary of State or Attorney General.

- Apply for 501(c)(3) tax-exempt status. This involves a federal Form 1023, as well as a written description of activities.

If you are concerned about the legal implications of these actions, talk to a lawyer. If you cannot afford legal counsel, you may be able to obtain it as a **pro bono**, or donated, service. Some law firms make a point of encouraging their attorneys to donate their services to nonprofits. Other organizations, such as Lawyers for the Creative Arts, exist specifically to help certain kinds of non-profits with legal issues. Finally, do not underestimate the vast amount of legal information available for free on sites such as **www.nolo.com**.

Resources for Legal Information and Consultation

- **www.nolo.com**
- Lawyers for the Creative Arts
- Industry associations, such as the American Medical Association

Resources

The good news about starting a nonprofit is that you are not alone. Many organizations exist specifically to help nonprofits accomplish their missions.

Many states offer a service called a Donors Forum, which helps connect nonprofits to donors and funding bodies. The Donors Forum can help you with paperwork, research, and grant applications. Donors Forum events may be a good way to meet prospective board members. Membership is typically free or discounted for nonprofits.

www.Idealist.org is a Web site devoted to the nonprofit world. It includes news feeds, Q&A forums, job boards, and a wealth of information on standard practices. If you are facing a problem, click through this site to see how other nonprofit executives have handled similar issues.

The Chronicle of Philanthropy is a periodical for the nonprofit world. Here, you can keep up-to-date on happenings at other organizations. As your organization grows, you will want to ensure you send press releases about your activities to the *Chronicle*; its audience comprises not only nonprofit executives, but also donors and corporate funders who read the *Chronicle* to find efforts they might want to support.

Your state and federal government can answer many of your questions. Remember to look at the IRS document "ABCs for Exempt Organizations" and related publications. Your state's Web site should offer useful information as well.

The National Council of Nonprofit Associations can help you find a **business incubator** in your area — someone who will share space, equipment, and other services to help you get your organization off the ground.

CASE STUDY: CASA OF COOK COUNTY

Mission: Advocacy for abused and neglected children.

Lanetta Haynes is in the middle of her second year as Executive Director of CASA, and her fourth year — including board service — in the nonprofit sector. She works with a staff of 12 and a board of 15, a working board that meets six times a year. CASA relies on 260 volunteers, who put in roughly 50,000-60,000 hours of work per year. Foundations and individual donors provide the funding.

Haynes says: "[Our] day-to-day challenges include technology and the retention of volunteers. Organizational challenges in a larger sense include trying to maintain an active and engaged board and fundraising.

"[My greatest personal challenge is] finding the appropriate balance between work and personal life and prioritizing tasks. To help cope with these challenges, I try and rely on my team by delegating more, and I also try and schedule time specifically for myself."

If you are just starting out in the nonprofit world, "Talk to as many people in the field as possible, find advocates among your board members who will help you help the board get tasks accomplished, and always try and find the positives in every situation."

CHAPTER 2
The Board

This chapter covers what to expect from working with a board and what the board can do for your organization. In most nonprofit organizations, the **board of directors** — sometimes called the **governing board, the board of trustees,** or the **governing council** — has legal and financial responsibility for your organization. When you are getting started, they are likely to be your main staff and donors. As you grow, they will still be the people who help you with new initiatives, provide financial guidance, recruit new donors and volunteers, and keep the organization on the right track. They can help you tremendously.

The board sets the organization's mission and helps ensure that the organization's actions support the mission. Typically, the board must approve programs for the organization — at a high level, not at the level of minute details. The board is responsible for the financial stability of the nonprofit. It may approve the annual budget, and in charitable organizations, it is responsible for a large amount of the fundraising and development efforts.

When you are the ED, the board of directors is also your boss. You will report to them at meetings; you will be accountable to them. They will set expectations for your performance, and they have the power to remove you from office.

...pect to be the main decision-makers of the organi-
...the board a fundamentally passive body that gives
rubber-st..mp approval to the ED's initiatives. Some boards
want hands-on involvement in the minutiae of running the organization. Each nonprofit must strike its own balance, and that
balance will change as the organization evolves. It is important
to remember that everyone is there to serve the same mission;
you will accomplish more through collaboration than through
individual efforts.

The dividing line between board and staff can be difficult to identify. In some organizations, the same person can be both a board
member and a staff member. The ED, for example, can be an **ex
officio** board member. Generally speaking, however, the board
guides the planning and organization — the business end of the
operation — and the staff puts the mission into action in the community. In a theater company, the board might need to approve
the artistic director's choice of scripts, but they will not sit in on
rehearsals or vote on costumes and blocking. Similarly, in a hospital, the board might set the equipment budget, but it is up to
the doctors and nurses — the staff — to take temperatures and
administer shots. In short, the board is responsible for policy, and
the staff is responsible for implementation.

Types of Boards

Elected Boards

The board of directors can be elected by the members of the organization. **Elected boards** are common in membership nonprofits.
The election may happen by mail — especially in an organization with far-flung membership — or at the organization's annual meeting. Sometimes the elections are actual contests in which

candidates campaign, and sometimes they are mere formalities required to make official the choice of the nominating committee.

The ED of an organization with an elected board must be prepared to deal with the major shifts in board direction and philosophy that can accompany an election. The relatively rapid turnover of an elected board can also be an obstacle to accomplishing the organization's long-term goals.

Voting Rights

Typically, members of an organization may not vote for directors unless they have served some minimum amount of time or made some other minimum contribution. For example, in an alumni association, voting rights might be limited to those alumni who give more than $100 annually. In a church, voting rights might be limited to people who have been through a six-month educational course and opted to become congregants. The intent in restricting voting rights is not to be unfair, but to ensure that those who are guiding the organization have a vested interest in a positive outcome.

Self-Perpetuating Boards

A self-perpetuating board, in which current board members recruit and select new board members, is what you are likely to find in most charitable nonprofits. It is more stable than an elected board and — in most cases — better suited to helping the organization execute its long-term strategy.

When you start your organization, you identify founding board members. They are then responsible for adopting bylaws that govern the board's operation. Depending on the organization, they may also be responsible for recruiting additional board members. The ED and other staff members may be involved in recruiting efforts as well.

Board Diversity

A hazard of the self-perpetuating board is that board members and staffers may draw too heavily on their own social circles in recruiting new board members. The board could turn into a close group of friends that no longer represent the nonprofit's community or that even alienates key constituencies. Additionally, groups of friends — though delightful to meet with — may become lax in their oversight of each other, which can lead to laziness or even the sort of gross misconduct that can endanger the organization.

Hybrid Boards

Public organizations, such as public libraries and universities, often have boards whose members are appointed by someone from outside the organization. The person in charge of appointments is usually a public official — a governor or mayor. Some private organizations, such as churches, work this way as well: A central ecclesiastical council might appoint several board members for the local church.

Few organizations have boards that are entirely appointed. Instead, they combine external appointments with internal elections and, sometimes, with models of self-perpetuating board membership, thus they are called "hybrid." In a **hybrid board**, the number of seats selected by each method must be clearly designated. For example, an organization might have each of the following:

- Four board members appointed every four years by the state's governor

- Six board members recruited and elected by the other board members, subject to two-year term limits
- Twenty board members elected annually by the organization's membership

In this example, the varying term limits and methods of election prevent the entire board from changing at once — thereby ensuring some continuity of long-term planning — but they keep its membership dynamic and in touch with the wishes of the organization's constituents.

Some hybrid boards have ex officio seats, which means that someone holding a given office, such as the dean of arts and sciences at a public university, automatically has a seat on the board. Ex officio board members may or may not have votes. They may also be inclined to see their board membership as a mere formality, which means their involvement can pose a special challenge for the ED.

The Working Board

A working board, as its name suggests, devotes its time and effort to the nonprofit. You might want a working board in the early years of the organization, when you have few staff members and a relatively small, unambitious budget.

A working board typically has a minimum monthly time commitment. You will need to make sure tasks are clearly assigned. As with volunteers, plan ahead to make sure board members have all the resources they need to execute their tasks. When people are donating their time, you do not want to waste it.

The Giving Board

A giving board typically devotes much less time to an organization than a working board does. Instead, it is expected to make generous financial contributions. Members of a giving board might even have been recruited specifically for their financial resources.

On almost every kind of board, members are expected to make a minimum annual contribution. This minimum might be significantly higher for a giving board. Alternatively, board members who do not meet a certain fundraising expectation — say, $5,000 worth of new donations — might be expected to make up the difference out of their own pockets. This is known as a **give-or-get policy.**

If your board is truly diverse, some board members may have difficulty making large minimum contributions; they may also lack the social connections that would allow them to meet the threshold of a give-or-get policy. In such a situation, you may want to tailor individual contribution thresholds to the means of each individual board member. Obviously, you do not want to impoverish your board members. But they should know that their contribution to your organization is supposed to be one of their highest financial priorities — ahead of all their other charitable giving, usually with the exception of their church.

The Advisory Board

An advisory board is not a governing board. It is a separate entity. Not every organization has — or needs — an advisory board.

An advisory board does not have legal or financial responsibility for the nonprofit. Rather, it functions as a council of experts, offering informed guidance and opinions on the governance of the organization. Some nonprofit experts suggest calling an advisory board an "advisory council" to avoid any misconception that this group has fiduciary responsibility.

Recruiting Board Members

If you have a self-perpetuating board, you will need to give some thought to its composition. As you build your board, think about what the organization needs. How much money will you need to raise? What professional skills and services will you need?

Almost every organization will need help with the following areas:

- Legal advice
- Marketing, graphic design, and related services, such as printing or electronic communications
- Accounting and bookkeeping
- Business structure and strategy

These services are expensive. If your budget is close to zero, begin building your board by recruiting professionals in these areas.

Depending on your field, you may also want to bring in a few specialists. A nonprofit clinic might want board members who are doctors or professionals in public health. A theater company might want a board member who is a respected playwright or director. An educational nonprofit might seek out board members who are retired teachers or professors. A nonprofit devoted to increasing literacy might recruit board members with connections to the publishing world.

Other questions to ask as you recruit board members include the following:

- What is this person's work ethic like? In nonprofit boards, the truism holds that if you want something done, it is better to ask a busy person. In volunteer groups, laziness can be contagious; in boards, it is deadly.

- How big is this person's social circle? Will he or she be able to recruit many new people to come to our events, donate, and get excited about our cause? Though it may be fun and rewarding to work with a close friend, do not overlook the benefits of recruiting someone whose social circle does not perfectly overlap with yours.

- Can this person donate generously or help us obtain generous donations? Board members are a major source of donations. Not every board member has the same financial resources, and it is reasonable for some board members to give in time and skill what others give in dollars. But every board member should have social or professional ties to people who *can* give considerably. And board members cannot be hesitant about using those ties.

- What sort of nonprofit experience does this person have? Will he or she be able to educate other board members about nonprofit strategy and policy, or will you need to help this person learn about the nonprofit world?

- Is this person enthusiastic? Will he or she be a champion of our group? A board member who shares your passion for your cause can be a natural — and therefore powerful — source of word-of-mouth advertising.

You may want to create a questionnaire for prospective board members. If you do, ask them to list skills they feel they can contribute. You may discover you have overlooked a potential source of help.

Make sure prospective board members are aware of the time commitment you expect. A board member must be able to make your organization a priority. You do not want to be surrounded by people who do only the minimum.

Setting the Bar

Michael Nameche, former ED of Rock for Kids and current ED of the Chicago Coalition for the Homeless, says that in his experience, a volunteer board is only as strong as its weakest link. That is, the person who does the least typically sets the bar for everyone else. People take their behavioral cues from what other people do, not what they say. That means that even if you have clearly spelled out high expectations in writing, you will get dramatically different results if you allow subpar performance in practice. If you notice underachievement, speak to that person immediately. Make sure he or she understands that a commitment to this organization demands more. If his or her behavior changes, fantastic. If not, it is time to let that person go.

Finding Prospective Board Members

Personal connections are important in building a board. People want to serve alongside people whose company they enjoy and whose ideas they respect.

That said, it is a good idea to step outside your immediate circle of friends. Make sure everyone — your parents, your hairdresser, your baby-sitter, your minister or rabbi — knows about your new organization. Friends, family, and acquaintances will be excellent recruiters; if they are proud of you, they will brag, and eventually, someone you do not know will hear about your efforts.

If you already have a solid volunteer base, look at your most active and enthusiastic volunteers. Could they be board members? Do not be hurt if they say no; many volunteers contribute precisely because they prefer direct interaction with clients. However, an active volunteer may know a good candidate for the board.

You may want to attend professional networking events. If you meet someone who seems like a good prospect, remember that your natural enthusiasm for your cause will be your best ally. You do not need to try for a "hard sell." In fact, if you start to feel as though only a hard sell will convince this person to join the board, abandon the effort. Your board should consist of people who instinctively grasp the appeal and worth of your mission — people who believe in it as strongly as you do.

Finally, you can use resources such as Idealist or BoardSource® to recruit board members. This is the least personal approach, and you may want to take some time to get to know people you meet this way. One option is to create a probationary six-month period in which the organization and the new board member can try each other out.

Board recruitment is, at heart, about building relationships. Like any human relationship, it takes time and maintenance, and it suffers setbacks. Do not be discouraged.

Board Officers

The titles of board officers may vary depending on organizational structure. You may not have all of these officers. In some cases, the same person may serve in more than one office at the same time. You may also want to create additional offices.

The **president** is the chair of the board. The president's responsibilities may include

- Making sure your organization adheres to bylaws and policies
- Speaking to the media about organizational activity
- Recruiting other board members
- Organizing and leading meetings
- Spearheading important organizational decisions or initiatives
- Overseeing all reports from different departments and addressing any problems

On the board, as in everywhere else, the **vice president** steps in if the president can no longer perform his or her job. The vice president may assist the president with any of the responsibilities listed above. Your board may also want to put the vice president in charge of certain committees or task forces.

The **secretary** keeps all records, including minutes of the board meetings. These records are important for legal compliance. Make sure your board secretary has a way to collect and distribute information, as well as a secure place to store paper records. The secretary may also assist the president as needed.

The **treasurer** handles the finances of the organization. Especially in a nonprofit's early stages, the treasurer may perform all the functions normally associated with a chief financial officer — budgeting and strategic planning — in addition to basic accounting duties, such as writing checks and purchase orders, and keeping the books.

A **director** may or may not be an actual board member. This person is typically an executive, such as the ED, or other staff member who works with the board. Regardless of who this person is, it is a good idea to have a staff representative present at all board meetings; it helps keep the board connected with the staff's day-to-day experience, and it helps the staff know about the efforts the board is undertaking on behalf of the nonprofit. You must decide whether you want to have this person be a voting board member or simply serve as a liaison between the board and the staff. If this person is a voting board member, you may want to waive his or her board donation requirements.

Board Meetings

Your board must, by law, meet at least once a year. Most boards, especially working boards, choose to meet more often. Monthly meetings can be a good option for working boards. Longer intervals allow the organization and its tasks to become lower priorities.

Board meetings must follow the policies and procedures outlined in the organization's bylaws. The secretary must take minutes and, afterward, distribute copies to board members. This is particularly important if tasks have been assigned, as the distribution of minutes can remind people of what they must accomplish.

How formal you want your board meetings to be depends on your organization and your board. Some boards will be more comfortable following strict parliamentary procedure ("Motion raised and seconded," and so on). Other boards may prefer a more relaxed procedure. Whichever procedure you choose, the bylaws should clearly reflect the decision.

The Board and the Bylaws

Your bylaws will outline:

- Specific responsibilities for board officers
- Term limits

- Rules of succession
- The size of the board
- How board positions may and may not overlap (For example, the president may not be the same person as the treasurer.)

Once you have incorporated, your board is legally bound to adhere to the bylaws. Make sure every board member has a copy of this document and understands it thoroughly.

You may modify the bylaws; for example, if your organization experiences immense growth, you may need to expand the board. Any revisions to the bylaws must be registered with your state. The board's secretary often handles this documentation and is responsible for knowing your state's compliance requirements.

Board Committees

Whether your board needs to form committees to address certain tasks or initiatives depends on the size of the organization, the size of the board, and how your board members prefer to work. Many nonprofits find it helpful to form at least the occasional **ad hoc committee** — a committee that meets only as needed to address a specific project or task.

Committees sometimes comprise only board members, but that need not be a rule. You may find it useful to bring in interested staff members or volunteers to serve on a committee, particularly if you have a volunteer with specialized expertise. For example, if you have a volunteer who works as a business consultant, enlist his or her aid in your strategic planning committee. You may even discover that some of your organization's clients are interested in serving on a committee. Channel that enthusiasm. It is almost always in your best interests to help people serve the organization.

Common Types of Committees

Not every organization needs every kind of committee. The following are some committees you may want to consider having.

An Executive Committee

This committee often consists of board members or chairs from other committees. The executive committee helps make decisions between board members and set policies. It does not require any funding.

A Planning Committee

This committee sets the long-range plans for the organization — the goals for the next three to five years. It is important for the planning committee to share the ED's vision. The planning committee should also work closely with the finance and development committees to ensure the organization will have the resources it needs to carry out its plans.

A Steering Committee

This may be separate from the planning committee, or the two committees may be combined. The steering committee helps the organization put the long-range plans into concrete action. It sets short-term priorities that support the long-term goals. It may spearhead a new initiative, such as a new program that reaches out to a different neighborhood or client base.

A Finance Committee

This committee handles all financing issues, controls the budget, and oversees financial statements. If you are audited, the finance committee will be in charge of preparing all required information for the IRS. The finance committee may start as a one-person effort, in the form of the board treasurer. When the organization's finances get too complicated for one person to do all the work — or when issues of ethics or transparency make it a good idea to have two people involved — it is time to create a finance committee. See Chapter 10 for more information about nonprofit finances.

An Auditing Committee

Some nonprofits establish an auditing committee separately from the finance committee to ensure that the finances are thoroughly reviewed on a regular basis. The auditing committee might work with an outside reviewer, whether that reviewer is a private consultant or an IRS auditor.

A Development or Fundraising Committee

This committee is in charge of obtaining the organization's funds. If you have a staff development director, he or she should be an integral part of the development committee. The work of this committee may go far beyond simply requesting donations and into strategic, long-term approaches to development; for example, if the planning committee has decided that the organization should move into a new facility, the development committee may govern the 24-month capital campaign that makes that possible. Conversely, it may be the development director who sets the strategy and the committee that does the legwork of carrying it out, such as assembling donor mailings or overseeing volunteer phone banks. Which division of duties is right for you depends on your organization, your goals, your resources, and your staff. Whatever you decide, though, make sure the responsibilities are clearly defined; nearly all of your budget will come through these channels, and your organization's ability to carry out its mission depends on having them function well. See Chapter 8 for more information about development.

An Events Committee

If you plan to have special events, such as an annual open house or event-based fundraising, it is a good idea to hand their management over to an events committee. Event planning is quite complicated, and it becomes far more complicated when a nonprofit is involved; your events must not only come off without a hitch but must also support the organization's mission and strategy. An events committee can probably meet on an ad hoc basis, coordinating its meetings with the event schedule. It is a good idea to enlist someone from the development committee to obtain appropriate donations for the event, such as food, equipment, performances, or printing.

A Programming Committee

The programming committee deals with the organization's real reason for being: the ways in which it reaches its clients. Your programming committee should help guide the planning of different initiatives, assess which programs are working and why, and keep in touch with clients about the services they are receiving.

A Hiring or Personnel Committee

This committee helps your organization decide when and how to bring in staff — and when to let them go. It handles salary administration and creates all employment policies, communicating them to employees. It also resolves all staffing issues, such as problematic performance or conflicts. If your organization offers benefits to its employees, the hiring committee may also oversee benefits administration and vendor selection. As the organization grows, you may find it advisable to replace this committee with a director of human resources. Remember, though, that the ED will always report to the board. See Chapter 12 for more information about human resources and employment policies.

A Nominating Committee

This committee nominates people — typically from within the organization — for specific offices, positions, tasks, and assignments. You may be able to combine the efforts of the nominating and hiring committees.

A Maintenance or Facilities Committee

This committee oversees repairs to property, buildings, and equipment owned and operated by the organization. If the organization does not yet own any property, this committee can be in charge of the search for appropriate facilities.

A Membership Committee

A membership committee is not necessary in every organization; not every organization has members who fall outside the designations of board, staff, clients, donors, or volunteers. For a nonprofit such as a church, however, or a neighborhood parents' association, a membership committee can be crucial. A membership committee helps the organization keep in touch with members — and helps members keep in touch with the organization. It might organize phone trees, e-mail lists, various excursions, or weekly meetings. It can lead recruitment drives and help the facilities and planning committees know when the organization is about to outgrow its current capacity. It can also keep members involved enough that they eventually become volunteers, donors, or board members.

Note that the line between "members" and "clients" can be blurry or sometimes nonexistent. The members of a church are its clients, as we use the term in this book; they are the people it serves. However, it is unlikely that they think of themselves as clients — they are members of the congregation. You probably already use the appropriate term instinctively, but your board may want to consider whether your organization has both members and clients, and, if so, whether it is adequately addressing the needs of both groups. See Chapter 5 for more information about client relations.

An Ethics Committee

After you have set ethics policies in writing, your ethics committee is likely to be an ad hoc committee that meets only to address possible ethical violations or to update policies as needed.

An Awards Committee

This may be an ad hoc committee that meets only once a year, if, for example, you have a standing award given at the annual open house. Or — if you are trying to create a culture that constantly recognizes excellent contributions — you may choose to have a standing awards committee.

A Volunteer Committee

This committee coordinates volunteer communications, division of labor, and sign-ups. A representative of this committee may be the person who directs volunteer efforts on site. As appropriate, this committee can also keep tabs on the skills and qualifications of volunteers and help them use those skills to meet the organization's needs.

Committee Governance

You can help your organization function properly by making sure the activities of committees are clearly defined. Each committee should:

- Decide how often it needs to meet
- Decide who is in charge of doing what

- Recruit personnel — from other committees or the volunteer pool — as needed
- Coordinate efforts with other committees as appropriate
- Set its own strategy and timetable to support the larger organizational goals and strategy
- Appoint a chair
- Appoint a person in charge of reporting the committee's activities back to the board

In short, each committee should function like a smaller, slightly less formal board.

Term Limits

You may want to set term limits for committee members — normally one to two years. Some people will come to your organization with the goal of learning and helping out in a variety of areas. Some people have a single, focused area of expertise and prefer to stay within that area. Committee policies should accommodate both styles of work, but they should also ensure that you can remove committee members who are not pulling their weight. One useful policy is to conduct evaluations at the end of the term and allow interested committee members to run for reelection to the committee.

Meeting Place

Each committee should find a place to meet that is, if possible, convenient to all members. You will notice a decline in performance from board members and committee members who cannot easily attend meetings.

Time Management

In planning committees, think about what is efficient for your board members as well as for the organization. No one likes to feel as though all their time is taken up with meetings, particularly rambling or unproductive meetings.

One useful strategy is the committee mini-meeting — a 15-minute speed session. A mini-meeting lets committee members touch base with one another without feeling overwhelmed, unproductive, or distracted from the task at hand. To minimize board members' commutes, suggest holding mini-meetings before or after board meetings, or via Web conference.

Agenda

The chair should enter every meeting with a written agenda. Several days before the meeting, he or she should solicit input from all committee members on what should be on the agenda. Not only does this ensure that every voice is heard, but it can also nudge procrastinators to finish up their tasks before the next meeting.

Minutes

Someone should take minutes at committee meetings, just as at board meetings. These minutes should be submitted to the board secretary and kept with other board records.

Work Load

Make sure work load is appropriate for committee size. One useful strategy is to let committee chairs call on the members of other committees — especially the volunteer committee — when they need help.

Spelling Out Your Expectations

Make sure the expectations for committees are clear and set forth in writing. As with the board, instruct committee chairs be alert to underperforming committee members and address these problems promptly.

Committee expectations need not be part of the organization's bylaws, but you and the board should revisit them occasionally to confirm that:

- They are still realistic
- They still support the organization's strategy and mission
- You still ensure that the board members and volunteers meet these expectations

An annual audit of committees should be sufficient to answer these questions. Have every committee assess itself — its actual, practical operations against its written expectations — and report to the board with any problems or recommendations.

An Annual Retreat

One way to keep the board and the staff in tune with each other is to hold an annual retreat. The style of the retreat is up to you. If the organization is struggling, you might want to have a retreat that combines fun with work so that people not only rediscover what they enjoy about collaborating with each other, but they also emerge with a new dedication to the mission and strategy. If the organization is in relatively good shape, you might hold a retreat devoted to a specific initiative, such as new development efforts or the raising of awareness in the community. Encourage creativity, openness, and collaboration. The best ideas come about when people are comfortable working with one another, when they know their ideas are valued, and when they trust that a good idea actually has a chance of being executed.

Working with the Board of Directors

As ED, you will work extensively with your board. As in any working relationship, you will likely encounter disagreements. Common sources of frustration include scheduling, meeting time and length, efficiency, whether board members are actually carrying out their assigned tasks, budgetary priorities, programming priorities, and committee work.

Be responsible and professional about these disagreements. If there are differences of opinion about how the organization should be run, discuss them calmly and diplomatically within the meeting. If they are true personality clashes, make sure the board president is aware of them and takes steps to resolve them before the atmosphere grows poisonous. It is the president's responsibility — not yours — to remove troublesome board members.

You can ward off many problems by instituting an annual review process. Once a year, have each board member conduct a formal, written evaluation of the company and of his or her own contributions. Questions to ask include:

- Were you aware of the organization's goals for this period?
- How did you help the organization meet these goals?
- If the organization failed to meet a given goal, why do you think that happened?
- Did you meet your fundraising requirements for this period?
- How many new people do you think you introduced to the organization in this period?

- Do you think the board meets too often, not often enough, or just the right amount?

- Are you satisfied with the way board meetings are conducted? Could the board make use of any new technology or techniques to make these meetings more efficient?

- Are you pleased with your level of contribution to the organization?

- What problems do you think the organization might have in the next 12 months? How do you think the board can act to prevent or fix those problems? What actions are you interested in leading?

These evaluations can take place when the board evaluates the ED.

Board Performance

There are many ways of evaluating board performance, some of them contradictory. One useful resource is BoardSource, which has created a list of 12 principles at work in effective boards:

1. Governing in constructive partnership with the ED
2. Being mission driven
3. Thinking strategically
4. Establishing a culture of inquiry in the nonprofit
5. Being independent-minded
6. Establishing an ethos of transparency
7. Complying with values of ethics and integrity
8. Sustaining financial resources
9. Working toward results and measuring the organization's performance by those results
10. Working intentionally, rather than reactively

11. Engaging in continuous learning about themselves and the organization

12. Revitalizing through planned turnover and recruitment

You can see a more thorough discussion at **www.BoardSource. com**.

Term Limits and Succession Planning

Board members, like anyone else, can become burnt out. Their commitment to the organization may be as strong as ever, but they may need a vacation or a change of pace from their ordinary duties.

Term limits are the standard way to prevent having a board full of officers too burnt out to work. Be careful, however, as term limits may have the opposite of their intended effect: They may oust someone who is not at all burnt out and who remains completely engaged in his or her work for the organization. A few standard practices can help you prevent this unintended consequence of term limits:

- Allow board members to bypass term limits if they complete an end-of-term evaluation that requires them to state — in writing — their commitment to the organization and to specific tasks for the next term.

- Allow a board member to bypass a term limit with the consent of the rest of the board, as expressed by a formal vote.

- Institute rotating term limits. Popular options include "serve two years, rest for one" and "serve any three of five years."

If a board member does step down, you will need to find someone to take his or her place. If the departure puts your board membership below the minimum specified in the bylaws, finding a new board member may be a matter of legal compliance, as well as healthy functioning. The end of a board term is entirely foreseeable, so an end-of-term resignation should not be a surprise; you can start recruiting and training likely replacements well in advance. The remaining board members may also want to reassign tasks to accommodate the new member's skill set.

Succession planning refers to ensuring that you will know someone qualified and ready to take over after a departing officer. There are several ways to handle this. The easiest is to elect new officers several months before the end of the current term. Give officers-elect the chance to shadow current officers, to observe them in action, and to ask questions. Not only does this help you train new officers and introduce them to the committee members they will work with, but it also creates an opportunity to improve processes. The new officer, watching with fresh eyes, may spot inefficiencies or chances to change organizational structures for the better.

The board may want to create a succession committee for the purpose of having a ready supply of candidates and making these transitions smooth.

Financial and Legal Responsibilities of Board Members

Typically, the board members are **fiduciaries** of the nonprofit organization. They are legally accountable for the actions of the organization. Ultimately, they must answer to public governing bodies — at both state and federal levels — for the legal correctness of the nonprofit's activities. They must also answer to the public — the nonprofit's constituents — for the appropriateness of organizational actions and decisions, and they must answer to donors for the responsible use of contributions.

The Legal Standard of Care, Loyalty, and Obedience

A 1974 court case, usually called the Sibley Hospital Case, gave us the legal standards that continue to define responsible board governance — **care, loyalty, and obedience.**

Care refers to appropriate attentiveness, due diligence, and prudence in board decisions. The standard of care requires board members to have a full understanding of the issues upon which they vote.

Loyalty refers to placing the organization above the board member's own personal interests. A board member attempting to use his or her office for private financial gain would be breaching the standard of loyalty. Additionally, this board member would likely be violating the organization's conflict-of-interest policy, but that, by itself, might not be grounds for legal action.

Obedience refers to the board's adherence both to law and to the organization's mission, as stated in its charter and other official documents.

Board members who do not abide by the standards of care, loyalty, and obedience may be subject to **intermediate sanctions.** Intermediate sanctions are personal financial penalties imposed by the IRS on individual board members. They typically apply in cases of a specific type of misconduct called an excess benefit transaction, which means the board member is being unduly rewarded for his or her service. An excess benefit transaction is a formal breach of the standards of loyalty and obedience.

If the nonprofit is **dissolved** — that is, it has somehow outlived its usefulness, its budget, or its ability to function, and everyone involved believes it is time for the organization to cease to exist

— the entire board of directors must give its consent in writing, often meaning that every board member must sign a form, which your lawyer can help you prepare.

CASE STUDY: CHANGING WORLDS

Mission: The mission of Changing Worlds is to foster inclusive communities through oral history, writing, and art programs that improve student learning, affirm identity, and enhance cross-cultural understanding.

Mark Rodriguez has been Executive Director of Changing Worlds for six years, and in the nonprofit sector for 15 years. He is the first ED of the organization, which now has six core staff and 16 contractual staff. More than 20 volunteers put in more than 5,000 hours of labor annually. Main sources of funding include individuals, foundations, corporations, and earned revenue.

"The organization's greatest challenges include meeting the growing demand for our programs, fundraising, and cultivating ongoing leadership and accountability on our board of directors," says Rodriguez. "Some of the personal challenges I have faced include clearly articulating my vision for micro areas and devoting more time for me to help prevent burnout."

If you are just starting out in the nonprofit world, "do your homework, Rodriguez says, "and be sure you are not duplicating existing nonprofit services. Also, build the best board of directors you can at the onset. With their support, they will help guide and grow the organization."

CHAPTER 3

Legal Requirements

This chapter covers the major legal requirements that apply to most nonprofits, as well as some policies and practices that are not required, but are advisable.

Much of your success in the nonprofit world depends on your ability to follow directions. Grant writing hinges on your completion of a relatively mundane checklist of documents. Legal compliance, likewise, is mostly a case of learning the rules and following them.

It may feel ironic that starting a nonprofit to support a cause about which you are passionate — one of the most individualistic, independent things you are ever likely to do — can involve so much mundane conformity. The truth is that few people will notice if you get the legal requirements right — but they will notice if you get them wrong. More to the point, noncompliance can endanger your ability to carry out your mission.

Articles of Incorporation

If you plan to apply for federal tax-exempt status under code 501(c)(3), you must first **incorporate** with your state. The federal government, understandably, is reluctant to grant tax-exempt status to individuals.

Incorporating also allows your organization to open its own bank account and own its own property. It may shield you — and your assets — from being personally liable in the event that anyone sues the organization. It makes your organization, officially, a legal entity that is separate from any of the individuals involved in its creation.

To incorporate, you file a document called **articles of incorporation.** You will need:

- A mission statement (see Chapter 1) that describes the work you intend to do and presents a clear reason for your organization to be a nonprofit.

- A list of founding board members. Your state should specify a minimum number of board members — usually three — required for incorporation. You will likely need to provide their names, addresses, telephone numbers, and Social Security numbers.

- A federal Employer Identification Number (EIN). You obtain this by either filing a form SS-4 or visiting the IRS Web site, at **www.irs.gov**, and completing the online application. The application is free.

You may also need to pay an application or processing fee, called a **startup cost.** This may be a steep fee — likely several hundred dollars. If you cannot afford it, you may be able to find an early donor — either an **incubator** program or a friend, colleague, or relative — who will help you pay. This is **seed money,** the nonprofit equivalent of venture capital. It is *not* a tax-deductible charitable contribution because your organization has not yet received federal 501(c)(3) status.

Bylaws

The term **bylaws** refers to the document that governs the activities of your organization's board of directors. As a rule, you must have a founding board before you adopt bylaws. See Chapter 2 for more information on how the bylaws govern the board.

You may modify the bylaws as needed. In most states, these modifications are a matter of public record, and you are required to file any changes with the state's attorney general or the secretary of state.

Bylaws typically address:

- The name and purpose of the organization
- The location of your office or facility
- The names of the board of directors
- The powers of the board of directors
- Organizational memberships
- Committees
- Officers
- Financial provisions
- Organizational indemnity

Bylaws protect trustees from liabilities and lawsuits. They create standards for behavior within the organization, allowing current and prospective staff and board members to know what is expected and the consequences of deviating from those expectations.

Typical Bylaw Structure

A standard bylaws document might contain the following sections, or articles.

- Article I: Name of Organization
- Article II: Purpose of Organization
- Article III: Limitations
- Article IV: Members
- Article V: Financial and Personal Liability
- Article VI: Dissolution
- Article VII: Incorporator

Resources for Writing the Bylaws

Your lawyer can help you draw up bylaws. You may also want to read the bylaws of similar nonprofits. Some organizations post their bylaws on their Web sites. Other online resources, such as the Foundation Center^{SM} and the Donors Forum, offer lists of sample documents. The Minnesota Council of Nonprofits, at **www.mncn.org**, offers samples and templates. Your state may have a similar council that can help you ensure your bylaws comply with state law.

501(c)(3) Status

You will apply for federal tax-exempt status with a Form 1023 (or, for certain organizations, a Form 1024). This is complicated, but not impossible. Once you have made a good effort at completing the form, you may want to spend an hour or two with an experienced nonprofit lawyer to make sure you have understood the requirements correctly.

The Form 1023 will ask you to submit a written "description of activities," a prose account of what you have accomplished as an organization so far. Keep a copy of this description; you may be able to use it when you are writing grants in the future.

Other requirements of the Form 1023:

- Financial activity sheets
- Articles of incorporation
- Bylaws

You should receive notice of the IRS's decision about eight weeks after you have submitted your Form 1023. They may grant your tax-exempt status immediately, or they may ask you to revise your application before they grant tax exemption. If they make such a request, submit your revisions promptly.

Your 501(c) status depends on the type of organization you are.

- 501(c)(3): Most charitable organizations; religious, educational, and scientific organizations; arts, culture, and humanities organizations; environment and animal organizations.

- 501(c)(4): Civic leagues, social welfare organizations, and local associations of employees. Apply for 501(c)(4) status with a Form 1024.

- 501(c)(5): Labor, agricultural, and horticultural organizations. Apply for 501(c)(5) status with a Form 1024.

In this book, we use 501(c)(3) to refer to all federal tax-exempt status, unless otherwise noted.

Policies

Conflict of Interest

A **conflict-of-interest policy** is designed to protect the organization and its donors from board malfeasance. It requires board members to not engage the organization in business transactions from which they could profit unduly as private citizens. The interests in conflict are the board member's; officially, a board member has an interest in the well-being of the organization; personally, he or she wants to turn a profit.

Sometimes, however, a board member may legitimately wish to enter into a business relationship with the nonprofit. For example, the nonprofit might need to print brochures promoting its new program. A board member who owns a printing company might offer the printing to the nonprofit at a discount. This could be quite an advantage for the nonprofit, and a good example of why you want to have a diverse board with connections to a variety of industries — but the board member's company is making money, so the issue is still potentially thorny.

One solution is to put the project through an open **competitive bidding process.** If the board member's company offers the lowest price, then it has earned the right to do business with the nonprofit. A conflict-of-interest policy may mandate a threshold amount over which all vendor expenditures must go through open bidding.

The conflict-of-interest policy may also specify that the board member in question — the "interested party" — may not vote in any board decisions regarding the board member's business.

A conflict-of-interest policy may also weigh the size of the expenditure against the organization's total related expenditures. In the example of the brochures, if the organization spends $50,000 a year on printing, and the brochures are a $700 job, that is less of a problem than if the brochures constituted the entirety of the organization's printing for the year, or if the price of the work would eat up most of the marketing budget.

Finally, a conflict-of-interest policy should take into account the **arm's length principle.** This requires that if a transaction happens between two people who have an existing relationship — whether their ties are business-related or familial — the transaction be conducted as though the two people were strangers. In a nonprofit, an **arm's length transaction** with a board member's company would mean that, even though the board is doing business with the board member's company, the board still conducts due diligence on the company; seeks the lowest price; exercises the standards of care, loyalty, and obedience; and maintains its responsibility to its donors.

Intellectual Property and Copyright

An **intellectual property policy** protects creative work. **Copyright** is the right of ownership to a given piece of creative work. Copyright need not be registered with the U.S. Copyright Office to be official or legally binding. A **patent** is the right of ownership to a given idea or technology; it does need to be registered with the U.S. Patent Office to be official. However, registering copyrights and patents is inexpensive and highly recommended.

For an arts organization, particularly one devoted to creating new work, an intellectual property policy is vital. You must clearly and unambiguously establish who owns the rights to all works developed. For many arts organizations, this is a relatively easy question to settle: the rights belong to the artist — the painter, the author, the musician, the choreographer, etc. — and the arts organization is merely licensing the work for exhibition, publication, or performance. However, arts groups that develop their work collaboratively must put some thought into their intellectual property policy, addressing questions such as these:

- Are collaborative works the property of the group of artists? Of the nonprofit organization?

- What happens if one of the collaborating artists wishes to allow the collaborative art to be produced elsewhere?

- If the work is produced elsewhere, how are its earnings — or royalties — to be divided among the collaborators?

Similarly, any organization that might develop technology — whether it is donor management software or a new device that helps a veterinarian operate on an animal— must be alert to the issues of ownership of these ideas.

In a typical employment relationship at a for-profit corporation, work developed by employees is considered **work done for hire** — also called **work for hire** — which means that if an employee develops a new piece of technology, writes an article, or creates something while on the clock, the creation is the property of the corporation. The employee has created it in the course of employment and, therefore, receives all the compensation to which he or she is entitled in the form of his or her regular salary.

Naturally, a work-for-hire intellectual property policy may run into problems at a nonprofit. If a teacher writes a lesson for his or her class at a nonprofit educational institution, who has the right to re-use that lesson — the teacher or the school? If a pastor writes a sermon, does it become the property of the church? By contrast, if you hire a grant writer, you likely *would* expect to be able to re-use some of what he or she wrote to describe the organization — without paying further fees or royalties. Each of these expectations must be clearly outlined in the intellectual property policy and clearly communicated at the time any person enters into a contract for work.

If your organization does adopt a work-for-hire approach to intellectual property, it must have well-defined boundaries. Furthermore, if your organization employs people who have their own creative pursuits in addition to their work for the nonprofit, a work-for-hire policy must state clearly that it applies only to work developed during employment hours — for example, that the theater company will not own the rights to the play an employee has written on his or her own time.

Data Integrity

A **data integrity policy** governs the uses of the information your nonprofit collects. For example, if you have a donor mailing list, a data integrity policy might prohibit donors' contact information from being shared with other nonprofits. It might prevent the nonprofit from making money by selling donors' e-mail addresses to interested organizations.

Another important aspect of data integrity is **client privacy.** Respecting client privacy may keep a homeless shelter from printing a brochure that shows the faces of the people the organization helps; it may ensure that the shelter changes clients' names when describing how it helps others. A client privacy policy also ensures that someone who goes to a church's peer counseling service can trust that his or her personal problems will not be discussed with other parishioners.

In some cases, client privacy is more than a matter of courtesy — it is a matter of federal law. In any medical organization, privacy of patient records is strictly regulated by the Health Insurance Portability and Accountability Act (HIPAA), and in a shelter for those who are fleeing domestic violence, client privacy is a matter of safety.

Regardless of the function of the nonprofit — whether it is a school, a church, or a shelter — you must respect the privacy of any clients under the age of 18. This includes obtaining consent from children's parents before, for example, listing their names in publicity for a youth gallery opening.

When you do want to use client information — such as when a client's inspiring story could help you reach prospective donors — have the client sign a **release agreement** or **consent form** that clearly outlines the information and its intended use.

Finally, a data integrity policy should address **privacy of information**. This information may contain data on the workings and procedures of the organization, and it may deal with the copyright on an upcoming creative production. For more on copyright, see the next section. A nonprofit is a public organization, and as such, it is subject to certain transparency requirements — that is, there is information about the organization's workings that should not be kept private. The organization's annual report is a matter of public record. However, some information manifestly should remain within the company. If the board of directors is considering several candidates for chief financial officer, these candidates' names and résumés should not be leaked. Most HR-related information raises issues of employee privacy.

Privacy is so important that many data integrity policies are simply called privacy policies.

Accountability and Regulatory Compliance

Policies of accountability and regulatory compliance ask employees and board members to take responsibility for their actions. They help ensure that the nonprofit's actions will be legal and that, if a problem happens, you will be able to trace it to its source.

Financial and Financial Management Policies

A financial policy is sometimes part of an accountability policy, sometimes separate. It can also be related to a conflict-of-interest policy. These policies require your board members and employees to make decisions based on a sound, responsible assessment of your organization's financial health, resources, and needs. It would be a violation of policy, for example, for a manager to purchase an expensive piece of equipment without ensuring the organization had budgeted for it, or for a project manager to allow overtime and expenses to balloon on what was supposed to be a modest initiative.

To some extent, you can enforce financial responsibility through other rules and common-sense practices, such as requiring board approval in advance of incurring certain expenses, limiting the number of employees who have spending authority, and requiring two signatures on checks over a certain amount. But asking staff to sign a financial policy reinforces the message of their ultimate responsibility for the solvency of the organization.

Volunteer Policy

Volunteering seems fairly simple, but it can turn into a regulatory minefield. The following are issues to consider as you draft your volunteer policy:

- Does your organization serve minors and receive state or federal funding? If so, you will need to conduct background checks on volunteers who deal with underage clients.

- What happens if a volunteer decides to apply for employment or board membership? Does he or she receive privileged consideration?

- What happens if a volunteer receives a gift in return for volunteering? Do you need to set a value limit on those gifts?

- Does any of your volunteer work require training, such as CPR training or instruction in using a proprietary piece of software? Volunteers should know what they may and may not do without appropriate training or skills. If your employee or board member will be taking the time to train volunteers, you may want to have the volunteers sign a commitment form pledging a certain minimum of volunteer hours. This way, you can build a dedicated group of volunteers and avoid wasting your employees' or board members' time. Next time around, ask one of your skilled volunteers to train the new volunteers.

- Do volunteers need to follow a dress code, for their own safety or the safety of others? For example, to serve food in a soup kitchen, volunteers will need to cover their hair and wear closed-toe shoes to comply with health regulations. To sort donations into the soup kitchen's warehouse, volunteers should have heavy-duty shoes, work pants, and perhaps jackets and gloves. Spell these regulations out in advance. If your volunteers arrive prepared, you can make better use of their time.

- Will any volunteers be asked to drive their own cars in the service of the organization? If so, you will need to spell out a reimbursement policy — if any. You must also clarify issues of liability and insurance.

- Will your volunteers have access to privileged information, such as client or donor databases, artistic submissions, or case studies? If so, they must sign and abide by your privacy policy. They will also need to maintain confidentiality about organization or employee information.

For example, if volunteers handle your marketing and PR, they will need to keep a new initiative or hiring announcement confidential until it has officially been announced.

- Do your volunteers understand the legal traits of their work? It sounds simple, but in our lawsuit-happy climate, it bears repeating: Volunteers must know that volunteering is not the same as being employed; that no workers' compensation, unemployment, or other benefits appertain to their work; and that they will not be paid for their time.

Employment Policy

Policies governing employee conduct are covered in Chapter 12. Your employment policy may also discuss issues of intellectual property regarding who owns the rights to what employees invent or create on the job.

Diversity

A **diversity** policy — which pledges the organization not to discriminate by gender, nationality, or other criteria in selecting board members — is not mandatory, but it is strongly encouraged. Diversity is frequently a criterion in grant funding; organizations that make a point to include women and minorities may have an easier time obtaining funds. And, more to the point, diversity can help your organization. Having a variety of backgrounds on your board means that board members will not all fall into the trap of operating on the same assumptions. Diversity can help your organizational guidance be more thoughtful and can also help you reach different populations with a better sense of empathy and understanding.

Ethics

Some organizations will want to plan and articulate an ethics policy with the belief that ethics should inform every organizational decision. Having a written ethics policy can be a smart move, especially if you rely heavily on a volunteer workforce who may be unfamiliar with your organizational culture. An ethics policy can also reassure donors that their gifts will go to good use.

Good ethics focus on building a stable, honest, strong, and trustworthy organization. In your ethics policy, you will need to define precisely what that means for you and your nonprofit.

Reporting

Regardless of your nonprofit's size, you must report its finances annually on a federal Form 990 or Form 990-EZ. The Form 990-EZ is permitted only for organizations whose annual budget is under $25,000. A Form 990 lists all income and expenditures for the year. If you file late, you will incur a $10 fee for every month you are late. You may file for an extension with Form 2758.

Some states also have annual reporting requirements. Check with your secretary of state and your state's attorney general. In some cases, failing to report to your state can cause you to be listed as an organization in poor standing, which could affect your ability to obtain donations and grants. Reinstating your good standing may involve paying hefty fees, and these fees can cost you in more than one way: They are not only expensive, but entirely preventable, and donors may resent seeing their donations go toward such expenses.

Insurance

The type of insurance your nonprofit needs depends heavily on the activities of the organization. Some kinds of insurance are mandatory for legal compliance, while others are simply smart moves.

Depending on your provider, you may be able to obtain a package of insurance policies called **business owner's policy insurance.** This often includes property, liability, business, bodily injury, and medical policies.

As with all business decisions, remember to shop around before settling on an insurance provider. Check with your attorney about your most likely liability issues — not just before you purchase insurance, but whenever anything significant changes within the organization.

Bonding Insurance

Bonding insurance provides protection from financial loss. Anyone who deals with organizational funding should be included in this policy.

Liability Insurance

Liability insurance protects you in the event of an accident or injury incurred during your organization's activity. You may maintain a standing policy, or — if your activities are relatively infrequent — you may obtain event-specific policies, often through the venue hosting the event. Most venues will demand some form of liability insurance before they consent to host your event, whether it is a theater performance or a gala fundraiser.

Commercial general liability insurance (CGL) provides coverage for a wide variety of acts that may result in injury or property damage.

Director and officer's liability insurance (D&O) protects the organization against wrongful management.

Accident insurance covers medical expenses for volunteers who are injured while serving the nonprofit.

Finally, **umbrella liability insurance** can help in a variety of circumstances that other coverage may not address. It can also help if you have already exhausted your other policies.

Malpractice Insurance

Medical nonprofits may need to obtain **malpractice insurance,** which protects the organization in the event of a patient lawsuit. Other organizations may want to look into **professional indemnity insurance,** which protects against professional negligence.

Property Insurance

Property insurance covers your facility and what is inside it. It is the corporate equivalent of a homeowner's or renter's insurance policy. Like a homeowner's policy, it may be void if you do not observe certain security precautions, so you must ensure that all employees adhere to these requirements.

Tenant liability insurance covers rented property. Whether you rent your main facility from a landlord or rent property to others (as in the case of a theater that rents its stage to itinerant companies), your tenant liability policy should spell out who is responsible for property maintenance and who bears the financial responsibility for injuries incurred on the premises, particularly when those injuries result from negligent maintenance. A tenant liability policy should also address injuries incurred on the premises by someone who is not an employee — such as a client, volunteer, or tradesperson.

Vehicle Insurance

If you own or lease a company vehicle, you will need to obtain **car insurance.** Maintaining a vehicle insurance policy may require you to ask for the driving records of any employees who might drive organization vehicles. A company vehicle will also be subject to mileage reporting requirements. See the full list of considerations in Chapter 3.

A **non-owned or hired auto liability insurance** policy applies to employees' or volunteers' personal vehicles when they are used in service of the organization. You may or may not need such insurance.

Employee Insurance

Until you have employees, you do not need **worker's compensation insurance** or **unemployment insurance.** Once you have employees, however, these protections become imperative.

Worker's compensation insurance helps you cover the medical expenses of an employee who is injured on the job. Unemployment insurance pays for unemployment checks for an employee who must be laid off. Chapter 12 discusses more of the insurance considerations related to having employees.

Note that these policies are distinct from the insurance policies you might offer to employees as benefits, such as life insurance or disability insurance. In those policies, the employee is the client; he or she is the person protected by the policy. In worker's compensation and unemployment insurance, the organization is protected.

Other employee insurance policies to consider include **employee benefits liability insurance,** which protects the company against neglecting employee benefits; and **improper sexual conduct/ abuse insurance,** which protects against legal costs resulting from violations of the workplace sexual conduct policy.

Permits

Solicitation Permits

A **solicitation permit** allows your organization to ask for donations. Many states, cities, and municipalities require solicitation permits for all fundraising activities. In some places, the permit depends on the type of fundraising activity. Having students or scouts ring doorbells to sell cookies and candy would likely demand a permit. Posting a "Donate here" link on your Web site might not. Using a phone bank to call prospective donors might require a permit, but you might not need a permit to send personal letters to friends and family who you think will support your new nonprofit endeavor. Check your local requirements before engaging in any fundraising activity.

Asking for funds without a solicitation permit could lead to fees — both for the organization and for the individual employees in violation of the solicitation law — an inability to collect donations, or even a revocation of your organization's charter.

To obtain a solicitation permit, you typically must submit the following:

- An application form, which may ask for information such as the names of people who will be soliciting for donations, the neighborhoods in which they will be soliciting, and the method and purpose of the fundraising efforts
- A copy of your IRS nonprofit determination letter
- A copy of your most recent financial statement

The government may ask for other documentation, such as proof of your good standing with the state's attorney general or sample donation solicitation materials. It is in your best interest to comply promptly with these requirements, as a charitable nonprofit that cannot ask for funds is dead in the water.

Nonprofit Mailing Permit

If you plan to send any amount of mail — whether you are mailing an annual appeal letter or you will rely on postcards to let your audience know about upcoming events — apply for a **nonprofit mailing permit,** which sharply reduces the costs of postage for bulk mailings. The application is available at your local post office.

Other Permits

Being a nonprofit does not excuse you from needing a **construction, or building, permit** on any major renovations to your facility.

For large public events, such as parades, protest marches, or concerts to raise awareness, you must obtain special **event permit,** and you may also be subject to special noise and traffic regulations.

State Compliance and Tax Exemption

Listing nonprofit compliance requirements for all 50 states is beyond the capacity of this book. Check with your state's department of revenue, secretary of state, and attorney general's office. Most of them will have the relevant forms and policies posted online. In some states, compliance may be relatively easy. In other states, compliance may have you longing for the simple days of the federal Form 1023. In no state are you excused from complying.

Obtaining **state sales tax exemption** is a must, regardless of the state you live in. Sales tax exemption allows you to make purchases without paying state sales tax. Not only does this enable you to spend less money, but it may also be a requirement of some donations. Donors, understandably, want their money to go to you, not the state government. Similarly, if you obtain state or federal funding, you may actually be prohibited from using it to pay for state sales tax. For a nonprofit, sales tax is an unnecessary and preventable expense.

Your city or county may also offer **property tax exemption** for nonprofits. This will require a separate application, but the benefits are obvious.

To apply for state sales tax exemption or property tax exemption, you will need proof of your federal 501(c)(3) status.

Where to Find Help

The IRS Web site at **www.irs.gov** offers a wealth of information for nonprofits.

Free Web resources, such as **www.Idealist.org** and **www.Nolo. com**, can help you make sense of legal and business terminology.

Check the Web site of your state's department of revenue, secretary of state, or attorney general for information about state and municipal requirements.

Finally, check your city's Web site to make sure you are not overlooking local compliance issues, such as building codes, zoning, and permits.

CHAPTER 4
Organizational Infrastructure

This chapter explores the day-to-day practical realities of running an organization — equipment and space, communications, and banking — and how to address these practical needs without losing sight of the organization's mission.

Brand and Mission

[handwritten note: BRAND = Σ IMPRESSIONS]

A brand is far more than just a name, tagline, or logo. Your **brand** is the sum total of impressions your public has of your organization. You add to your brand every time the following occur:

- The organization's name appears in the news ✓
- You hand out a business card ✓
- Someone you have helped tells someone else about it ✓
- Someone puts your bumper sticker on their car
- Someone drives past your sign
- Someone sees your poster on the subway
- You introduce yourself as the executive director ✓
- Someone volunteers for you
- A potential donor gets a phone call from you

- You come into contact with any member of your community ✓

Each of these interactions can be positive or negative, and you do not always have control over whether an interaction is good or bad. For example, you might have a successful volunteer day, but this means your parking lot is full, and a volunteer arriving late potentially cannot find a spot. If the volunteer must walk three blocks, is cold and grumpy when he or she does get there, and has missed orientation, the volunteer might perceive the organization as disorganized and lacking appropriate resources. *EXACTLY.*

Brand management is the continuous process of manipulating the aspects of branding you *can* control to create the most positive impression possible. Those aspects include publicity materials and press releases, the way you answer the phone, how quickly you respond to e-mail, and the way you personally interact with others. If you have employees, you will need to build an organizational culture (see Chapter 12) that leads to behavior that reinforces that brand.

Brand identity is the official way you present the brand through the messages and images you send, and the look and feel of your communications as a whole. Brand identity is closely tied to graphic identity (see Chapter 7, as well as the discussion later in this chapter). Imagine Nike® without the swoosh, one of the most famous logos in the world. Think about the number of people who have purchased clothing bedecked with the swoosh and you will have a good idea of strong brand equity; think about the number of people who associate the swoosh with sweatshop labor, and you will have a good idea of the lasting damage that a public controversy can do to an organization's identity.

Nonprofit Brands, Emotional Associations, and Mission

Take a moment to think about some well-known nonprofits. Chances are, you associate a logo and a color or color scheme with each one. Think about the Goodwill® dove, the Red Cross, the extended hand of United Way, or the pink ribbons of the Susan G. Komen Foundation.

How much do these images matter? On the one hand, not much. As long as you get a mammogram, does it matter what color the ribbon is? Of course not. On the other hand, you likely cannot see the pink ribbon without thinking — perhaps proudly, perhaps sadly — of a friend or relative who has fought breast cancer or gone on a fundraising walk. Or perhaps you see the ribbon and realize, guiltily, how long it has been since your last self-exam. Your personal emotions have become intimately tied with the graphic identity. The logo is doing its work because it causes you to feel, on an immediate, emotional level, the personal relevance and merit of the mission. If the logo succeeds in convincing you to have a check-up, then it is carrying out the organization's mission. In that respect, brand identity — and its graphic representation — can be one of a nonprofit's most powerful tools.

PERCEPTION

Brand is important because if your organization exists to serve your community, then how your community perceives your organization is crucial. If they see you as amateur or inadequate, then your ability to reach them is limited. If they see you as deserving of support, they will likely give you more support, which will increase your ability to serve them. In such ways, a brand is often self-fulfilling. Branding is something to think about immediately, as you will be building a brand from the moment you name the organization.

SELF-FULFILLING

Brand equity is the worth of your brand in terms of public goodwill and earning power. For for-profit companies, earning power is selling power; for nonprofits, it is the brand's power to attract donations. You can likely think of a few nonprofits with strong brand equity.

Brand recognition is the ability of your brand to inspire recognition — not just of the brand itself, but of the organization and the mission behind it.

The Relationship of Brand and Mission

If there is one lesson we will emphasize repeatedly, it is this: Go back to the mission. The mission can help you when you are burnt out; it can help you recruit donors and volunteers; it can help you help your community; and it can help you now as you develop your brand. You cannot create a good brand without thinking about your mission.

Contemplating how to form a brand requires you to think about how you want people to feel about your organization. What instant reaction do you want people to have when they hear your name or see your logo, before logic has even entered the picture? This reaction should be instinctive and emotional; it is all right to describe it with a gesture. You may want people to place a hand on their heart and sigh, to get misty-eyed, or to exclaim, "Oh, I *love* them!" But you need to know what reaction you want. This is the relationship you are going to try to build. People build their identities in part on the brands they choose to support, and you want your brand to be something that people will be proud to consider their own.

Many of us, fairly or not, associate marketing and branding with slick gimmicks, cheap attention-getting, and bait-and-switch tactics, which might be because we have fallen for them before. In the for-profit world, branding often entails building up a set of associations and values that may have little to do with the actual monetary worth of the goods or services that the brand is associated with. Think of the typical logo T-shirt: There might be a $30 gap between its retail price and its actual worth; think of the lengths to which petroleum companies will go to portray themselves as green. In the nonprofit world, branding also entails building associations and values, but it *must* be associated with real worth. The worth is the change you create in your community and in the lives of your clients; there can be no slick fakery here. The messages you are sending must be real, as disingenuous branding will come back to haunt you in the nonprofit world after people perceive the gap between your promises and your deeds. Once your community senses this sort of dishonesty, you will have to battle your way back to respectability. Your mission must be central, and your messages must be honest and consistent.

If the organization and the brand identity share a clear purpose — as drawn from your mission — you will have an easier time spreading your message and carrying out your work. If there are gaps between the organization structure and the brand identity, the disconnect will rapidly become visible, and you will have a problem with credibility.

With that in mind, let us look at some aspects of nonprofit infrastructure. As you read this chapter, think about how each aspect of organizational structure relates to your organization, your resources, your goals, and your mission.

Office and Equipment

Virtual and Physical Offices

Some start-up nonprofits do not have an office and, instead, work from the homes of the founders or from donated spaces in libraries and conference rooms. They may establish a virtual office, in which they use online conferencing and Web-based information storage to carry out their missions.

A virtual office has distinct advantages. Not every nonprofit needs its own office space, particularly not in its early years. If the nonprofit has not yet begun to pay staff, it may be premature to pay for rent and maintenance of an office space. Some nonprofits — such as arts organizations — are concerned with creating intellectual property. They may prefer to pay for rehearsal space, performance space, or display space on a project-by-project basis, rather than maintain a standing facility.

However, there are also disadvantages to a virtual office. Some grants — including those given by the federal government — are contingent upon a physical inspection of the nonprofit's facilities. That is, you will not be able to receive the grant money if the inspector determines that your facility is not sufficiently professional or suited to your activities. An ED whose office comprises a couple of crates of file folders under the dining table, for example, is unlikely to make a good impression.

There is more at stake than federal funds. At some point, the growth of the organization will demand that you introduce new people to your operation, and a physical introduction is far more powerful than a virtual one. To cultivate new donors, invite new collaborators, serve new clients, or recruit new board members — eventually, you will need your own space.

Other Facilities

Some nonprofits, such as clinics, educational institutions, and churches, depend on having a physical facility; they cannot execute their mission without a location. Start-up costs will be significantly steeper for these organizations. Nonetheless, it is important not to skimp on the requirements of maintaining a business facility. Check with local government. Comply with requirements about inspections, accommodations for people with disabilities, fire safety, and any other relevant issues. Being a nonprofit is not an excuse for noncompliance.

Almost every nonprofit, regardless of its other facility needs, will need some sort of office or administrative space. If you maintain a specialized facility — such as a gallery, kennel, clinic, or shelter — you will need to decide whether to keep these functions separate or integrated. Depending on your situation and your resources, it may be cheaper to rent a small office suite in an administrative building than to get a rural animal shelter wired for Internet service. You should weigh considerations of these costs against the considerations of efficiency that come from having all staff members in one place — as well as the intangibles, such as a shared sense of mission or a collaborative culture — that come from having the organization's core work visible to the administrative staff.

Office Equipment and Furnishings

When you start a new organization, it is tempting to deck out the office elaborately and furnish it as you have always imagined it would be. However, especially on the shoestring budget of your early years, this may not be the wisest way to spend your organization's money. What matters most is function, not form.

Furnishing for Your Clients

If your clients will frequently visit your facility, it is a good idea to think about their comfort. An organization that helps people deal with mental illness, for example, should attempt to create a soothing, reassuring environment. An organization that offers legal counsel to the underprivileged should take steps to make its facility professional to ensure clients know they are receiving qualified, professional help. An animal rescue organization must have a clean, safe, animal-friendly facility with appropriate restraints and utilities. Outfitting a facility in this fashion may cost a bit more, but this expenditure clearly has a purpose that is directly related to the mission of the organization.

You can frequently obtain office furniture and equipment — even computers and photocopiers — from donations. Other low-cost options include garage sales and community bulletin boards, such as **www.craigslist.org**. You must decide how much effort to put into saving money in this area. Would you rather have a free copier that jams on every tenth page or a new one that will set you back several thousand dollars but can function without constant supervision? Different EDs will have different answers.

One way or another, you should have the ability to print documents, make copies, and send and receive faxes. You should also have a safe place to store paper documents.

You will need to obtain up-to-date software for any office computers. This does not mean you need to behave like an ordinary consumer, however. Organizations such as TechSoup^{SM} can help you use software at low costs. For-profit businesses, such as Microsoft®, have major giving programs. Plan your purchases and explore your options.

At a minimum, a well-equipped nonprofit office computer should have:

- Microsoft Word® or a similar word-processing program to handle correspondence and grant writing
- A Web browser
- An e-mail program
- Anti-virus software
- Microsoft Excel® or a similar spreadsheet program
- Microsoft PowerPoint® or a similar presentation program
- A bookkeeping program, such as QuickBooks™
- A contact management program, such as Microsoft Access® or eTapestry℠, to handle donor relationship management
- A way of handling online content management; this could be a Web 2.0 application such as WordPress® or a program such as Macromedia™'s Contribute®
- A basic photo editing program to handle your photo archives
- Calendar or scheduling software

You may additionally want to consider:

- Layout software or desktop publishing software, such as Adobe InDesign™
- Web design software, such as Adobe Dreamweaver®
- A specialized database for client or member information (particularly crucial for medical organizations)
- Project management software
- A grant application calendar
- A firewall or virtual firewall

Telecommunications and Utilities

For optimal communication, you will need an **Internet Service Provider (ISP)**. Conduct research to find the one with the best offering for your organization. You may be able to obtain high-speed Internet service bundled with your telephone service.

You must set your own budgetary priorities, but it is a safe assumption that you will conduct much of your organizational research online; that you will need to maintain a Web site and an e-mail newsletter; that you may be applying for grants online; and that you may be dealing with online print services for your promotional materials. For all these reasons, invest in high-speed rather than dial-up Internet service. You can probably find high-speed service at a comparable price, and the savings in time and convenience will be well-worth what you spend.

If multiple employees will be using your Internet service, it may be a wise idea to implement an Internet policy governing reasonable standards of use, whether any personal use of the Internet is acceptable, and what sort of communications may be sent from organization e-mail accounts.

As the organization grows, you may need to move beyond simple Internet service; you may need a dedicated server or T-1 ring for the office. It is a good idea to bring in an IT consultant to help create a robust technology solution that meets your needs. Organizations such as Tech Soup offer low-cost or pro bono technology solutions for nonprofits.

The variety of phone service you need depends on your organization. Some nonprofits may find a cell phone more expedient than a land line. This may be a good solution, for example, for a new organization without a physical office, or for an itinerant performance company that works in many different performance spaces rather than at a single, fixed venue.

Other utilities you may need to pay for include electricity, water, waste management, recycling, and gas; include these costs in your estimate of the monthly cost of maintaining a facility.

Maintenance and Security

Who is responsible for cleaning your facility? Does your building rental include maintenance, or will you be responsible for it? If the budget is low, you may want to assign clean-up duties to staff on a rotating basis. For certain facilities, however, that may not be an option. For example, a medical clinic or a shelter for recovering addicts will create a certain amount of biological waste; it may be not only unreasonable, but also unsafe for untrained employees to handle this sort of waste disposal and clean-up.

A rental may include building security services. In a low-budget building, tenants may be responsible for the security of all the offices. If you are uncomfortable with tenant-controlled security, consider talking to the building's other tenants about pooling resources to pay for a security service.

Permits and Tax Requirements

Some facilities require special permits. Many performance venues, for example, have special requirements regarding parking accommodations, fire exits, and the number of restrooms. An organization that does not meet these requirements might not be able to obtain a permit or may have its permit revoked; this could mean, for example, that a nonprofit arts organization loses its ability to charge admission to the performances it has created. A nonprofit that sells food and drink will need to comply with local health codes and inspection requirements, and failure to comply could result in all operations being shut down.

At a minimum, maintaining an office may require that you obtain a business permit. Check with your state and local departments of revenue to find out what other permits and licenses you must procure.

Insurance

You will need to carry a property insurance policy on your facility — see Chapter 3 for a more thorough discussion of insurance policies for nonprofits. You may want to talk to other business owners in the building or other nonprofit executives in the community about their insurance providers. This can give you a good idea of standard premiums and practices for your area.

Bank Accounts

A bank account is a money management tool for the organization. You will need a plan for the monies involved. Every transaction must have a clear **paper trail** — a document or series of documents explaining who spent or received the money and what the money was exchanged for. An organization that cannot account for its money is at risk for an audit and will almost certainly have a harder time obtaining donations from corporate donors or charitable foundations.

You may want to talk with banking consultants at several local banks regarding your options. Make sure the bank knows you are a not-for-profit organization; bring a copy of your IRS determination letter. Ask your bank about:

- Special offers for nonprofits — for example, accounts that waive certain fees or permit a greater number of monthly transactions.

- Sponsorship programs. They may feature a different local nonprofit every month and encourage their other customers to donate.

- A reciprocal sponsorship program, in which you include advertising about the bank in your lobby or printed programs, and the bank donates a few dollars to your account for every new customer it acquires through you. See Chapter 9 for more information about reciprocal relationships with for-profit companies.

If you are considering banking with an institution that offers such programs, ask the bank for information about typical returns for participating nonprofits. Evaluate your options. If you are understaffed, a sponsorship program may not be worth the extra cost in time and effort of visiting a bank with no convenient branch locations.

Other questions to ask before you choose a bank include:

- How many branches does the bank have in your community?
- Does the bank have **FDIC insurance**?
- What fees accompany different kinds of accounts and expenditures?
- What kinds of accounts can the bank offer you? This may be important for your long-term financial strategy. You may want to start with a basic business checking account and graduate to more sophisticated investment offerings.
- When is the bank open?
- How is the customer service?
- Can you check your account online?

Some banks offer useful consumer education services, such as classes in financial planning and management. Even if you are not personally responsible for the finances of the organization, it may be a good idea to avail yourself of these services. An ED should be financially literate.

Checking

You will likely need a **checking account** for the organization. To ensure funds are spent responsibly, many nonprofits establish a policy of requiring two signatures on every check. One signature is typically that of the board treasurer, and the other may be that of the ED, the chief financial officer (CFO), the managing director, or another staff member. If the organization is too large, or this is too much of a hassle, you could only require two signatures if the check is more than a certain amount, such as $2,000.

When other staff or board members need to make a purchase for the organization, they must obtain a check in advance or complete a **purchase order**, which is a form requesting funds for a specific purpose. You should set a **purchasing policy** before obtaining a checking account; it is easier to establish behavioral expectations from the start than to impose them on people who have become accustomed to laxness.

Inconvenience and Financial Responsibility

Purchasing policies and paper documentation may seem like a waste of time, particularly if you are used to conducting your personal banking online or with a single swipe of a card. However, it is easier to document your activities now than to attempt to reconstruct them in a month from a handful of crumpled receipts. Deliberately instituting roadblocks to spending helps your organization ensure that every expenditure is responsible. How you define responsible spending depends on your strategy, but typical criteria might require that:

- The expenditure is within the budget
- The expenditure will not detract from the organization's core programs
- The expenditure is documented
- The expenditure supports the mission
- The expenditure is consistent with the organization's financial strategy

The expenditure does not violate any organizational policies, such as the conflict-of-interest policy

A checking account will likely come with a **debit card.** Using a debit card can be convenient, but for precisely that reason, it may not be advisable. It is easy to pay for purchases with a debit card, and it is easy to make deposits at ATMs and withdraw cash. But cash expenditures can be impossible to trace. At many banks, ATM deposits are not recorded the same way in-person deposits are recorded — they may not include itemized listings of the checks within a single deposit, and the records may not be kept for as long a period of time. If you do decide to use your debit card, be sure to save receipts and record expenditures daily.

Savings

A savings account helps you set aside funds that you do not need for the day-to-day operation of the nonprofit. You might create a savings account for a specific spending goal or program.

Savings accounts come in different varieties. Some are relatively straightforward **interest**-bearing accounts; some are tied to market performance; some are actually **investment vehicles** and therefore do not carry FDIC insurance, even if the bank is federally insured. Know what you are getting into.

Your board treasurer should carefully evaluate all your savings options against the organization's financial strategy and long-term goals. You may indeed choose an investment vehicle for some of the organization's funds. But because the organization is a not-for-profit, it is subject to stringent documentation requirements, and investments with substantial returns may receive special scrutiny, especially if those returns do not immediately go toward the organization's programming.

Petty Cash

Petty cash is cash on-hand at the organization's main location that goes toward such small expenses as deliveries, office supplies, postage, food, and drinks.

One person — ideally, appointed by the board — should be in charge of the petty cash. This person must keep records of money added to the store of petty cash as well as money paid out. Each record must include time, date, amount, the purpose of the expenditure, the vendor, and the staff member involved. The staff member should be required to sign the record. The petty cash box should be kept locked and secure.

Periodically, the petty cash records should be audited — by the board treasurer, the board finance committee, the board auditing committee, or the CFO — to see whether spending patterns reveal any savings opportunities. For example, you may have many small expenses for supplies that would be cheaper if you bought them in bulk, or the food for monthly volunteer meetings could be donated by a local restaurant rather than purchased.

Borrowing

Borrowing, loans, and credit cards should be a last resort. Before acquiring any **debt,** take a long look at your organization's financial health. Ask yourself the following questions:

- Where can you cut costs?
- In the long run, are you serving the mission by acquiring debt?
- How long will it take to repay the debt?
- Have you already exhausted your other options, such as a special donor appeal, a board appeal, or a fundraising event? See Chapter 8 and Chapter 14 for more information about emergency fundraising.

If you do decide to borrow, your options include:

- A **line of credit**
- A **credit card**
- A **loan** from a bank

The Small Business Association, at **www.sba.org**, can help you find sources of loans and grants.

It sounds self-evident, but in the wake of the credit crisis, it bears mentioning: Borrowing means you must eventually pay the funds back to the lender. Applying for a loan can be a time-consuming process, involving a great deal of paperwork. A credit card may seem more appealing, but convenience requires responsibility. A purchase made by credit card is essentially an **unsecured loan** — that is, a loan for which you have submitted no collateral. It is a greater risk for the lending institution and, consequently, it carries higher penalties for the borrower, typically as higher interest rates and fees. If the credit card carries a balance from month to month, it could wind up incurring substantial long-term costs for the organization.

The board must approve any decision to borrow. The board members, after all, have financial responsibility for the organization. Expect them to resist the idea of borrowing; they are simply being responsible, as borrowing is rarely a good idea for a nonprofit.

If you do borrow, treat these funds as what they are: emergency funds. They do not permit greater financial freedom; on the contrary, they should mandate greater discipline. You are not obligated to spend every penny of a loan.

Graphic Identity and Promotional Materials and Standards

A **graphic identity** is the visual way you present your organization to the world. Graphic identity encompasses considerations such as:

- **Logo**. The logo is, in essence, the visual symbol of what you do. It may be concrete, like the United Way hands or the TechSoup soup bowl, or relatively abstract, like the Project: Philanthropy colon. With the logo comes questions about its graphic **treatment**: Is it ever OK to display your logo without the company name below it? Is it permissible to have text overlap the logo? Can you add a shadow to the logo because you think it would look more eye-catching? Can you distort the logo to fit in this layout? Different companies will have different answers to these questions. Google™ maintains a playful new-economy image by changing its logo often, with illustrations that reflect holidays and other special events.

- **Color palette.** For example, your two main colors might be dark blue and light blue, to match the colors of your logo; your secondary palette might include a wine red and a soft gray, the colors you use for subheads in your print documents; and your tertiary palate, which you use for occasional emphasis, could have pine green, a lighter red, and charcoal gray.

- Standard **typefaces** and **fonts**, and how they are used. What font do you always use for letters and informational text? Are your main headers always 14-point Garamond Bold and navy blue? You can reinforce these standards by creating standard styles or templates in your organization's word processing software. Remember to address both print and Web communications. Because of differences in Web users' browsers and system defaults, the variety of fonts you can reliably use for informational Web pages is considerably smaller than the variety you can use for printed communications.

- Standard **paper stocks**. This can be difficult to enforce, particularly for organizations that rely on donated materials and printing.

- Standard layouts. Do all your brochures have a two-column page setup, for example? Are they as instantly recognizable as brochures your organization has produced?

- Images. Do you use only photographs, only illustrations, or both? How do you handle informational diagrams, such as pie charts and bar graphs? What information must be included in a caption?

Typically, you will develop a graphic identity with a graphic designer, who can help you answer all these questions and find cost-effective ways of executing the results. The designer should know your organization's goals and be thoroughly familiar with your mission and brand. Good design supports the mission; bad design can sabotage it by confusing your organization's official messages.

A graphic identity is often enforced with a **brand standards manual**, a document that communicates the different components of the identity to employees and volunteers. For example, a brand standards manual can show your volunteer Web designer that it is not OK to distort and animate your logo. It can also tell your assistant not to use clip art in this month's newsletter. Having a brand standards manual answers many questions about design before they come up, often saving hours of time from well-meaning employees or volunteers turned amateur designers. Brand standards also keep your organization looking professional.

Many organizations supplement their graphic identity with an editorial identity — an organizational voice for written materials. This means there are certain words and phrases the organization prefers to use and certain words it prefers to avoid. For example, an organization that serves the developmentally disabled might officially avoid the word *handicapped*. An organization devoted to nonviolence might try to avoid even subtle references to violence, as did one educational organization that never used the term *bullet list* to refer to its layouts. Editorial standards might be communicated and maintained with nothing more than a list a few pages long, and the organization — or its marketers or communication consultants — might take the time to develop an editorial style manual.

Promotional Materials

Every piece of printed material is an opportunity to reinforce — or weaken — your organization's brand and message. Few organizations can afford to have every kind of material printed at the same time, so you must look at your likely activities, communications, and audiences and choose the materials that will be most effective for you. You can add other materials gradually.

Sometimes printers and paper companies donate materials to nonprofits, so even if you cannot have everything printed at once, it may not be a bad idea to have everything designed at once. That way, you can be sure your brand is consistent, and you will be able to take advantage of donated printing if the opportunity presents itself.

Stationery

Letterhead may include separate sheets for formal business letters and more casual thank-you notes. You may want to have printed envelopes to match. Good designers can help you use these materials for double duty. For example, your standard envelope may be the right size to accommodate not just business correspondence, but also the brochure that provides an overview of your organization. If you have a color printer, you might be able to save on printing costs by creating a Word letterhead template rather than having reams of stationery printed.

Business Cards

Business cards are the simplest — and most important — means of exchanging information in face-to-face networking. They do not have to be expensive, but they should reflect your brand. And they must show people how to get in touch with you — in person, on the phone, and online.

Exchanging Business Cards

Often, professional networking leads nowhere, and business cards wind up doing nothing more than gathering lint in your pockets. Set yourself — and your nonprofit — apart by following up on networking contacts. When you receive a business card from someone else, do yourself a favor: Immediately write on the card the date and the event where you have met this person. You may also want to include a note or two about what he or she does or aspects of your organization in which he or she is interested. In the next few days, send a quick follow-up e-mail to that person, saying "Nice to meet you!" and addressing one of the specific items you talked about. A little effort now can pay off down the line — whether in donations or in a lasting professional relationship.

Newsletters

Newsletters can be a good way to keep people in the loop about what your organization is doing, as well as any large recent donations, public education initiatives, and more. See also the section later in this chapter on online newsletters. For some audiences, print newsletters are more effective than electronic ones. They need not represent massive printing costs. As with your letterhead, your designer can help you create a Word template in which you simply update content while keeping the design intact.

Signs

If you maintain a public facility or office, visibility is crucial. A good sign is a worthwhile investment. Remember that you can be creative with its materials and location; however, take care not to violate the terms of your lease or your zoning code.

Brochures

Brochures are especially useful if you offer multiple programs or serve multiple constituencies, as they give you a way to tailor different messages to different audiences. Take pains not to let the messages get *too* different, however; all the brochures should recognizably come from your organization. One way to differentiate them is to use essentially the same layout, but to assign a different color palette to each program or initiative.

Posters

You may or may not need posters and fliers to raise community awareness of your programming. Arts organizations tend to rely on them heavily, although a single good review — which costs nothing — can often do more than a city block plastered with posters. Before investing heavily in posters, talk with other area nonprofits in your field about their successes and failures with such promotions.

Stickers

Stickers can be printed for relatively little money. They have several advantages. First, they last a while; your message is seen repeatedly. Second, they allow your supporters to feel like active participants in your cause and to advertise for you. Third, they can be specific, effective, and memorable statements of your beliefs (how many times has your attention been arrested by a well-worded bumper sticker?). If you can't cover the expenses of printing a large batch of stickers, look into online merchandise stores, such as Cafepress® or Zazzle®, which allow you to upload designs that are then printed when users order them.

Other Materials

Marketing professionals often refer to other promotional materials as **tchotchkes** — from the Yiddish word for "trinket" or "toy" and pronounced *chach·ka* — or **swag**. Tchotchkes might include T-shirts, caps, tote bags, magnets, pencils, calendars, mugs, and related items. As with stickers, if money is a concern, you can create tchotchkes through print-on-demand Web vendors.

If you are hoping to drive behavioral change in your community, you may want to consider creating tchotchkes that relate directly to that behavior. For example, a children's literacy initiative might give away branded pencils and writing pads. Recycling programs often offer canvas tote bags to reinforce the message of using non-disposable materials. Just make sure the tchotchke is closely tied to the behavior in question. If you want to promote safe sex, handing out branded condoms is likely to be more effective than handing out branded postcards.

Web Presence

Your **Web presence** is the way your organization is represented on the World Wide Web. It is more than just your Web site, although that is a vital component. Web presence also entails:

- Your organization's use of social media and blogging
- How often your organization and its activities and members are mentioned in online publications and discussion forums, and whether these mentions are complimentary
- How easy it is for someone to find information about your organization online
- The accuracy of online information about the organization

To understand what it takes to build a good Web presence, abandon the idea that the Web is an impersonal, faceless technology. The Web is a community. Building a good Web presence involves the same work that you would have to expend to become a prominent citizen in a physical community. You must be active, available, helpful, trustworthy, reliable, vocal (in a positive way), supportive, and ethical. These may sound like old-fashioned values for a high-tech endeavor, but they will stand you in good stead. The challenge is to let technology assist, rather than hinder, your efforts.

Web site

Your **Web site** is likely the first place people will go when they want to know more about your organization, whether they are prospective clients, volunteers, donors, or board members. Members of younger demographics are more likely to use the Web than the Yellow Pages, even to find a phone number. Your Web site's job is to anticipate and meet these users' needs.

A Web site is no longer an optional part of doing business. You may want to create at least a basic site even before you apply for 501(c)(3) status.

Chapter 7, on marketing and public relations, covers researching markets, creating strong messages, and meeting your audience's needs in more depth. In this section, we will look at some of the essential components and structures that support those messages.

Considerations of Web Design

Information Architecture and Navigation

Information architecture is the arrangement of information in a Web site. Typically, you plan information architecture with a diagram called a **site map.** For a sample arrangement, see the exhibit later in this chapter.

Posting an E-Mail Address on the Contact Page

If you put your e-mail address on your Contact page, you will likely receive spam, or unwanted junk e-mail, at some point. Depending on your Web security software, spam can be an occasional nuisance or a serious, productivity-sapping problem. In any case, you may not want to post your personal e-mail address online; particularly in some settings, clients can overstep their bounds, and you may need to maintain a measure of privacy.

Even if it is not your e-mail address, there should be an e-mail address — or a fill-in-the-blanks message form — on your Contact page. Popular choices for these general-purpose addresses are info@yourdomain.org, questions@yourdomain.org, or talk-tous@yourdomain.org. You may want to have staff and volunteers answer these messages on a rotating basis; make sure they are checked at least once a day.

Most Web hosts will let you create e-mail addresses that use your domain name. These may be Web-based e-mail accounts, in which the host dedicates an amount of server space to each account — usually charging you an additional annual fee. Or they may be **forwarding accounts**, which are simply e-mail addresses that automatically send mail to another designated address. You can create, for example, yourname@nonprofit.org, and have it send messages directly to your Gmail^{SM} account.

Most Web sites contain certain types of pages, such as:

- A **home page** is the first thing users see when they visit your domain. It is the Web equivalent of your mission statement; it might even feature your mission statement. It should, at a minimum, have your name, your logo, and a brief description of what you do, along with a clear way for users to obtain more information.

- A **news page** — sometimes not separate from the home page —that provides the latest information about your organization.

- A **contact page** shows users how to get in touch with you via e-mail, snail mail, or telephone. It may also allow users to sign up for your e-mail newsletter.

- A **press page** allows members of the media to learn about your latest activities and download your press releases and press photos. As always, make sure you have obtained releases from all the people in the photos, and be alert to legal issues involving photographs of minors. You may also want to post links to favorable media coverage you have already received.

- A **Frequently Asked Questions (FAQ) page** provides the information users are most likely to want. Whom do you help? How do you do it? Do you have religious or political affiliations? What kind of donations do you need? Do you need volunteer labor? Think about the questions you typically answer in conversations about your nonprofit; post them all online, along with thorough answers.

- A **donation page** allows users to give online, frequently with a service such as PayPal. It may also include the organization's **donor roll** — the list of donors and sponsors.

- **Informational pages** — such as About Us, History, Who We Are, and What We Do — tell users more about your organization and programs. Depending on the breadth of your offerings and the age of the organization, you may have just one or two informational pages, or you may have 20.

- **Forums** or **discussion boards** allow users to participate in public dialogue relating to your activities. Not every site has — or needs — these. Forums may be particularly useful for nonprofits that offer client-support groups, provide online education, or wish to maintain close relationships with donors, volunteers, and clients. However, creating and maintaining a forum demands a skilled programmer, a large amount of bandwidth, and a reliable way of safeguarding users' privacy and personal data.

- **Navigation** is the way users get between different parts of the site. Before building your site, take some time to click through your favorite sites, as well as the sites of other nonprofits you respect. Pay attention to how they work. Are they predictable? Are they well-organized? Can you find what you need on the first try?

The Importance of Design

The nonverbal messages we send are even more important than the verbal ones. Human beings, when faced with two conflicting messages, tend to trust the nonverbal one.

What this means for your branding and marketing materials is that it does not matter how noble your mission is or how worthy your organization is; if your brochures are riddled with typos and your Web site design looks amateurish, people will assume your organization is unprofessional, overhasty, untrustworthy, disorganized, or worse. Likewise, if your Web site is impossible to navigate, you are sending users the nonverbal message that you do not really care how frustrated they are. Conversely, good Web site design can reinforce your concern for and attentiveness to your clients' needs.

Many aspects of Web design focus on the user. Chief among these aspects are **intuitiveness, usability,** and **accessibility.**

Intuitiveness

Your Web site should be intuitive — that is, someone using it for the first time should be able to figure out where to click in order to get the information he or she needs. This means that:

- Items in menus should be clearly named and labeled
- Information should be where users expect to find it

Usability

Your Web site should be usable, abiding by certain conventions of Web design, such as the convention that once a user has clicked on a link, the link changes color. Links should take users where they expect to go. If your site includes features such as JavaScript™ — for example, in cascading menus — they should be carefully tested and timed to ensure that users will be able to click where you want them to.

A component of usability is **readability.** It is more fatiguing to read on a screen than it is to read a printed page. That means that your online content should be briefer than your printed materials — even if it conveys the same messages. It is a good idea to break Web content into short paragraphs —**chunks,** in Web development lingo — and bullet lists. Web writing expert Crawford Kilian recommends that you think about your site not as a brochure, but as a résumé.

Many Web developers now recognize that Web audiences break into three major groups:

- Those who want to be able to quickly skim a page and get the main pieces of information

- Those who are looking for comprehensive, in-depth information
- Those who prefer audio or video content

Ideally, your site will meet the needs of all three groups. However, before you fill your site with video content, look at the next section on accessibility. Think about offering a featured video or podcast that plays when the user clicks on the Play button, rather than automatically.

Learning More About Web Usability

Web usability is a fascinating combination of cognitive psychology, market research, and graphic design. One guru of Web usability is Jakob Nielsen, whose Web site, **www.useit.com**, offers a wealth of information on effective site design and information architecture. Donald Norman's book, *The Design of Everyday Objects*, is a classic look at the way people interact with the things and systems they use, and the surprisingly strong influences such systems can have on our behavior.

Accessibility

Your Web site should be accessible. Web accessibility takes into consideration factors such as:

- Users' sight impairments, like blindness or colorblindness
- Users who may reach your site on slow Internet connections or from public computers
- Users with old or unconventional Web browsers
- The default fonts and colors available on most Web browsers

Intuitiveness, usability, and accessibility go hand in hand. The more straightforward and intuitive your site is, the easier it will be for all users to get around. Sites that use numerous whistles and bells — such as animations, pop-ups, and sound effects — risk distracting users from what matters most: the content. In fact, in some cases, the problem goes beyond distraction and into alienation. A user who must wait too long for your site to download is likely to move on to another site, and may give up on your site — and your organization — altogether.

Other aspects of Web design must reflect your organization's needs.

Brand

Web messages should be consistent with messages you are sending in other media. Web communications should be branded, just like those in other media.

Purpose

You must know the purpose of each Web page you publish. Is it simply to inform users about your activities? Is it to convince them to volunteer or donate? Is it to coax them to sign up for your e-mail newsletter? Is it to educate them? The desired behavior must be either explicit or implicit in the Web page's content and design.

Goals

If you want to raise $10,000 from new donors this year, your Web site must make it easy for prospective donors to learn about your mission and support it. If you are an arts organization striving to increase attendance, your Web site must show audience members how to find you and why they should.

Sample Nonprofit Site Map and Navigation

Here is a sample site map for a nonprofit that provides music education to underprivileged kids on the South Side of Chicago. The organization has four programs: a summer youth music camp; after-school classes and concerts — which meet at the organization's main building and at several Chicago Park District facilities — an instrument donation service, which provides musical instruments to needy kids and schools; and a program that sends professional musicians into area schools to teach semester-long classes. The organization is 15 years old and receives about 50 percent of its funding from donors. Another 20 percent comes from government and private grants, and 30 percent comes from events like an annual concert featuring student soloists and ensembles, and another featuring high-profile music celebrities who donate their performances.

To understand how that translates into the online arrangement of information, let us first look at the site map (*See Figure 1: Site Map*). As you can see, it is much like a typical organizational chart because it presents a hierarchy. Each box represents a separate page. The pages with titles in bold type are the **main navigation** — the categories of information. You can think of the main navigation as a table of contents for the Web site.

Now let's look at how a Web page might reflect that hierarchy. (*See Figure 2: Site Hierarchy*).

Figure 1: Site Map

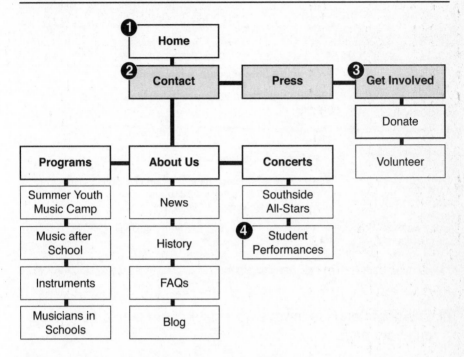

1 Everything starts with the home page.

2 The shaded pages are special. They are calls to action — that is, they represent actions the organization wants users to take. Because they are so important, they will be available from every page in the site.

3 Each main navigation page functions as a mini home page for its section.

4 Notice that most of the detailed informational pages are sub-pages. The main navigation pages contain only the basics, for users who want quick information at a glance. Users who are looking for more in-depth coverage can find it here.

Figure 2: Site Hierarchy

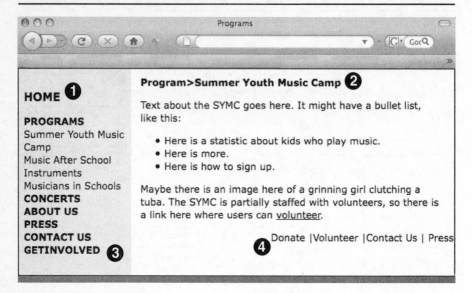

① The home page is always accessible from the same place on every page.

② This path — often called bread-crumbing — lets users know where in the site they are. Not every Web site uses this feature. Many use the top bar for navigation. However, users must have some way of knowing where they are and where they can find other pieces of information.

③ The left-hand navigation contains the main headings, as well as the subheads for this section.

④ Calls to action are clearly visible. Donations and volunteers are important to this organization, so they have opted to emphasize each call to action rather than use the umbrella link of "Get Involved." Because the calls to action are so important, it is okay that they are repeated here and in the left-hand navigation.

Domain Registry and Hosting

Your Web **domain** is the name of your Web site. For example, the domain of Atlantic Publishing is **www.atlantic-pub.com**. Nonprofits traditionally use the .org suffix rather than .com, but this is by no means universal. It is also not a reliable indicator of the integrity or structure of an organization, as few domain registries require proof of 501(c)(3) status before registering a .org domain.

To use a given domain, you must **register** it — that is, secure rights to the name. Domain registration is inexpensive; it can cost as little as $5 or $10 a year. Many companies, called domain registries, offer this service.

A Web **host** provides the data storage and retrieval that enables your Web site to function. Your Web host has a data server. You pay monthly, quarterly, or annual fees to rent space on that server. Web hosts typically regulate the type and amount of data and activity they permit. If a new program or event causes your Web traffic to surge, your host may require you to pay more for the extra **bandwidth,** or server space, your organization is using.

Many companies offer both domain registry and hosting in bundled service packs.

Domain Registration

Some domain registries are reputable; some are less so. Well-known services include **www.GoDaddy.com**®, **www.DotEasy. com**®, **www.omnis.com**, **www.directNIC.com**®, **www.register. com**®, **www.webdomain.com**, and **www.BuyDomains.com**SM.

If this is your first time registering a domain, know that some companies make their profits by "squatting" or "hijacking," which refers to the practice of cheaply registering domains they think other organizations will want, then selling the domain rights for a premium. If this happens to you, there are a few options: You can use **www.Whois.net** to discover who has the rights to the domain you want and try to negotiate with them; you can re-name your Web site and try again with a different domain; or you can pay the premium. Naming rights are strictly first-come, first-serve. For the same reason, be sure to renew your domain registry promptly and regularly. If your domain's registration expires, the domain is likely to be snatched up by one of these profiteers.

Search Engine Optimization

Search engine optimization (SEO) is the practice of ensuring that your Web site is findable. For example, if you are running a Los Angeles nonprofit that offers free music education, you want to be one of the first sites that appears when someone Googles "LA free music ed."

There are multiple methods of SEO; some are ethical and some are not.

- It is entirely ethical to have a clear, well-written Web site whose text frequently uses the **keywords** with which potential clients are likely to search. It is an essential part of Web planning to think of those keywords and incorporate them into your site's design — the menus, links, and other features.

- It is also ethical to offer many **links** to related sites, and to ask — but not require — your partner organizations, donors, and clients to post links to your site.

- It is not ethical to embed repeated keywords in your site's graphics, so that they are invisible to users but visible to search engines. This practice can get your Web site disqualified from some search engines.

Good Web writers and designers will know how to handle SEO; this is one of many reasons to trust your Web site to the pros.

Blog

A **blog,** or Weblog, is a Web page that you update frequently — something like a cross between a journalistic column and a diary. Individual blog entries are called **posts**.

Blogs are typically personal, and corporations have used them with mixed results. As noted above, your Web presence is your citizenship in a community, and the blog is where such hard-to-quantify factors as personality and humor can play a big role. Many Web users balk at the first whiff of corporate speak or phoniness. Your blog should not read like a press release. Information that does read like a press release belongs on the News page of your Web site.

Instead, use the blog as an opportunity to share the personal experience of your nonprofit work. After reading your blog, a Web user should feel that he or she knows you and your organization better. That personal connection is key: It will keep readers coming back to your site, and it will make them feel more involved — which leads to donations and volunteer work.

At the same time, you must take care not to make it *too* personal. Respect employee and client privacy; change names if you need to tell an anecdote. Keep the language clean — it may be informal, but it should not be crude. A good rule of thumb is to make sure your potential donors would not be embarrassed to read your blog from their work computers.

A few tips for effective blogging:

- Update content regularly so users have a reason to keep coming back to your site and feel involved in the day-to-day goings-on of your organization.

- Involve readers. If you are struggling to name a new initiative or program, ask for suggestions. If you would like to create an effective thank-you gift, ask readers what they would most like to receive in exchange for volunteering. Make your blog a place where discussions happen and community grows.

- Do not be afraid to discuss the negative things, like a regulatory blow, a loss of funding, or a client's heartbreaking circumstances. Nonprofits deal with societal problems, so don't pretend the challenges do not exist. Your organization is defined by how it meets these challenges. Readers who can witness the ways you handle problems may be more moved to donate or volunteer. They may also be able to help you solve the problem in a way you have not considered.

- Invite board members, donors, volunteers, and clients to participate as guest bloggers. This is a good way to build readership; guest bloggers are likely to tell their friends about what they are doing.

- Occasionally, post a few snapshots from recent events.

- Take a tip from print journalism — create a regular column or department, such as "Client of the Week."

Getting the Most from Your Blog

Look at sites such as **www.ProBlogger.net** for articles and information about using your blog to its full potential. This can in-

volve relatively complicated technical know-how, or it ca
simple as knowing how to write a good title.

Social Networking Sites

If you have not heard of Facebook®, MySpace®, Twitter, or Linke-
dIn®, odds are good that your computer is currently too dusty
to be used. These are **social networking sites** — also sometimes
called **social media**. They are places where people connect with
one another online — sometimes for casual socialization, sometimes for professional networking.

Opinions are divided on the business effectiveness of social media. Certainly, there are good ways and ineffective ways to use
these resources. They can be a fantastic tool for connecting with
different constituencies — or they can be a waste of time, depending on which sites you use and how you use them.

Public opinion shifts quickly — never more quickly than on the
Web. As of this writing:

Facebook

Facebook is the accepted juggernaut of social media. It has its detractors, particularly among those who feel that it still conveys an
unprofessional image due to its origins among college students.
Facebook does make a point of being fun. It offers numerous
applications, some user-created, such as online games and activities. These features may not be such a drawback, however;
they keep users so involved that many refer to the site as "Crack-
book." From a marketing perspective, this means that Facebook
has already done much of the work of ensuring that people will
want to visit your page. And for a youth-focused or arts-relat-
ed nonprofit, fun may be exactly the image you want to project.
For businesses, Facebook also offers advertising and "fan pages,"

which give users the opportunity to declare that they are fans of your organization. Fan pages — used to tremendous advantage by the Obama campaign, among others — allow you to inform your fans of special events or initiatives and make it easy for you to help your supporters feel that they are members of a privileged group. Fan pages also provide an automatic, effective version of word-of-mouth advertising: As soon as someone becomes your fan, most of his or her friends will know about it through the main page's newsfeed.

LinkedIn

LinkedIn is seen as the more strictly professional networking site. It too has its detractors, many of whom call it stodgy, boring, or conservative. But if "conservative" is the appropriate image for your nonprofit, this may not be a drawback at all. Precisely because of these conservative, formal overtones, LinkedIn may be the most useful site for recruiting corporate donors or board members. It allows members to endorse one another and recommend people to others. These recommendations are typically more thoughtful and formal than Facebook. LinkedIn also offers the useful feature of discussion boards; if you want to create, say, a volunteer forum, but do not have the tech resources to do it on your own Web site, a LinkedIn group may be a good option.

MySpace

Professional use of MySpace is largely limited to musicians; increasing quantities of ad content and solicitations have driven social users to Facebook. A music-related nonprofit would do well to maintain a MySpace page; however, Facebook has been increasing its music-related utilities and may surpass MySpace in this arena as well.

Twitter™

Twitter™ allows you to provide multiple brief updates, called "tweets," throughout the day. Opinions are divided on the value of these updates. If you need to build connections with a far-flung community, or if you are working to raise awareness, Twitter may be a lifesaver. If you find yourself struggling to think of new updates, Twitter may be a waste of time.

Some tips for using social networking sites:

- As with your blog, remember that the key component of these sites is "social." Your messages here must be genuine, with no hint of corporate-speak or advertising. The sites are about building relationships — professional relationships, in some cases, but nonetheless, relationships among people.

- Update your status relatively frequently — several times a week, at a minimum.

- Social media can easily eat up a full-time work day. Delegate status updates and other maintenance — such as posting news about events, writing recommendations, and making and accepting friend requests — to staff members or volunteers who already use these sites regularly and are familiar with their social standards and mores.

- Include links to your social networking pages on the Contact page of your main blog. This is an easy way to bring your content to users. You can be certain that users check social sites more often than they check your home page.

- Use the sites' event features, which often automatically publicize respondents' RSVPs, to create invitations and generate word-of-mouth for your events.

- Offer small prizes to online friends in order to reward friendship and keep users involved. For example, an arts organization might create a Facebook-only ticket discount for a given night's performance. If you sell merchandise, either to fund your efforts or to publicize your organization, you could offer a Web coupon. If you need to raise funds for a special initiative, make sure you post that in your Facebook status — and keep updating your status, with both numbers and thank-you messages, as you receive donations.

HTML Newsletters

An online newsletter is a fantastic, cheap way to keep in touch with your clients, donors, and volunteers. Services such as Constant Contact are the easiest way to create such newsletters. These services offer:

- Mailing list maintenance and database storage; prices are typically based on the size of your mailing list, with discounts available for nonprofits

- Automatic mailing list sign up; you will need to insert the service's sign-up field on your Web site's Contact page, which is easier than it sounds

- Protection of user data

- Easy layout and graphic interfaces — as with everything else, make sure what you create here is consistent with your brand; stock layouts can diffuse your message

- Automated sending

An online newsletter is almost always less expensive than a printed one. It can facilitate calls to action, letting readers click directly to your donation page, your box office, or your online volunteer sign-up sheet. It lets you inform your audience of late-breaking news — "Elton John is going to make a surprise appearance at tonight's benefit concert!" — and special milestones. You can also use it to gather information about your constituencies by occasionally asking readers to complete simple online surveys.

Online Giving

Online giving is an increasingly important component of development efforts. See Chapter 8 for a full discussion of development. The ability to accept online donations is fast becoming de rigueur. Having this ability lets you tie the action closely to the message; a prospective donor may stumble across your site and decide immediately to donate. Online donations also allow you to collect and monitor donor information. You can set user information fields on your Donation page to feed directly into your donor database.

PayPal® — currently the industry leader in online transactions — allows you to install a payment button on your site. Crucially, this may allow your organization to accept credit cards, which can otherwise be an expensive proposition.

Sponsored Search Engines

Some nonprofits become partners of search engines such as GoodSearch® at **www.goodsearch.com**, which donate a portion of their per-user advertising revenue to your organization. The per-user revenue is minuscule, but, of course, any donation is better than nothing. If you become a partner of a sponsored search engine, remind all your users to use that engine, and make it easy for them: Post the link on your Web site, and include it in an e-mail newsletter.

Web Content Maintenance

Content management — the regular updating of online information — can take many forms.

If you have consulted with an outside Web designer for your site, and no one in the organization is truly a designer, you may be best served with a simple piece of content management software, such as Contribute, which was first developed by Macromedia, now available through Adobe®. Contribute lets you change text as needed while leaving the site's design intact.

If you do have a good designer in the organization — either a staff member or a regular volunteer — he or she can handle content updates with the regular Web design software, most likely Dreamweaver.

Some organizations are now turning to **Web 2.0** interfaces, which work something like collaborative blogs. As with Wikipedia® and other collaborative sites, this approach relies on the wisdom of the group and trusts that individual members will recognize and correct inaccuracies. For some nonprofits, this approach is perfect. More traditional organizations may find it problematic.

A **Webmaster** is the person in charge of keeping Web sites up to date, making sure your content is current and your technology continues to function smoothly. Often, the Webmaster is also responsible for enforcing brand standards and editorial standards online. It is essential to designate someone to handle these jobs. Web sites, like sharks, die when they stop moving.

CHAPTER 5
Your Clients

This chapter covers the nonprofit's true reason for existence: the people it serves. Clients are the people who receive goods or services from your nonprofit organization. They may be a needy community; they may be an audience; they may fall into several different subgroups. Without knowing them and what they need, you cannot serve them effectively.

Knowing Your Clients

Learning how to assess your clients' needs is important — perhaps more important than anything else your organization does.

Learning about your clients involves asking plenty of questions. You will need to conduct demographic research about your community — with your library, your census bureau, and other relevant organizations. You will also need to talk directly with prospective clients and their families and friends. Finally, you should talk with other nonprofits that serve your community. Questions you should be asking include:

- What services can you offer to your clients?
- What services are your clients already receiving from other nonprofits? How could those services be improved?

- Which clients need which services?

- Where are those clients?

- How do you reach those clients? How do you find them, advertise to them, and talk to them?

- What else do they need? What do they value?

- Do their needs follow a seasonal pattern? Will you need seasonal volunteers or employees to accommodate this pattern?

- Do their needs follow a predictable economic pattern?

- Do their needs follow a weather pattern — as for disaster relief organizations or homeless shelters?

- Do you need emergency response services?

- Who do you need to target? Who are the people whose lives could substantially improve if they knew about your organization? Where are these people? How do they get most of their information?

- What hazards do you want to prevent or avert?

- Who can you educate?

Understanding your clients' needs is where your marketing strategy intersects with your business plan. It is the key to running an efficient organization — and to accomplishing your mission.

Chapter 7, on marketing, discusses how to tailor messages to your clients' needs in more detail.

Making Clients Aware of Your Work and Your Mission

Talking to Clients

Just as you would for prospective funders or board members, prepare an elevator speech for prospective clients. This speech may be a bit different from the others because it is not about why the community needs your organization or why someone should support your organization — it is about how you can help the person directly in front of you. Make sure everyone in your organization knows what to say in such a situation.

Because this chapter focuses on raising the number of clients you serve, it is easy to become distracted from your real purpose — to see clients as numbers and nothing else. But each one is an individual, with individual goals, hopes, dreams, and problems. In the end, you will be far more effective if you pay attention to individuals than if you focus on raising the numbers.

Recruiting Clients

Surveys

Conducted properly, a survey of your clients' needs can be your first step towards recruiting clients. Not only are you reaching out to your target audience, but you are communicating the message that you care about what they need. You do not need to make this a hard sell. Just make sure prospective clients understand that you are conducting research because you want to open a business that helps them and responds to their most pressing needs. Make it clear that you do not want to make any assumptions about your clients — you want the facts so you can respond to the real situations and help the real people. If you have a rough idea of when you will be starting operations, give prospective clients a postcard, flier, or sticker that informs them of this date.

Events

Hold an open house or orientation event and publicize it widely. Allow current and prospective clients to come and sign up for services they think they might need. Ask them to write down something they personally need help with.

Once a month, have a bring-a-friend night — a casual, no-pressure evening when people can come and meet your staff and get to know your organization. Ask current clients to bring friends who they think could benefit from your services. These nights need not even be formal events. For example, much of the business of Chicago's hallowed fringe theater community takes place in dive bars, as actors, writers, directors, and audience members relax over beers after a show.

If you charge for your services — perhaps you give some services away, but charge tuition for your education program — offer a referral discount to clients who bring friends. This strategy is particularly effective for arts organizations that are trying to build audiences. Talk with your CFO to make sure a discount is feasible, and establish a way of monitoring which clients take advantage of the discount. You may discover that one or two clients are doing a good deal of your recruiting. Find a way to say thank you — and to involve these clients in volunteering for the organization.

Publicity

These events do not matter much if nobody knows about them. You may not have a giant advertising budget for promoting yourself to prospective clients. In the absence of funding, you must plan carefully. Make every effort strategic; make it count.

See Chapter 7, on marketing, for more ideas about strategic communications. For now, think about ways to meet prospective clients in person. Can you or a board member visit a church in your target community? Can you ask the pastor to remind the congregation about your services? Your client network will be stronger if you build it on a foundation of real, personal connections, not slick advertising.

Involving Current Clients in Your Efforts

Have you had an early success? Have you changed someone's life so much that he or she has become a passionate advocate for your organization? Make that person a part of your organization. Invite him or her to become a volunteer, entrusted with key responsibilities.

In making a client a trusted volunteer, you will be continuing to help that person. It is common knowledge in the nonprofit world that volunteering is therapeutic — it makes us feel better about ourselves and puts our problems in perspective. You are also ensuring that your most effective spokesperson — someone whose life you have changed — remains involved with your organization. Your client volunteer can help you spot signs of social problems with an insider's eye. And because of his or her experience, he or she may be able to talk to people you cannot reach directly.

Make it easy for such people to help you. Organize perks, such as group transportation or child care, on days dedicated to volunteering. See Chapter 13, on working with volunteers, for more ideas.

Assessing Clients' Needs

Apart from encouraging past clients to volunteer, talk with them regularly ← at least once a month → about their current plans and struggles. Do they face any new problems now? What current problems stem from their past problems? Perhaps these conversations can point you in the direction of a new service you could offer. Starting a support group for past clients is a good way to facilitate these conversations. You need not even call it a support group; it could be tied to your monthly casual social event.

Responding to Changing Needs

Your community changes — perhaps even because of your work — so you must not assume that the same services you offer now will be adequate or successful in five years. Assess your community's needs and your responses to those needs periodically — at least once a year.

There are multiple ways to conduct this assessment. You might want to create an annual survey. Team up with another nonprofit. Yours is probably not the only organization interested in this information. See Chapter 6 for more information on building coalitions of related nonprofits. If your survey develops into a community institution, consider sharing the results with other nonprofits who serve the same community. They will help you publicize the survey to ensure that more people will participate and that the results will be accurate.

To reach the most people, you will likely need to conduct the survey through multiple media. Online surveys are easy and inexpensive, but not every client will have Internet access or the inclination to spend ten minutes on an Internet survey. For some clients, a quick telephone call is the best way for you to obtain answers to your questions. Others that prefer having time to think about a written response might instead like snail mail better.

Think about ways, such as the following, to combine your survey with other messages so that it feels less like an obligation for your clients.

- If your activities have a box-office or reservation format — whether clients are seeing a performance or making appointments for services — include a survey question in these telephone calls. Before you finalize the reservation, ask your clients how they heard about you. This way, you will know which marketing methods are working.

- If your activities include petitions, letter campaigns, or other written activism (see Chapter 6), include a self-addressed client survey postcard, or e-postcard, with the written materials people will be sending to lawmakers.

- If you send an annual donor letter (see Chapter 8), include a couple of survey questions on your response card.

- If you have an annual open house, you can conduct the survey as part of your event. One popular method is to put a brief survey on a postcard-sized raffle ticket; attendees must complete your survey in order to be included in the drawing.

Arts organizations frequently employ the raffle approach with audience surveys. Organizations and events with audiences have an advantage in that everyone in the audience gets a program. This way, it is very easy to get a survey into the hands of a client, someone who is specifically there for your organization's event. When the clients are in your physical presence, it is easier to encourage them to complete a survey and turn it in. In contrast, a mailed survey runs the risk of languishing among clients' junk mail.

Nonprofits that provide specific social services, such as mental health assistance or drug and alcohol rehabilitation, know that follow-up is the key to making a lasting change and preventing relapses. Use these follow-up visits and communications as a way to assess your organization's continuing effectiveness. Former clients may face new problems now. They will provide the most honest picture of daily life in your community. Ask them for ideas about new services that could help them continue to improve their lives.

Assessing Your Effectiveness

Assessing your continuing client effectiveness does not end with your client survey. It also demands that you assess the organization itself. If your clients' needs are changing, you must look for ways to make the organization change along with them. See Chapter 11 for more information on conducting SWOT analyses and other assessments of your nonprofit's effectiveness.

Nonprofit guru Peter Drucker advises that the moment to reassess your organization is immediately after a big success — precisely when you think you know what you are doing. If you wait until you do not know what to do, you will need to do far more work to catch up.

(handwritten note in margin: REASSESS IMMEDIATELY AFTER BIG SUCCESS)

After a year of operating, you should be able to answer these questions:

- How have you helped your clients?
- Can you measure and document the results quantitatively or qualitatively? A quantitative result is measurable in numbers — for example, "There is 15 percent less violent crime in our neighborhood." A qualitative result is described in words — for example, "I feel safer." In business, it is tempting to ignore qualitative results, but in the nonprofit world they are no less valid than the numbers.

- Where are your clients now?
- Who are your future clients?

The answers to these questions will help you help more people in the future. They can help you secure funding and recruit volunteers. More to the point, they let you know that you are doing what you set out to do: You are making a difference.

CASE STUDY: PAY-IT-FORWARD HOUSE, NFP

Mission: To provide a place of respite and inexpensive overnight lodging to the families and friends of patients in the hospital in DeKalb County, Illinois, with Kindred Hospital-Sycamore as our primary focus.

Mary Lou Eubanks is Executive Director and cofounder of the Pay-It-Forward House. She has been ED for four years and in the nonprofit sector for a little longer. The organization hired its first part-time person, at ten hours per week, just six months ago. More than 100 volunteers provide services to families with a patient in the hospital. Between continuing volunteer commitments and "special hands" or "single project" volunteers, the organization receives about 5,300 hours of volunteer labor annually.

The board, which is both a working board and a giving board, has a two-tier structure: a Board of Directors that was initially just three people, now expanded to five, and a Steering Committee of 12. The Board has general oversight. The Steering Committee is involved in the day-to-day decisions and policy making. The goal is for the Board to meet three times a year, but, Eubanks notes, "We have only done so once out of the four years of operation." The Steering Committee meets once a month, though according to Eubanks, "In the last two years, we have not met in July, (or August) and December." Donations are the main source of revenue.

Eubanks says: "Day to day, the issue is juggling space to accommodate the greatest number of people while maintaining a calm, soothing atmosphere. In the larger sense, the paperwork and administrative requirements of running a very successful operation are far greater than I could have ever imagined, and figuring out how to go from a 100-percent vol-

CASE STUDY: PAY-IT-FORWARD HOUSE, NFP

unteer organization to a entity that has payroll and related costs is difficult, from a fundraising perspective and in terms of managing our image/reputation.

"Our organization's primary mission is to provide a place of rest and respite to people with a loved one in the hospital in our county. However, a secondary mission began to evolve from the very first presentation to the zoning commission: The Pay-It-Forward House also provides community local residents a place to volunteer. Our organization is blessed with wonderful community support, but for me, as Executive Director, it means a great deal of my time is spent on volunteer and community relations.

"The other unexpected challenge has been the attendant paperwork and liability-related issues that have to be addressed (such as insurance, worker's compensation, and payroll taxes)."

If you are just starting out in the nonprofit world, "know your own strengths and weaknesses," say Eubanks, "and let other people help you, especially in your areas of weakness. Be prepared to be surprised in more ways than you can count, and don't be afraid to say, 'I don't know' or 'Let me look into that.' Be flexible and enjoy the synergies that other people's contributions will make to the organization."

CHAPTER 6
Reaching Out and Spreading the Word

This chapter covers ways to expand your nonprofit's message and scope — building awareness, working for change in the political arena, and creating community programs. It also discusses important federal restrictions on spending in relation to lobbying efforts.

Creating a Public Policy Plan
Dedicating Resources

Changing public policy involves a commitment of equipment, energy, and time. According to the Center for Lobbying in the Public Interest, you will need one person working a minimum of three hours a week to effect the change you want. This person can be a volunteer, an employee, or a board member. You will also need to make sure those hours are spent effectively — so the person should have access to efficient equipment — such as a telephone, computer, fax, Internet connection, and a dedicated e-mail address — and appropriate materials — such as research books and subscriptions, organizational marketing pieces, and brand standards manuals. Make sure the person knows whom to contact, both within the organization and outside it, to get information or assistance.

Identifying Legal Issues

What laws affect your organization's efforts? What regulations interfere with or impede your success? As you craft your public policy plan, remember to look beyond the usual suspects. Some social problems might be the unintended consequences of well-meaning laws.

For example, if you are seeking to prevent childhood obesity, do not just look at the most obvious culprit, which may be budget cuts to local schools' physical education programs. Think of other causes, such as the following:

- The law that allows vending machines stocked with unhealthy snacks to be on public school campuses, and the related provision that lets food companies sponsor the health curriculum. Both of these laws were likely written to offer schools additional fundraising options, so you will need to think of ways to help schools replace the funds they would lose by forgoing such sponsorships.

- Federal laws dealing with food packaging and additives

- The absence of bike trails and recreation centers in your city

- Awareness problems, such as widespread ignorance of sound nutritional practices, or a culture that eschews physical activity

Next, rank these regulations according to several different criteria. Which ones have the greatest impact on your mission? Which ones do you have the greatest chance of changing? Which ones will make it easy for you to recruit public support?

Finally, conduct research. When you enter the world of public policy, you are dealing with taxpayer dollars. State the business case of your lobbying efforts. How would life in your community change? What will be the budgetary consequences of the changes you propose? What will be the costs of doing nothing? In our example of childhood obesity prevention, you can point to the thousands of dollars each child is likely to cost the state — in emergency-room trips, Medicaid, and lost productivity due to poorer health — when he or she grows into an obese adult. A coalition can be an invaluable source of such research and information.

Identifying Your Compliance Requirements

Before you do any actual lobbying, file a federal 501(h) lobbying election. Guidelines for this election will help you identify your organization's spending limits and what expenditures count toward them.

If you expect to spend considerable money on lobbying, consider creating a separate 501(c)(4) organization.

Deciding on the Most Effective Actions

Identifying the most effective lobbying actions involves matching the actions — and goals — to the audience. Consider the following questions:

- Which legislators are likely to respond to certain tactics or information?
- Who is likely to be sympathetic to your cause?
- Who is likely to want your budget numbers?
- Which board members, donors, clients, and volunteers are best qualified to talk to which legislators?

- Will an in-person visit work best, or can you accomplish your goals with a few phone calls and e-mails?

Take the time to tailor your approach to each legislator. Keep your purpose firmly in mind — you may need to accomplish some small goals before you can approach the larger ones.

Community Coalitions

A **community coalition** is an alliance of independent nonprofit groups coming together for a common cause. It may be a formal, legally recognized body or a more casual gathering.

There may be a number of reasons to form a coalition:

- To attack a widespread social problem, such as drunken driving, that is larger than any one nonprofit can tackle

- To raise community awareness and motivate widespread change

- To make a concerted mass effort to influence public policy

- To raise many funds or resources quickly for a specific cause

- To share resources, ideas, or information on related topics

- To boost organizational credibility

The first step in forming a coalition is to ensure your plans and goals are clear (see Creating a Public Policy Plan). It is fine for the different organizations to hang on to their individual missions — no one is asking them to forsake their reasons for being — but everyone must be united on the purpose of the community coalition. Disagreement about your goals will sabotage your efforts.

You will need to come to an agreement about how to share the expenses and workload of the coalition's activities. As with any transaction involving money or resources, it is a good idea to get this agreement in writing. If there will be printed or electronic materials supporting the coalition's efforts, you will need to agree on a way to share credit — for example, making sure that the logos of all participating organizations receive equal space in the layout.

Coalition meetings, like meetings within your organization, should be efficient. Come to each meeting with a set written agenda. Appoint an effective, energetic person to lead meetings. Try to keep representatives of different groups interacting; do not let the coalition turn into a loose affiliation of cliques. Encourage representatives to sit next to people they do not know. Social interaction can fuel commitment to the common cause. The coalition or meeting leader should make sure every voice is heard and every disagreement is resolved civilly and amicably. You may need to create a set of bylaws — formal or informal — to govern coalition meetings.

A **coalition consultant** can help you coordinate these efforts and avoid likely pitfalls. Some of your volunteers may have previous coalition experience as well. You may also want to talk with other nonprofits that have experience in forming coalitions, and find out what worked for them, what did not, and what they would do differently this time.

Nonprofit Partnerships

You may want to take a step beyond creating coalitions. You may want to find organizations with missions similar to yours and approach them about creating **partnerships**, in which you share certain expenses and coordinate efforts to make both operations more efficient. Naturally, do not jump into such an arrangement blindly. With the ED of the other organization, conduct a SWOT analysis (see Chapter 11) of the prospective arrangement.

Lobbying

Lobbying is a way of gaining legislators' attention when you want to change something in your community. It counts as lobbying when you — acting as a representative of your organization, rather than as a private citizen — state your position on a piece of legislation. It counts as lobbying when you involve the public in attempting to sway legislation one way or another.

Before you lobby, you *must* get the facts on state, local, and federal restrictions on lobbying for nonprofits. Lobbying without regard to regulations can jeopardize your tax-exempt status. Federal restrictions prohibit spending more than a certain percentage of your organization's budget on lobbying:

- No more than 20 percent of the first $500,000 of your yearly expenditures
- No more than 15 percent of the next $500,000

These limits include amounts you pay someone else to lobby for you. Additionally, 501(c)(3) organizations are not permitted to work for the election of specific candidates. This rule is not designed to curtail your freedom of speech — it is meant to prevent campaign finance abuses. Your state and municipality may have further rules.

Form 5768

Before lobbying, fill out IRS Form 5768, which informs the IRS of your lobbying activities. Private foundations are not allowed to make expenditures for lobbying.

You should also take the time to learn how your legal system works. Some questions to ask include:

- What committees make recommendations on the legislation you are hoping to change? Which senators and representatives serve on those committees? What are their voting records?

- What process must a proposed legislative change go through before it becomes a law?

- Which elected representatives have pet causes and projects similar to your mission?

- Where does the state get funding for similar initiatives? Be prepared to suggest a funding source — or multiple ones.

- What possible objections might a representative raise to the change you are proposing? How will you defend your cause against those objections?

- Will there be any public meetings, such as town halls, related to this cause? Such a meeting can provide an opportunity to educate lawmakers and citizens all at once.

You will also need to know about the resources you can commit to lobbying.

- What is your annual budget? What legal limits apply to how much you can spend on lobbying efforts?

- What can you afford to spend on lobbying? Lobbying costs may involve not just the cost of communication materials, transportation, and employees' time, but also the expense of research and the dissemination of information (see Advocacy and Activism, following).

- Do you think lobbying will be the most efficient way to accomplish your agenda?

- Do you have the people and technology you will need to support your lobbying efforts?

- Who can you call on for help?

- Are any of your donors or board members influential members of the community? A phone call from such a person could carry more weight than a month of expensive lobbying work.

- What are the consequences for your organization if your lobbying effort fails?

- Does your board back your lobbying efforts?

- How far are you willing to go in support of this cause?

- Is now a good time to lobby? What is public opinion like in terms of your cause? Is the current legislative climate receptive to new initiatives and expenditures?

More Information on Lobbying

The Center for Lobbying in the Public Interest® (CLPI®) can help you learn more about the most effective ways to lobby. You can also talk to a lobbying consultant — or your lawyer.

You may want to form a lobbying committee comprising board members, employees, and volunteers.

Direct Lobbying

Direct lobbying is face-to-face — or occasionally, telephone or mail — communication with legislators. Many people assume lobbying is aggressive and confrontational, but that is not necessarily the case. Treat it as an opportunity to educate your lawmakers. Share the facts of the cause. Take a lesson from your development materials (see Chapter 8) and start with the specific individual case: Introduce your legislator to one of your clients, someone whose life could be dramatically better if an unreasonable law were revised. Assume the best of your public servants — that they really do want to serve the public — and show them new ways to help.

Legislators are busy people. Before you meet with a legislator, write the elevator-speech version of your lobbying effort and practice it. Work hard to find the quickest, most effective method of stating your case. A long, rambling presentation may do more harm than good.

If you try direct lobbying via mail, remember that more than 200 million pieces of mail go to the U.S. Congress each year. Make sure your letter looks important. It should not look like part of a campaign. Make it personal. Handwritten letters may get attention — although letters should not look deliberately amateurish in an effort to excite pity. Keep letters respectful and polite. Keep them short, under a page, and get your main point across in the first paragraph. Check for proper formatting, grammar, and spelling.

Finally, keep track of your efforts and their results. Maintain a list of legislators you have contacted, methods you used to reach them, messages you sent, dates, and results.

Why Does the Individual Approach Work?

Nonprofit professionals and psychologists are becoming aware of a phenomenon known as compassion fatigue — the exhausting state of being asked to care about too much. Donors and legislators are equally subject to it. It happens whenever we are pelted with negative news stories, whenever we see a number that reveals the scope of a social problem — especially if the number is so large as to seem insurmountable — and even when we have just heard dismaying news from four friends in a row. What it does not affect is our basic interpersonal instincts — our ability to become interested in the circumstances of someone else. That is why a smart development approach leads off with the individual.

Grassroots Lobbying

Grassroots lobbying influences legislation by influencing public opinion and asking the public to contact legislators on behalf of your cause. If your topic is one likely to create public outrage — for example, removing the legal loophole that allows a local corporation to dump toxins less than a mile from an elementary school — this may be the most effective tactic. But you must be specific about the behavior you hope to provoke. Do not just raise alarmist warnings. Provide the specifics — the telephone numbers and Web sites of your legislators' offices, a simple script for phone calls, a preprinted postcard bearing the legislator's name and address, a few facts about the situation, and a place where community members can write their own brief messages.

Advocacy and Activism

Advocacy and activism can be related to your lobbying efforts. **Advocacy** includes research, data-gathering, and other efforts you make to support your cause and refute opposing viewpoints. Advocacy may support direct or grassroots lobbying efforts; it may also be part of community education activities.

Common forms of **activism** are boycotts, petitions, rallies, picketing, and sit-ins. Activism is typically related to grassroots lobbying and works best when it involves large, "hard-to-ignore" groups of people.

Government Relations

Not all government relations involve working for legislative change. Other forms of government relations include:

- Providing impartial research and information
- Serving on panels
- Giving advice or information to a legislative body or its committee
- Offering public forums and discussions of the impact of legislation on the community you serve

These activities can be ways to raise the profile of your organization and build public support for your mission without actually lobbying — or even spending marketing money. Of course, if you are brought in as an impartial consultant on an issue, you must do your best to be impartial, acknowledging both sides of the issue and being honest about personal bias.

If you receive government funding, you might also spend a fair amount of time working with government representatives to ensure that you are spending government funds responsibly. Some nonprofits that receive a high percentage of their funding from the state describe acting almost like a state agency, being expected to follow the state's directions without question.

In any case, if you anticipate much work in either direction, it may be a good idea to designate an employee or board member as your key **government liaison**. This can streamline relations — letting legislators and their staff know whom to talk to when they need help a given issue — and ensure that you are giving accurate, consistent information to your elected representatives.

Educational Programs

Sometimes the best way to change a social situation is with information because educating the public can support your mission. For example, if you are trying to help struggling teenage parents, you may be able to accomplish much by offering a GED program or a class on personal finance. Furthermore, many donors look favorably on educational outreach, which takes a proactive, preventive approach — rather than the triage approach many organizations take — to social problems.

Audience

Educational programs can be for donors, volunteers, employees, clients — anyone. As with any program, begin by evaluating the intended audience and determining the best way to bring them the message they need. Look at your audience's life style: What time of day would be the best time to offer your program? What location would be most convenient for them?

Budget

Set a budget. Include the costs of classroom facilities, teaching materials and equipment, marketing, and, if you are not working with volunteer labor, teacher fees. If this amount is larger than what you can afford, consider holding a dedicated fundraiser for your educational efforts.

Staff

Select an educator. Who has appropriate expertise? Who has the skills to work with a classroom of strangers? Are there teachers or retired teachers among your volunteers or board members? They may not wish to teach your program, but they may be willing to offer consultation or training in effective teaching methods to the person who will teach the program.

Also consider whether effective classroom management might involve having a teacher's assistant (TA) as well as a main educator. The TA might be a volunteer or someone who hopes to work more in the educational program one day.

Format

Set a program format. Some information is best delivered in a one-day workshop. Some can be conveyed in weekly or nightly classes. Ideally, your program format will complement the needs of your audience as well as the structure of the information you are delivering.

Location

Choose a location. Can you hold the class in a conference room at your main facility? Would a local public school be willing to donate a classroom on weekends? What other, less orthodox options are available? For example, is there a local corporation with a training center for its employees, and could it be persuaded to let you use a room there?

Relevance

As you develop your educational program, always consider its relevance to your mission. Educational programs can easily acquire a life of their own, and though there is certainly nothing wrong with education for the sake of education, your donors and funders will wonder why you are spending their money on efforts unrelated to your main goals.

Sponsorship Programs

Sponsorship means allying your nonprofit with a for-profit corporation in order to expand your efforts and raise your profile within the community. You can learn more about relations with the for-profit world in Chapter 9.

Sponsorship takes many different forms:

- A business may choose to make monthly or yearly donations.

- A business may offer its support to a special event or initiative. Support may come in the form of publicity, in-kind donations — as in an event venue, equipment, prizes, or food — or money. The business may expect naming rights or other promotional consideration in return for its support; for example, "United Airlines® is proud to present the Steppenwolf Theater Holiday Gala". You may be asked to display its logo prominently; if you have ever seen the numerous corporate logos adorning the back of a T-shirt from a charitable fundraiser, you know how this works.

- Some businesses strongly encourage employee volunteerism, rewarding it with additional paid time off or other perks. If a business supports a certain cause, it may sponsor an employee volunteer day for a related nonprofit.

Most corporations want to publicize sponsorship somehow; their public image improves when they are seen to contribute to the community. This publicity can help you raise your profile.

But, as with all alliances, there are other considerations. Chief among them: Will association with this sponsor improve *your* public image? For example, if your organization promotes pacifism and nonviolent conflict resolution, it would not make sense to enter a sponsorship arrangement with a defense contractor.

Media Sponsorship

Radio stations, newspapers, or other media outlets may be interested in sponsoring nonprofits by helping you spread the word about events and programs for free or at reduced rates. Newspapers often call a nonprofit at the last minute if there is a hole in the layout that could easily be filled with an ad; the newspaper donates the ad space and solves its layout problem, and the nonprofit gets free advertising. Even if you do not plan to do print ads, it can be a good idea to have your designer create a few general-awareness ads in standard sizes so you can take advantage of media sponsorship opportunities if they arise.

Sponsorship Resources

If you run an arts nonprofit, take a look at Fractured Atlas at **www.fracturedatlas.org**, an alliance of arts associations that can help you find local media sponsorship, as well as sponsorships that cover other supplies. And you do not have to be in the arts to get sponsorship from public media. Many public radio and television stations offer media support to nonprofits as part of their charters. Talk directly to the station where you are hoping to get media coverage. Many for-profit media companies also see themselves as serving the public interest and therefore are quick to offer airtime or print space to nonprofits.

Outreach Programs

Outreach is a loose term for the act of expanding the number of people you reach or the way you reach them. In the sense of community outreach, it often involves entering a new geographic area or trying to send a message to a new demographic.

Your reasons for outreach may be varied:

- You may have just learned of an underserved community that could benefit from your organization, and you are trying to find ways to bring the service to them or them to the service.

- You are worried that the organization is not growing enough. You need to expand your audience or your pool of clients.

- You are trying to engage in activism or advocacy and want to involve a large group of people from your community.

- Your mission is related to awareness, and you want to expand your educational efforts.

Methods of outreach involve the same careful research and attention as marketing. Once you have a good sense of the people in the community, you can choose the media that will help you communicate with them. To start with, there may be no better outreach method than simply taking a walking tour of the area, introducing yourself and your mission to everyone you meet, and taking the time to listen to their questions and concerns.

CHAPTER 7

Public Relations and Marketing

This chapter covers the specific tools and techniques of communicating with the public and spreading your message. Marketing depends on filling needs in the community, not simply selling. Planned and positioned properly, it advances the organization's mission and complements development efforts. But adhering to a marketing strategy has its own set of challenges when you are working with limited funds.

Many people assume that marketing is the same as selling or advertising. This is not true. **Marketing** is a way of developing a product or service to meet a need, then showing the public and the community that what you have is what they need. Marketing is the business activity of presenting your services to the community that needs them. It can be as complicated as a multi-thousand-dollar effort involving surveys, billboards, and handouts or as simple as a conversation.

Market Awareness and Research

Without evaluating your community, you will not know how much your organization is needed until it fails, thus, you must conduct **research.**

Research involves different methods. You might start with a recent community census. Questions to ask include:

- What sorts of households are in your community? Who are the people you are trying to help?

- How does your community break down by household size, marital status, neighborhood, income, age, health, education, political leanings, religious affiliations, national traditions, and leisure activities? Different groups will need to hear different messages in different ways — possibly even in different languages.

- What forms of transportation do your community members use? Will their transportation affect the way they get services from your organization? Maybe you need to make sure people know you have a parking lot, or maybe it is not a bad idea to bring the services to the clients, the way The Night Ministry® does. On weekends, the Night Ministry drives its trademark white bus into Chicago's problem neighborhoods. Inside the bus is a clinic where people can be tested for HIV and other STDs.

- Where and when do your community members work? If your target clients are mostly shift workers who have trouble taking time off, you might need to consider starting a 24-hour help line or another way of accommodating their workdays.

- What kind of work do your community members do? What kind of work do they want to do? If you plan to offer educational programs, they will have an easier time succeeding if they match your clients' aspirations and goals.

- What are your community members' greatest problems? Who is already helping them solve these problems? Perhaps your clients receive considerable spiritual guidance from a local church — or weekly food from its food pantry. Perhaps many families in your area have quietly turned to grandparents for child care. Make sure your service does not prevent your clients from receiving this other assistance. Plan coordinating schedules or promotions with the other organization — or, if your missions are similar, create a community coalition, as explained in Chapter 6. Research these other lifelines and try to structure your offerings in a way that does not interfere or create other problems to be solved.

- What are your community members' greatest hopes and fears? How can you help them realize their hopes and put their fears to rest? This is essentially why we work in the nonprofit world. Do not start a marketing campaign unless you can answer these questions.

- Who is already being served by a nonprofit? What nonprofit is helping these people? Are the services adequate? Knowing what groups are already being served helps you find the groups that may be overlooked. Serving a particular niche — such as single moms without high school diplomas — may make it easier for you to get funding. It may require you to narrow your mission, and therefore your mission statement; see Chapter 1 for suggestions on revising mission statements.

In narrowing your mission, you may feel as though you are excluding potential beneficiaries of your services. That may be true — at first. As your success grows, you can expand. Of course you want to save the world; that is natural and admirable. But no one has yet been able to do it. It is no less admirable to save one or two people.

Tailoring the Message to the Audience

If you have listened to your clients, you will have an easier time creating a message that reaches them in the right way. Advertising and marketing campaigns fall apart when they operate on arrogance — the assumption that because a campaign is slick, funny, or well-executed, the audience *must* respond. No campaign is slick, funny, or well-executed enough to salvage a bad product. And not every audience wants a slick, funny campaign in the first place.

Talk to your clients. Nothing can substitute for that qualitative experience. Get a sense of the way they have experienced your organization — the good and the bad — and the way they experience life. Get to know them as individuals.

As you plan your marketing, temporarily go against the conventional wisdom that advertising is mass communication. Break your audience into as many different subgroups as possible: single moms, veterans, families without kids, families with kids in school, families who have lost kids, families using grandparents as caregivers — the list should be long. You should know, roughly, how many clients are in each subgroup, but for the time being, you do not need to do anything with those numbers.

For each subgroup, think of a representative individual you have met in your community. Tell your marketing team about that individual, as if you are making an introduction: "This is Ann. She works nights as a physician's assistant. She takes the bus to work. She has a little sister who is battling alcoholism and a father who just lost health insurance coverage for his dialysis treatments. She listens to hip-hop and knows everything there is to know about Aretha Franklin. She goes to church when she can. She gets her hair done regularly." Already, your team knows that Ann has a few problems with which she might be able to use your help. And your team has at least four good ways to reach Ann: advertisements on city buses, as well as on hip-hop and Motown radio; fliers or announcements in church; and conversations at the beauty salon. Some of these messages may be startlingly inexpensive — would it cost anything to send a volunteer to the salon to talk to women about a dangerous new STD epidemic?

As you develop your different marketing messages, ask your team to think — carefully and empathetically — about how each of these individuals would respond to this message: "What would Ann say to that? Will she even see that ad?" Do not make the mistake of trying to create one message that will speak to all these individuals. Instead, look at the different messages they need to hear. If your organization and brand are consistent, it is all right — even advisable — for the messages to vary by audience.

You may also discover some problems with your mission. Maybe there is one population whose needs are entirely different from everyone else's. Is it efficient for you to keep serving them? Can you enlist the aid of another organization that is better equipped to help them? This, too, is all right. Communities, people, and organizations change. It is better to acknowledge the changes than to ignore them.

Now, go back to the number of people in each subgroup. Which groups are largest? Are they the same groups that have the most pressing needs? If so — you have just found your highest-priority marketing messages.

Connectors, Mavens, and Salespeople

In *The Tipping Point,* a now-classic work on the ins and outs of word-of-mouth marketing, Malcolm Gladwell identifies three types of people who are chiefly responsible for the spread of ideas.

Connectors are exceptionally social people. They are the people who remember everyone's birthday, who have Rolodexes thick with business cards, and who can introduce you to the nephew of a colleague who happens to be looking for work in your area of expertise. Connectors, in short, bring people together. They create the social networks that allow ideas to travel.

Mavens are experts. They are friends whose opinions you automatically trust. You can probably think of someone whose taste in music is exceptional — someone who has always heard of four new bands you do not know but would probably like; who spends hours poring through used CDs in the local record store; and who is happy to spend a Friday night in a dingy bar, listening to a musician who is about to be discovered. This friend is a maven of music. Mavens' expertise comes naturally from their passion for the topic at hand. Whereas connectors create breadth — ideas widely disseminated — mavens create depth.

Salespeople are not what you may think — smarmy, fast-talking, or untrustworthy. Gladwell uses "salesperson" in the sense of "advocate." A salesperson is naturally charming and enthusiastic. You have so much fun talking to a salesperson that you have more positive associations with the ideas he or she supports. Performing arts organizations typically have plenty of natural salespeople in their ranks, particularly if they work with improvisers. Whereas connectors give ideas a path to travel and mavens give them weight, salespeople give them energy and excitement.

Some people fall into more than one of these categories. It is possible to be both a maven and a salesperson, for example. The real point here is that, even in the age of the Internet, word of mouth still relies on personal connections and human personality traits. Word-of-mouth marketing is the most reliable and the most useful because it is the hardest to fake. It depends on genuine emotion, genuine enthusiasm, and real social connections.

Consistency of Messages

If you are talking to multiple audiences, you will be unlikely to say the exact thing to each of them. There is a best way to reach each audience and, in some cases, the message will need to change a bit. You can go into much more detail in a grant proposal than in a 140-character Twitter tweet, to take an extreme example. If you post a video podcast on your Web site, it may communicate a level of human warmth that simply does not come across as well in a brochure.

However, there is a big difference between tailoring the message to the audience and simply telling each audience what it wants to hear. The former is effective; the latter is dishonest. See the section on brand in Chapter 4 for a discussion of the problems of credibility that can arise when there is a perceived gap between the message and the truth. Tailoring the message means leaving the fundamental truths untouched, but choosing the words and the medium that are most likely to carry them home to your audience. If you know with certainty what you want to say, and if you have done your market research and stayed true to your mission, your messages will be consistent. If you do not know what you want to say, it is better to wait until you do know.

Press Releases

A **press release** is one way to let the public know about what you are doing. It is a mass mailing — or sometimes an e-mail or a fax — that you send to the members of your local press community who might be interested in covering your organization's activities.

Writing a Press Release

In essence, you write the story you want a newspaper to write about your organization. Remember the questions a journalist will ask:

- What is happening?
- Why is it happening?
- Where is it happening?
- Who is involved?
- When is it happening?
- How is it happening?

Remember, too, that journalists are *always* looking for a good story. Start your press release with the most interesting part. And think hard about what that part might be — not from your perspective, but from the perspective of the average reader of the periodical. The most interesting part is probably not the bit about "nonprofit organization holding event." It might be "Your Organization [always use the specific name] helps record number of homeless in frigid January." Records pique interest, as do specific details. Look for an individual angle similar to one that you used in a successful development campaign. Spend more time on the first paragraph — and especially on the first sentence — than on the rest.

Sending a Press Release

Are you sending the press release yourself? If you do not already know how to use Microsoft Word's Mail Merge, you are about to learn. Mail Merge draws names and addresses from a database to automatically fill in address labels, delivery addresses on cover letters, and whatever other components of a mailing might need to be customized.

You will need to time your press release to give journalists enough time to contact you with follow-up questions and to write their stories. Ideally, the stories should appear in print just before your event, so that they will focus maximum attention — and perhaps maximum charitable donations — on your activities. Some publications may not need more than three or four weeks; six weeks is fairly standard.

Some journalists prefer to be e-mailed rather than faxed or mailed hard copies. You can usually find this information out in advance. Try to honor these preferences, as you are more likely to garner interest and coverage from a journalist who is not annoyed — and it is cheaper to e-mail than to send a hard copy.

If you do choose to use hard copies, remember to use your postal discount to send your press releases.

Creating and Maintaining a Press List

Remember that "press" extends far beyond daily newspapers. Weekly and monthly publications should also be on your list. Remember that monthlies often need significant **lead time** — the time between their receipt of the information and the time it appears in print. Some local magazines need as much as three months' notification in order to include your event in their calendars.

If you are near another large city, or if you operate in a metropolis that routinely gets visitors from other cities, you may want to include the newspapers from those cities in your list. And if there is a publication that is not local, but whose coverage is considered the gold standard for your area, include it as well. For example, many Chicago theater companies send their press releases to *The New York Times*®; and a nonprofit gallery would probably send a release to the national publication *ArtForum*®.

Do not forget about local radio and TV news shows. Nonprofits can often provide exactly the human-interest angle local anchors are looking for; make sure you highlight those activities.

If you live in a larger city, with multiple newspapers and other press organs, sending press releases can be expensive. Do not add to the expense by sending them to writers who no longer work at certain newspapers, writers who do not cover your topic, or periodicals that have ceased to exist. People often change jobs regularly in journalism, and it can be difficult to keep track of everyone. As you build relationships with various journalists, some will inform you when they are changing jobs and beats, but it is not a bad idea to conduct an annual purge in which you remove information that is past its expiration date. A volunteer can help you by calling local newsrooms to verify which names are current.

 ## PR Services

A PR service handles press releases and public relations for you. PR professionals likely already have strong working relationships with many local journalists; they already know different writers' preferences and perspectives and can get your story into the hands of the person who can tell it best. They may also be adept at spotting stories where you did not know you had them — digging interesting media angles out of your day-to-day operations.

PR professionals may submit you or your organization for various awards or other recognition. Many community organizations like to recognize local leaders or philanthropists, for example. The more you receive such recognition, the higher — and more respectable — your organization's profile.

PR professionals can also help you communicate bad news. See Communicating Bad News, later in this chapter, for a fuller discussion of how to handle those messages.

In-Person PR (INTERNAL PR)

Sometimes it is important to offer individual PR as well as mass messaging. Remember that major decisions and events affect individuals as much as they affect your organization. Do not let these individuals find out from your broadcast e-mails or the TV news; contact them personally. Even a good surprise, such as the announcement that your play has won an award, will generate certain feelings of betrayal if a cast member hears about it from a newspaper story before getting a personal call or message from the director. The personal call reinforces the message that this person's contributions are a recognized, valued part of the organization's success. This is important for the continuing health of your relationships with your collaborators, staff, and volunteers, but it is important for your word of mouth as well. When people feel that they have been part of a success, they feel empowered to brag about it.

In-person notification is equally important for the delivery of bad news if you hope to work with someone or receive his or her donations again. For example, if you have lost a major government grant and must now stop research on a certain initiative, the researchers in charge should all get personal notifications from the ED. These notifications should come before anyone has to ask, "Hey, what happened with that grant?" If you do not deliver this news proactively, you create the impression that you are attempting to hide it from the people it affects.

PR and Development

We have already discussed the value of timing in PR. For development, it is important to time press releases so that stories about your organization will appear just before your big fundraising event or its RSVP deadline. If possible, try to place a feature article about your organization's activities just before your donor letters go out as well. An inspiring piece about the people you serve can lay the groundwork for your donors.

Use PR to celebrate development triumphs such as when your organization receives a major grant. Success breeds success. Furthermore, the community you serve is legitimately interested in your plans to serve it in the future. Announcing a grant or bequest is a great way to generate interest for future programming — particularly if you might need a few more donations to make that programming come to fruition.

You might not want to call attention to problems your organization is having, but you *can* use PR to help solve development problems. This is one area in which there is a dramatic difference between what works for for-profit businesses and what works for nonprofits. Tell the press about the gap between your vision and reality. Explain how many more neighborhood children could have reading materials if you just had a working copier. Describe the ways in which the poor economy is affecting the people you serve, and how you could help those people if the economy had not affected your donations, too. If you have built up goodwill in the community, people want to help you. PR can let them know that now is the time their help will matter most.

Strategic Marketing

Strategic marketing is much more than spreading the word about your newest program. In fact, it begins long before the debut of the program, with careful research to ensure that such a program will be the best way for you to serve your community. The research should also look at the ways your community prefers to receive messages. It should look at different demographics within the community and the different ways they typically behave, as well as the ways you hope to persuade them to behave. Finally, all of this must be in support of your mission and your long-term plan for the organization.

Listening to Your Clients and Donors

Every interaction with a donor or client is an opportunity to learn more about how you can help them. In our rush to serve, we sometimes become entangled in a "holier than thou" mentality that operates on the assumption that we know our clients' needs better than they do. Combat these assumptions by cultivating an organizational culture of humility, respect, and continuous learning.

You may also want to conduct more formal market research. This can involve surveys, polls, examination of local census records, perusal of attendance or service records of nonprofits with missions similar to yours, and research into the business patterns of for-profit companies in the area. It makes sense to examine your clients' and prospective clients' buying patterns, particularly if you hope to start a cause-related marketing initiative sometime in the future (see Chapter 9).

Finding out what your clients want and satisfying that need does *not* mean telling them what they want to hear. In fact, for some organizations — such as those that work to raise AIDS awareness in communities that are in denial about the severity of the problem — that approach would be quite detrimental to the mission. Your real challenge is to find the community's true needs — which may not be the same as its articulated needs — and satisfy them, and let people know about what you are doing in a way that makes them receptive to your messages. It might be better summed up as "telling them what they *need* to hear, in the way they *want* to hear it."

Qualitative and Quantitative Research

Quantitative research involves measurable numbers and can be important, particularly as you work to establish financial goals or prove the effectiveness of a given program. In marketing, qualitative research is just as important. Overheard bits of conversation about a favorite song or a terrible subway poster provide insight into the feelings, thoughts, and preferences of your audience. Marketing traffics in feelings and opinions to deliver facts, so you must understand each factor.

Measuring the Effectiveness of Your Messages

As noted in Chapter 5, when anyone contacts your organization, ask them how they heard about you. Whoever is answering your phone should maintain a running log. If you maintain an "info@" or "questions@" Web address for general inquiries, the same practice should apply. They have found you on the Web, but what brought them to your site?

At the end of each week or month, gather this information and analyze it. Some questions to ask include:

- Have calls or e-mails spiked after the appearance of a particular advertisement? If so, which one? If not, why not?

- Have other events, such as a highly publicized case of animal abuse, triggered calls to your organization? Do you have a way of following such news stories with a quick message to let people know of your availability?

- Where do your clients remember seeing your ads?

- Which periodicals do your clients read, if any?

- Which television channels do your clients watch, if any? What time of day are they watching?

- Which radio stations do your clients listen to, if any? When?

- Which people seem to be the source of your word-of-mouth referrals? Send thank-you cards to anyone who refers a new client to you. It is a small, inexpensive gesture, and it goes a long way toward maintaining the loyalty of your vocal advocate.

- Have you had any surprises? Are people learning about you in unexpected ways? Is there a way you can use those unexpected channels to distribute more information?

Other ways of tracking your effectiveness include:

- **Coupons** always show their origins. Put a small coupon code in the design of each coupon, and make sure the code is different for each periodical. For example, if you are running a coupon ad in the Times, the Daily News, and the Post, the coupon should be slightly different for each paper.

- Offer a small discount based on a **promotional code**. You can use codes in almost any medium — print ads, online ads, even TV and radio spots — but the codes should differ based on the medium. For example, a theater company offering discounted industry tickets might promote the rate three ways: first, in the theater trade paper, which tells actors to bring a head shot to receive a $10 ticket; second, by word of mouth from the cast and crew, who tell their friends they can get in cheap by telling the box-office person the code word "paper;" and third, to the company's e-mail list, who receive a printable coupon they can redeem at the box office. If, at the end of the weekend, the company has 14 new head shots, three printed coupons, and no record of the "paper" code, it knows several things: The trade paper works, the e-mail list works somewhat, and the cast and crew may be too embarrassed about the show to tell anyone to see it. (Again, this is an example of why genuine enthusiasm should not be faked. It is rarely a good idea to ask someone to fake enthusiasm for a subpar product.)

- Most e-mail services track your **click-through rate (CTR)** — the number of users who click on one of the links in your e-mail message. A good CTR for an **opt-in mailing list** is around 6 percent.

- CTR is also the measure of the efficacy of ads on Web sites and sponsored links on search engines. A good CTR for sponsored links is around 10 to 15 percent.

- E-mail services can also tell you your **open rate**, or the number of users who have opened your message. For an opt-in list, this rate should be between 20 and 40 percent.

A good e-mail marketer can go beyond tracking this rate to find ways to automatically customize your users' online experiences and your messages, based on the ways they interact with your e-mail. When a user clicks on one link instead of another, the marketer learns something about that user's preferences.

- Response rates for direct mail are typically about 2 percent for the first contact, but for second contacts, they can jump to 5 to 35 percent. If your first-contact response rate is higher, some element of your campaign is working well. Try to figure out specifically what it is — listen for clients' casual comments and jokes about "that face on the envelope" or other elements of the piece. Rather than attempt to duplicate the success, try to build on it, following up on the element and giving your clients recognizable continuity.

Repeat, Repeat, Repeat

Sometimes it takes a while for the message to sink in. The poster gets someone interested in your theater company's show. The stack of postcards at the bar reminds him that he has been meaning to make reservations for your show. The mention on *NPR*™ jolts him awake: The show closes in two weeks!

As you analyze your marketing effectiveness, do not despair. Even if one message seems not to be getting through, it may not be a crisis. MULTIPLE MESSAGES, MULTIPLE MEDIA

You need to send multiple messages in multiple media. You cannot assume that one exposure to your message is enough to produce the results you want. At least one study indicates that for nonprofits involved in development efforts, e-mail and direct mail seem to work better when used together than when used alone.

When to Change the Message

First, conduct careful analysis to make sure that the problem is, indeed, the message, not the medium. Are you reaching the right people through the right methods and telling them what you think they need to hear? Are people getting your message and still not responding? If so, then the message itself may be flawed.

Fixing the message could be a simple matter of tweaking your tagline, including your physical address on the subway poster, correcting a word you did not realize was offensive to a certain population, or abandoning the wordy print ad in favor of a single, arresting image. With these changes, a marketing professional or graphic designer can help you strengthen — but not abandon — the message.

But what if your message has a more complicated problem, one related directly to your mission? If your mission is somehow inappropriate for your clients, no amount of tweaking is going to fix it. You need to reexamine the whole organization. Is the mission still relevant, but for a different group of clients than you previously thought? Is the mission itself out of date? Have you lost touch with the clients who used to need your services? Has a better service entered your community? Correcting problems on this scale requires a SWOT analysis (see Chapter 11) and some hard, honest decision-making. You will almost certainly need to adjust the strategy, and the problem may go so deep as to need a mission-level adjustment. You will probably need to think about **rebranding**, which we discuss in more detail later in this chapter.

Marketing Tools

Chapter 4 outlines some of the essential tools for letting people know about your organization, such as a Web presence and various print materials. After reading this chapter, you should have a good idea of how to put those tools to work in the service of your message and your audience.

Because people need to be exposed to your message multiple times in order to remember it, the combination of posters, postcards, stickers, and radio is more effective than posters alone. It can also be more expensive. Later in the chapter, we will discuss some ways to advertise on the cheap.

As we explore different methods of marketing, remember that, as Marshall McLuhan said, the medium is the message. Your choice of advertising media says something about your organization. A young nonprofit with a young, tech-savvy client base would naturally use Internet marketing. A shelter trying to reach the homeless might not have reason to reach its clients with the Internet; it might instead opt for a poster campaign in local bus shelters. It would not make sense for a nonprofit art museum or literary magazine to use a TV ad because many people in their audience might feel that the organizations' reputations would be tarnished by association with the "lowbrow" medium of television. A giant advertising budget is no protection against a poorly chosen message — or an alienated audience.

Radio and TV Advertising

Radio and TV advertising can cost a few hundred dollars — for a single "drop-in" on your local public radio affiliate — or thousands, even millions, of dollars for a TV commercial with a national audience. Prices are high because national TV advertising is a hot commodity: It gets noticed, and it reaches an immense audience. However, before diving into this medium, make sure it reaches *your* audience, and that it delivers your message to them effectively.

The components of good broadcast advertising are themselves the subject of numerous books. Opinions vary on which tactics are most effective — and, indeed, which tactics work likely depends on the broadcast's time of day, the show in which the ad appears, and other factors you cannot entirely control.

Broadcast efficacy is usually measured in **CPM**, which means "cost per thousand" — the M is a Roman numeral. The "thousand" means a thousand viewers. CPM is a ratio between the number of people who see your ad and what it has cost you to reach them.

Direct Mail

Direct mail is marketing material that you send to your clients at their homes or workplaces. Direct mail can be something as simple as a postcard but can also be a more complicated affair, such as envelope containing multiple components, such as a "Dear Friend" letter, a reply card, a reply envelope, a freebie magnet or sheet of address labels, and a "Don't throw this away" slip of paper.

Direct mail has some advantages. For one, as a physical object, it is harder to ignore than e-mail or other virtual advertising methods, and unlike a poster, billboard, or sign, it is actually in your client's possession. Your client can use your postcard as a reminder to him- or herself. If you are handling all the direct mail in-house, your mailing is probably relatively small, and you likely know many recipients. Encourage staff and volunteers to hand-write brief personal messages to recipients they have met; even a "Hi!" and a signature will suffice. Handwritten notes have the effect of turning mass mail into personal mail, which is far more memorable and effective.

But direct mail has disadvantages, too. The fact that it is a physical object means it is more expensive to produce than many other forms of marketing. Printing a postcard can be fairly inexpensive, but the larger, more elaborate pieces of mail are pricey, and assembling them is time consuming. Many organizations and marketing firms turn to **fulfillment services** to handle the printing, assembly, and mailing of these materials. As a nonprofit, you can receive a special U.S. Mail permit that gives you a discounted postal rate on mass mailings, but the price is still going to be high if you send a large quantity of mail. And, finally, direct mail can be impersonal. It might reinforce your message, but it should not be the only way you reach out.

One important thing to remember when you decide whether to use direct mail: You may have something of a generational divide in your audience. Older clients may respond better to physical mail than to e-mail, feeling that it is more personal or trustworthy — or, in the case of development efforts, a more secure way of transmitting payment. Before you decide not to use direct mail, look at your client demographics and make sure that your decision will not be alienating any groups.

Telephone Marketing

Telephone marketing, or **telemarketing**, is subject to the same Federal Trade Commission act that created the federal Do-Not-Call registry. Although there are certain exemptions for nonprofits, there are still rules your organization must abide by; make sure you are familiar with them before you begin.

Some nonprofits opt to outsource their telemarketing to solicitation firms. Some advantages of outsourced telemarketing are immediately evident. A solicitation firm has the technology and the staff to handle your campaign, and it can widen your reach. However, this approach may not be as efficient as it seems. Once again, it comes down to personal relationships. By outsourcing, you are taking your message away from staff, board, and volunteers — the people most passionate and informed about your work — and putting it in the hands and mouth of someone whose job is simply to deliver a message, regardless of its content. This means that, although you are using one of the more personal marketing mediums available to you, you are losing a chance to build a personal relationship with a potential client. For national and international nonprofits — organizations so large that they may have abandoned the idea of building meaningful personal connections between staff and clients — this may not be such an issue. But a fledgling organization might be better served by keeping the telephone marketing in-house, even — perhaps especially — if each call takes longer.

If you keep telemarketing in-house, abandon the idea of one-size-fits-all telemarketing. Treat the calls as personal phone calls. Give your callers talking points, but do not require them to adhere to a script, which many clients and prospects will find off-putting and impersonal. Remember to follow up; this is what turns connections into relationships. Keep records of success, and — if possible — have the same staffer call the same client the next time you have a phone campaign.

Finally, tailor your telemarketing efforts to your marketing goals, as telemarketing is not the most effective medium for every message. Arts nonprofits frequently use telemarketing to build their subscriber bases. Nonprofits offering other types of social services — particularly those that do not depend on sales — may be less likely to rely on this tactic. However, quite a few organizations use telephone solicitations in their development efforts.

Solicitation Permits

Do not start marketing efforts such as direct mail, telemarketing, or posting fliers until your organization has a solicitation permit. Otherwise, you could incur fines or jeopardize your tax-exempt status.

Advertising in Public

The term **signage** refers to your publicly visible signs: billboards, posters on the train, signs on the backs of bus benches, even the logo on the door of the company vehicle. Every one of these signs is an opportunity to strengthen your message.

It seems self-evident, but the front door of your facility should be easy to locate. Look at the section on Web usability in Chapter 4: The same principles of intuitiveness, usability, and accessibility apply to your physical building. If the door is not easy to find — or if your visitors routinely assume they have walked into the wrong office — you need better signs.

Ad space on billboards, or on the side of buses and trains, can be expensive, but it is often worthwhile — especially if you are trying to target a specific geographic region. For such ads, remember that either the viewer or the ad will be in motion. Typically, you have no more than one to three seconds to make your point. Try to keep the message under four words.

Ads within mass transit vehicles are a different story. They reach a captive audience — often working commuters — and they include the possibility of having a **take-one**, a coupon or flier that commuters can remove and take with them for future reference.

Because such advertising methods can be expensive, try a limited campaign, if possible, and test its effectiveness before you sink thousands of dollars into a major rollout.

Print Advertising

Print advertising includes ads in newspapers and magazines. The effectiveness of these ads is hotly debated; it depends heavily on such factors as:

- The ad's placement on the page
- The timing of the ad (Some of this is beyond your control; your ad may have strong layout and a favorable spot on the page, but because of the photos of yesterday's grisly car crash, no one will see the ad.)
- The audience of the periodical
- The other ads on the page (again, beyond your control)
- The visual impact and effectiveness of the ad itself

Print advertising can be risky and costly, but it can also be effective. Try to do as much as you can with the factors over which you *do* have control.

You cannot change the news of the day, but you can change the section of the paper in which your ad appears. For example, if your organization offers social services, maybe you will do better if your ad appears next to the story about the grim new statistics on unemployment. Similarly, if you run a theater company, you cannot change whether the newspaper's critic gives you a good or a bad review, but you can ensure your ad appears in the same issue as the review — to reiterate the basic message that your company is presenting a play, which is all you must do.

It is crucial that you choose your periodical carefully; this is where knowing your audience — and their reading and shopping habits — can pay off. It may seem impressive to have your ad in the large daily paper, but is that the publication your audience is reading? They may get their news from the smaller neighborhood daily — where, incidentally, ad space is much cheaper.

On a similar note, is the large daily paper the best way for you to achieve your goals? If one of your goals is to get a large corporate sponsor, you might be better served by advertising in the monthly *Chronicle of Philanthropy* — or by skipping advertising altogether and speaking directly to the CEOs of ten likely companies.

E-mail

Before you enter the world of e-mail marketing, take a look at the federal CAN-SPAM act, which took effect in 2004. You can see the full text on the Federal Trade Commission's Web site, at **www.ftc.gov**. The act imposes certain restrictions on all commercial e-mails:

- You must always offer recipients an easy way to opt out of receiving e-mails in the future.
- You must always identify your messages as advertising messages.
- You must represent yourself and your organization honestly. The e-mail's subject line must accurately reflect the message's content. The "from" field should reflect the actual sender. The message must contain your organization's physical mailing address.
- You may not use automated programs, such as **spiders, crawlers,** or **spambots,** to collect e-mail messages online.
- You must never send mass, unsolicited e-mail messages to people who have not signed up to receive them. Similarly,

it is not a good idea to purchase a mailing list from another nonprofit.

Consequences of spamming can range from being dropped from your Web and Internet provider's service to federal penalties, including fines of up to $11,000 per violation and imprisonment.

If you are using a service such as Constant Contact, you have some safeguards in place already. For example, every Constant Contact message includes an opt-out link. Some mass e-mail services require that a verification e-mail be sent to every new address to ensure that the recipient did want to sign up. Others use a **captcha,** a graphic that shows a sequence of letters and numbers, to prevent spambots from automatically signing up e-mail addresses; human eyes can read a captcha, but spambots cannot.

Even with these safeguards in place, be careful. Your messages may not technically be spam, but they can still be annoying. Keep them brief and necessary; always know why you are sending them, and time them strategically. To get a sense of whether your messages are annoying, monitor your "Unsubscribe" rates, which most e-mail services will track automatically. If many recipients unsubscribe after a message goes out, you have become annoying. Go back and look at your timing and quality of messages. Can you identify a pattern you do not want to repeat?

Online Ads

Certain carefully chosen Web ads may be useful for you, but you must be alert to your online audience, the goal and format of the marketing, and the sites on which your ads appear. If you have a young target audience, a Facebook ad may help you reach them. Facebook, as discussed in Chapter 4, has the advantage of showing users not just your ad, but also the names of their friends who support your work. This makes its service considerably more precise and less impersonal than most banner ads.

If you have partners, or if you are part of a coalition of nonprofits (see Chapter 6), mutual online advertising — sometimes called a **link exchange** — may be one of the fringe benefits of such an arrangement. Link exchanges work in two ways: they show your name to your partner's Web users, and they make search engines — which base results partly on the number of links to and from a given site — more likely to notice you.

Sponsored links are related advertising links that search engines return along with users' other search results. For example, if you run a domestic violence shelter and you pay for a sponsored link, a link to your Web site could appear in a special box at the top of the search results if someone Googles "domestic violence help." Different search engines have different success rates with sponsored links, but Google, Bing, and Yahoo!® all hover in the 10 to 15 percent range.

Banner ads are the ads that appear across the tops of Web pages. Often, they blink, flash, or use other animation to catch attention. The effectiveness of banner ads depends on their location and format, but there is evidence that Web users are increasingly inured to banner ads — that is, online readers are likely to ignore these messages altogether. As of 2006, standard click-through rates for banner ads had fallen to 0.3 to 0.5 percent. Marketing professor Tim Richardson notes that not every click-through represents a completed transaction. Richardson is referring to sales, but the same applies to clients who sign up for services or prospects who choose to donate. At these rates, a banner ad may need to be viewed 10,000 times before it leads to one completed transaction. Because many Web advertising services charge you by the number of times your ad is viewed, this can turn into an expensive, inefficient proposition.

Furthermore, the Web users who do not ignore banners altogether may think worse of the companies that use them, associating such messages with cheap products, late-night impulse buys, and spam. This means that, with certain audiences, your banner ads could damage your reputation. Do not use banners unless you are certain they are the only way you can reach an important audience.

Marketing Initiatives

Launching a New Brand

Sometimes an image just gets stale. Maybe your designer used a typeface that now looks dated, or a color palette that seemed fine at the time now screams "1985." Maybe the needs of your community have changed, and even though you have changed to meet those needs, your old communications do not reveal that fact. It may be time to **rebrand** — to create a new brand.

Rebranding can be a dicey business. You may encounter loyalty in the community that you had not accounted for — people who adore the old logo or, worse, people who are afraid that the new brand is the beginning of a move to a more corporate structure that will alienate or neglect the old community. Marketing is not just what you tell your community — it is what they tell you. If you know it is time for rebranding, involve your community. Begin with focus groups, open houses, surveys, and discussions. Talk about your plans for the future, and ask what people would like to see you offer. Make sure it is clear that the new brand is part of an effort to serve the community better, not to leave it behind.

Finally, do not assume that you have to jettison the old brand in its entirety. Perhaps you just need to update it. Find out which aspects of it people like — perhaps the colors are fine, but the logo could be simpler. Or maybe the tagline should be changed to reflect the updated mission, but the logo is part of your instantly recognizable sign — a community landmark. A good designer or marketer can help you create a new brand that incorporates the parts worth keeping.

Raising Awareness of New Services or Facilities

If you are introducing a new program or service and you are happy with your organization's brand, you must keep your new messages consistent with the old images of your organization. Many arts organizations, in particular, struggle with this dilemma every time they present a new show: The publicity for *The Nutcracker Suite* should not look or feel the same as the publicity for *Rite of Spring*, but devoted dance fans must know that both performances are the work of the same ballet company.

All the press releases about the new program should state clearly that the new initiative is being presented or rolled out by the existing organization. The names of the organization and the program should be associated from the beginning.

One good option is to create a **sub-brand**: a separate graphic identity for the new program that is still recognizably related to the overall organization's brand. For example, keep the type treatments the same, use a narrower color palette — perhaps a couple of the tertiary palettes already established for the organization — and, rather than creating a new logo, use the main organizational logo and tagline on all communications. Or create a tagline that echoes the organizational tagline, but adds a word or two — a twist that tells people this is something new from a trusted entity.

Let us look at an example of an organization that helps people with mental illness. It offers two programs, a clinic and a job training service. If it also decides to introduce a crisis hotline — a service that clearly relies on publicity to be successful — it is smart not to treat the hotline as an entirely new entity. People will be more inclined to call it if they understand that it is part of a brand that has already established itself as a trustworthy source for mental health care. At the same time, the most memorable part of the communication should be the number itself — say, 888-HELP-NOW. If people look at the posters and remember the name of the organization but not the number, the communications will not have the desired effect.

The organization then looks at its existing brands. Its blue-and-white logo appears on everything. The clinic's communication materials also use blue and white, with turquoise as a secondary color. The job training materials are blue and white, with green as a secondary color. To communicate that the new hotline is related to these services, the organization clearly needs to use the blue-and-white logo and color scheme in the hotline communications. But to show that it is a new service, the organization uses red — an established color of urgency — as the secondary color. The organization knows that the real goal of 888-HELP-NOW is to reach people who are in real trouble, people who might not otherwise call. So, in its publicity campaign of subway posters, the organization relies on stark, arresting photos, far different from the reassuring images it has used in its clinic and job-service publicity. But — as in those other materials — across the bottom of each poster is a bar of the secondary color and the name and logo of the organization.

Of course, that example is quite simple, as branding involves far more than posters. However, this should help you understand the value of the name you have already built up, and how to use your new program to solidify and extend that value.

Marketing on a Shoestring Budget

All of the methods we have discussed so far are relatively traditional: that is, they involve paying for the service of letting people know about your organization. Payments for such services can be fairly low, depending on the quality and timing of the service.

In this section, we will look at some different ways to raise your profile in the community without spending anything. They are not, of themselves, advertising; rather, they are best used in conjunction with advertising, to reinforce and reiterate your messages and improve your credibility. Nonetheless, they can be effective.

Publishing

Boost your status as an expert in your field by writing an op-ed or other article for your local newspaper. Whenever your organization's cause is in the news, write a letter to the editor. Your board members and other staffers can contribute to these efforts. Just make sure your organization is named in the byline.

Ghostwriters

If no one in your organization is a good writer, hire a ghostwriter. You may feel as though this is somehow dishonest, but it is no different from working with a graphic designer to strengthen the layout of your advertising. A ghostwriter does not fundamentally change your ideas; he or she simply states them more eloquently than you can. If writing is a burdensome, difficult task for you, working with a ghostwriter may also be more efficient than writing something on your own. If your article is brief, the ghostwriter's services are unlikely to be too expensive.

Public Speaking

Speak regularly at schools, trade associations, and other assemblies. Think beyond your immediate cause. For example, a female ED can speak to associations of women business owners, regardless of whether those business owners operate in the nonprofit world. Look at opportunities to speak at the luncheons of general philanthropic organizations, such as the Rotary Club or the Elks. Some churches and libraries may offer regular lecture series.

Panel Discussions

Appear regularly in local panel discussions related to your cause. If there do not seem to be any such discussions, host your own, and invite the EDs of other related nonprofits to join you on the panel.

Events

If you are hosting a special event, call a radio station to request a song. Be sure to let the DJ know that you are playing that station at your event; he or she is likely to mention your event and location on the air. You may also be able to get the radio station to visit your event and promote it on the air in exchange for certain sponsorship rights. See Chapter 9 on relationships with the for-profit world for a fuller discussion of sponsorships.

Guerilla Marketing

The term **guerilla marketing**, possibly coined by marketing expert Jay Conrad Levinson, refers to inexpensive tactics that rely on clever strategies, surprise, and nimble responses to individual situations. Guerilla marketing is not, therefore, separate from your other marketing efforts; it is simply at the far end of the continuum. It demands maximum audience awareness and personal attention. One of Levinson's examples of a guerilla marketing tactic is to pay the toll for the car behind you in line at the tollbooth — making sure you leave a business card for the tollbooth operator to pass along to that driver. This would be an excellent tactic for a nonprofit that works to improve highway safety, but could be relatively meaningless for an animal shelter.

Sit down and think creatively about your goals, your budget, and your audience. Ask yourself: When was the last time you got a nice surprise? Why were you surprised? How could you offer someone else a nice surprise?

Guerilla marketing is *not* sneaky or deceptive. Never give your audience a reason not to trust you.

Working with Donated Labor and Ad Space

Good graphic design and marketing copy are rarely cheap. They are, after all, professional services. However, you have a few options for minimizing the cost.

Whether you can or cannot afford professional services, you can control your costs by knowing your audience before you start. If you enter the design process with a clear sense of your clients, your messages, and your goals, you will remove much of the guesswork from the process, enabling designers to complete the job more efficiently. For the moment, forget about your tiny budget, and plan as though you are the client of a professional — which you are. Approach your marketing as a for-profit company would; the result is likely to be far more satisfactory.

Pro bono Design and Copywriting

One way to get good design and copywriting, even on a startup budget, is to find professionals who are willing to work pro bono — that is, to donate their services to you. Likely candidates are recent graduates from design, communications, and marketing programs — new professionals who need to build their portfolios. Talk to colleges, universities, and design schools in your area about talented students who might be able to help you.

Some nonprofits, such as the Taproot Foundation, recruit professional designers, writers, and programmers to offer their services to nonprofits. The scopes of these organizations are sometimes limited to certain cities, but their Web sites may still give you some ideas for obtaining pro bono services.

Pro bono marketing services have a few challenges, but you can meet them with careful planning and forethought.

Timing

When you are operating on donated time and labor, it can be difficult to insist on a project schedule. The nonprofit world is full of stories of pro bono marketing projects that take years to complete because an ED decided to wait for the next board meeting to obtain approval on the brochure revisions, and, by the time the board approved, the designer had started work on a 60-hour-a-week paying project. By the time the materials are printed, they are out of date.

Prevent problems of timing by knowing your goals when you start the project and communicating them clearly to your designer and writer. Agree in advance upon an arrangement that makes the most of the donated time — perhaps you or one of your volunteers can shoulder the burden of setting up a photo shoot so that the designer can arrive and quickly take pictures. Set deadlines for each stage of revisions and agree on a process for communicating these revisions to one another.

Coherency

Over the years, pro bono design and copywriting may ultimately involve the efforts of a series of professionals. Each of them may have different ideas about the best methods of communication — and, even more confusingly, they may all be effective. How do you ensure that your central messages stay recognizable and coherent, and your brand stays intact?

This is exactly the sort of situation in which brand standards manuals and editorial style manuals come in handy. Have your first designer assemble a brand manual for you — see Chapter 4 for an overview of the typical issues covered in a brand manual. This early manual may be basic — no more than a list of the stylistic choices your designer has made — but if this design works for the organization, maintain these standards.

Give the list to your next designer. If that designer makes any additions, he or she can augment the manual. For example, perhaps the second designer is the first person to create an HTML newsletter for you, so there is a whole new set of stipulations for that medium. Similarly, ask your first copywriter or editor to create a list of the verbal standards he or she is maintaining. Does your organization spell *nonviolence* with a hyphen? Will the *Chicago Manual of Style* or the *AP Stylebook* decide questions of punctuation?

Style and brand manuals have the added bonus of speeding up the marketing development process because, as you progress, many of the decisions will already have been made.

Note that pro bono services may not remove *all* the costs of marketing; printers and paper companies may be willing to offer you printed materials at cost, but rarely for free. There are a few charitable design competitions, often sponsored by paper companies, that cover printing costs as a prize to the winning design, but they are often quite competitive, and it would be a mistake to build expectations of winning the prize into your marketing budget.

The Charrette

To streamline your pro bono marketing, you could borrow an idea from Project: Philanthropy, a Chicago nonprofit that ceased operations in 2008. I served as a board member and volunteer for most of the organization's life. Project: Philanthropy used the architecture world's charrette model to provide efficient pro bono design and copywriting to charitable nonprofits. A charrette is an intensive design session.

In a Project: Philanthropy charrette, a group of 20 to 25 designers and writers gathered at a design studio, which donated its space and equipment for the day. The morning began with the charity's presentation of its mission and goals, followed by a group brainstorming session that resulted in decisions regarding brand, tagline, and color palette. Then the group split into smaller groups, with the writers each tackling a small brochure or other print piece and the designers breaking into teams to handle brochures, letterhead, and the Web site. By evening, the charity had a comprehensive, coherent brand, and final drafts of the materials that would support it. The printed materials usually arrived during the middle of the following week.

The great advantage of the charrette is that it requires a finite, easily definable amount of volunteers' time, and it is an inspiring, enjoyable way to volunteer — you typically get good work from people who might otherwise be too busy to help. The disadvantage, of course, is that decisions can be hasty; if you do not know what you want, the process cannot help you.

Client Privacy and Other Issues of Sensitivity

In all marketing materials, you must be alert to the needs of your clients and community. It can be a good idea to include a client profile in your marketing materials: Nothing better illustrates the impact your organization has on individual lives. But you must be aware of situations when telling your organization's story that might compromise the work you are doing with your clients. Some cases, such as job training and rehabilitation, represent continuing struggles for your clients, even if your organization's involvement has ended. Be alert to situations in which featuring your client's profile could help the organization but hurt the client. If you work with victims of domestic violence, protecting their anonymity may be part of keeping them safe. If you work with children, you face additional legal restrictions on how you may use their names and likenesses.

It is perfectly acceptable to create a pseudonym for your client in your marketing materials, but make sure you have his or her explicit statement of consent on a **release form** before you use their name or image.

Safeguarding client privacy extends beyond individual profiles and into any documents that discuss your clients' population. Does your brochure include a bar graph that shows, say, your clients' income levels, broken down by the neighborhoods you serve? Would it be possible for someone to use this information to interpolate data about an individual client — for example, if in a given neighborhood you have only three clients? Be sensitive to the needs and lives of the people you have served.

Communicating Bad News

Some nonprofits — such as halfway houses, needle-exchange programs, legal defense providers, and organizations on either side of the abortion debate — naturally generate controversy. Some, from time to time, are inevitably tied to human tragedy. Sometimes organizations become controversial themselves, as in the case of layoffs, grave financial losses, fraud, or radical changes of mission. These incidents will generate media coverage whether you want it or not. A PR professional can help you craft an appropriate official response.

Crisis communications, as they are typically called, should not attempt to make light of the problem, to cover it up, or to trivialize the concerns of the people affected. Crisis communications should be honest, serious, straightforward, and reassuring. Make it clear that you — both the organization and its leader — understand the gravity of what has happened and are doing as much as possible to address and rectify the situation.

CASE STUDY: ILLINOIS TECHNOLOGY DEVELOPMENT ALLIANCE

Mission: The ITDA is dedicated to creating the next generation of better, faster, smarter technology entrepreneurs by connecting, organizing, and educating entrepreneurs while catalyzing seed and early stage investment within the community.

John Noel is the President of the ITDA. He has spent a year as president, after 16 months as interim president. He has a staff of five full-time employees and two part-time employees, and a board of eight that meets on a quarterly basis. The board is a working board, and the organization does not currently have volunteers. The ITDA's main sources of funding are government grants and membership dues. Noel has worked in the nonprofit sector for eight years.

Noel says: "Our challenges are probably very similar to most other nonprofits. How do we continue to bring in funding and how do we effectively communicate our value to our benefactors (because the people we provide the most value to are not necessarily the ones who fund us)? Another challenge is trying to do more with very limited resources, not only from a cash standpoint but [from one of] personnel as well.

"Probably my greatest personal challenge is balancing work/family time. Many of our activities and the activities in the community occur after normal business hours. My response is to put a hard limit on the number I am willing to attend in a week/month. So far, that seems to work, and my family has a good expectation on how often I will be home.

"The advice that I would give to someone just starting out in the nonprofit world is that managing and running a nonprofit is very similar to running a for-profit. You have to have operational efficiency, treat your employees fairly, be creative about how you create value for your stakeholders, and, most importantly, you have to close the sale. Most nonprofits do not see asking for donations or applying for grants as selling, but it is."

CHAPTER 8
Development and Fundraising

This chapter covers the nonprofit's primary source of income: development efforts. How do you find the funds to do what you set out to do? How do you keep donors involved with the efforts of the organization? How do you find other sources of funding, such as foundations and government grants? How do you find non-financial donations, such as pro bono services or supplies? Most importantly, how do you keep development — which many nonprofits say is their biggest challenge — from taking precedence over the mission of the organization?

Funding the Mission

There is a point in the life of every nonprofit — usually near the beginning — when you recognize the size of the gap between your goals and the resources you have to achieve those goals. This moment can be dismaying, frustrating, or inspiring — sometimes all three. It is time to figure out how to fund the mission — how to acquire the resources you need to effect the changes you want.

To fund the mission, there are a few things you must have:

- A mission. If you are not 100-percent clear about it, you are not ready to start your development work.

- A budget. You must know how much money you have now, and where it is going. Every source of waste detracts from your ability to accomplish your mission.

- One-year, three-year, and five-year plans for the organization. See Chapter 11 for information on creating these.

- A sense of your community — your clients, your volunteers, and your donors. You would not bring a bake sale to a crowd that wanted a black-tie gala — or vice versa. If you have not done some sort of assessment of your market, now is a good time to do it.

- A way to conduct research on available sources of funding. This may mean purchasing an organizational membership in a service such as the Donors Forum, or it may mean partnering with a grant writer who already has such memberships. In terms of the time you can save by using these centralized sources, these memberships tend to be well worth the cost.

- A way to monitor the success of your efforts. We will explore some of these systems later in this chapter.

- Creativity. Many nonprofits use essentially the same methods to chase after the same donations and foundation dollars. There is good reason to pursue these sources of funding, but that does not mean they are the only ways to fund your mission. Be open to other possibilities.

- Flexibility. Your plans may have to change, depending on the success of your development efforts. This can be exceedingly frustrating, or it can be an opportunity to discover new efficiencies, different ways of serving your community, and different ways of running a business.

- A development strategy. We will explore what goes into that in the next section.

Mission Creep and Development Work

Mission creep — the gradual expansion or shifting of your mission — is a hazard for every business and project, but it can be a special problem if you are a new executive or are beginning your first foray into development work. There are a few reasons for this. There can be a shiny-new-toy quality to having your first office and realizing you have created an organization. Also, as you search for sources of funding, you will come across many grants that are related to your mission — sort of. Maybe you work to promote teen literacy. So when you come across a grant that provides funding for music programs for youth, you think, "Hey, writing lyrics could promote literacy." And then you spend considerable time and effort trying to present your organization as suitable for this grant, and then — if you get it — rearranging your literacy program to accommodate music teachers, and retooling your marketing messages to let people know about the new offering. In the process, you may alienate some funders who thought they were supporting literacy and perhaps see music as less essential. Make no mistake: there *is* room to expand and revise your mission, but it should be a decision born of careful planning and community research, not a desperate grab for more money.

Creating a Development Strategy

Your development strategy is your plan for acquiring the funding and resources needed to carry out your goals. Creating a development strategy involves many considerations, such as legal requirements, availability of people, timing, and other events.

Get started by looking at your five-year plan for the organization. How many people do you want to be serving? How do you want to serve them? Make a detailed estimate of the costs that will be involved. At this point, you are trying to find ways to cover costs, not eliminate them, so do not be conservative in your estimates. If anything, be liberal; that way, if the actual costs are less than your estimates, you will have a budget surplus. Some questions to think about as you assess your goals include the following:

- Will you need to hire more staff to reach this goal? Will that involve recruitment and training costs? See Chapter 12, on having employees, for a look at some of the other possible expenses.

- Will you need to move to new facilities, or expand or renovate the existing facilities?

- Will you need to acquire new equipment or replace current equipment?

- Will you need to acquire new permits or licensing?

- Will you need to conduct marketing work in conjunction with your efforts? A safe assumption in the for-profit world is that a strong marketing campaign will cost about 10 percent of the total project budget.

- Will you need to involve more volunteers to reach this goal? What will be the cost of recruitment and retention?

- Will you need to take on more board members? What will be the costs, including your time, of board recruitment?

- Will you need professional services? At some point, you will likely need to consult with a lawyer and an accountant. What about an IT professional to create the tech infrastructure that supports your outreach efforts? What about a lobbying consultant?

After answering all these questions, you should have a rough idea of the amount of money you need to raise to meet these goals.

Let's call that amount B, for budget. Is it a daunting amount? If so, that means you have some ambitious plans. The amount might be initially intimidating, but do not let it immobilize you. Recognize it for what it is — a way to change many lives — and let it inspire you.

You are still not quite done: you have not yet factored in the cost of raising the money. You might need to hire a contract event planner, a freelance grant writer, a phone bank service, or a graphic design and fulfillment company. You will need to account for the costs of your own time, as well as that of your development director, if you have one. You may need to rent a space or hire a DJ service for an event.

It can be tough, if not impossible, to estimate development costs before you have figured out the methods you will be using. Right now, we will make a rough estimate. You cannot spend more than 20 percent of the budget on fundraising if you hope to receive money from United Way; that is a reasonable starting benchmark of efficiency. To come up with a total budget that includes development efforts, and to get a rough idea of your five-year development costs, use the formula $D = 1.25 \times B$, in which B stands for your estimated five-year budget *without* development costs, and D stands for your budget *with* development costs. To find your estimated five-year development costs, divide B by 4.

Now that you have a rough idea of how much you will need to spend, it is time to look at when you will be spending it — the year-by-year plans. This is necessary to know so you can time your development efforts and anticipate your spending needs.

In writing, begin to work out the likely dates of your plans. What things will happen when? When will you introduce new programs? Are you coordinating your efforts with any immovable dates? For example, an organization devoted to promoting racial tolerance might plan important programming around Martin Luther King Jr. Day. A symphony might time several gala programs to coincide with a major anniversary of a composer's birth. An environmental organization will always observe Earth Day. Your budget must observe these holidays as much as you do, and that takes planning. Work backward from the dates to figure out what monies you should have in place when. For example, you will be sending press releases three months before a certain event, so you will need to have the PR portion of the event's budget covered by then. You might have to put down a deposit on a rental space — and the related liability insurance — as much as a year in advance. The more you think about these expenses now, the less you will be surprised by them as you carry out your programming.

Wall Charts

A whiteboard or a large, self-adhesive pad of poster-sized writing paper can help you figure out your year-by-year plans and development strategy. At first, just designate one piece of paper for each year in the five-year plan. Write the different benchmarks, programs, and events on the appropriate sheet of paper. Once you can see all five years at once, you can start to understand how events and tasks are interrelated. You will see the direct line between the donor letter that goes out in November 2010 and the performance project that opens in July 2011. The process can be exhilarating and inspiring, as when your major goals are broken down into smaller increments, it is simpler to see that your giant plans are, in fact, achievable.

Timing is especially important if you will be relying on government or foundation funding; applying for these monies is itself a lengthy process, and months may elapse between the application and the day you actually receive a check. As you conduct funding research, remember to work these application periods into your long-term schedule.

This is hard work, and it can seem overwhelming — especially if you are the only employee — to be staring at five years' worth of tasks to be accomplished and five years' worth of money to be raised. Remember to get perspective and help from your board members; you are not alone in this effort. Keep in mind your mission, and understand that few things will turn out exactly as planned. A strategy is a process, not a rulebook. You are beginning something that will continue for the entire life of the organization and will evolve as you gain more information. Let it evolve.

Now you know, more or less, how much money you need and when you need it. The next step: Where is all that money coming from?

Let us start with a quick reality check. Many founders start their organizations with big dreams of corporate benefactors and giant government grants. There are indeed organizations whose budgets come largely from state and federal agencies but, on average, most nonprofits receive 85 percent of their funding from individual donors. Just 11 percent comes from government sources, and a mere 4 percent is from corporations. 85% indiv donors 11% govt 4% corp

Take a moment to let that sink in. Go back to the earlier formula and multiply D times 0.85; the answer is the amount of your budget that relies on the charity of individuals. If you were not convinced before of the value of strong community relations, you should be now.

All of this means that you need to engage in some serious donor outreach — and soon. It takes considerable time to convert a person from a stranger to a committed, engaged donor. You probably do not currently know enough potential donors to carry your organization to the place where you want it to be in five years.

Before trying to work donor acquisition into your five-year strategy, read this chapter so that you have some idea of the options available to you. Think about your marketing strategy; many of your awareness campaigns can perform double duty as development efforts. Make an educated guess about the amount of donations you can expect to receive for each of the next five years. You can use this estimate to revise your expectations for board members — maybe, to achieve this goal, each board member is going to need to introduce ten new people to the organization every year — and for yourself. You can also use it to set smaller goals that will let you know, as you progress, whether your strategy is on track.

One more word of caution: When you are aware of the scope of your development efforts, it can be easy to fall into the trap of having something of an adversarial relationship with donors — "All I want is a little money! I need it now! Why won't you give it to me?" — but that is dangerous. A donor can be someone who helps you once—or someone who helps you for the long term. Much of this decision is up to you and how you respond to the donation, how you stay in touch with the donor, and how you keep the donor feeling involved with the organization and its mission. A new donor can be one of your most powerful allies — someone who will voluntarily spread the word to a whole new circle of people. But a donor who feels as though you have treated him or her as a short-term, disposable source of cash is not likely to help again.

Your donor relations are not just a question of building a reputation; they have practical implications for your development strategy. It takes less time and effort to get a donation from a repeat donor. If you take care of your donor relations, eventually, you will not need to battle for every dollar and you will have one of the best experiences it is possible to have: the knowledge that you have created a community of dedicated individuals who are all working for their own betterment and the betterment of the world.

Setting and Communicating Short- and Long-term Goals

You will need to set clear development goals with numbers attached — not just amounts of donations, but also number of donors. You will also need to make goals pertaining to foundation, government, and corporate income — for example, in March, I will find and research ten new sources of funding. These goals must be related to the organization's mission and goals. The ED and the board should know about them, as should development staff and volunteers.

Finding Different Sources of Income

Diversifying your development efforts is important. For one, you do not want to keep relying on the same group of friends and family members who helped you start an organization. Overreliance on these people can lead to guilt that you keep asking them for help, which brings you and your staffers dangerously close to begging. For another, expanding the pool of available donors is a smart strategy for the overall financial health of the organization.

Development Efforts in Response to Specific Short-term Needs

You may occasionally have to create a development campaign in response to a budget shortfall or an immediate opportunity. See the section on crisis communications in Chapter 7 and the section on budget shortfalls in Chapter 14 for suggestions on how to handle such situations.

Correlating Development Work to the Mission

If you have set a careful development strategy, the development efforts should be closely linked to the organizational mission, but you may want to check regularly to ensure that the connection is still close. Development efforts are particularly prone to "chasing the money," which can lead development goals quite far from the organizational strategy.

Involving the Board

As discussed in Chapter 2, it is common to have a minimum fundraising requirement for each board member, but do not look at this minimum as the only way your board can help your development efforts.

One of the most valuable ways your board members help your organization is by getting their personal social and business networks involved — as volunteers and as donors. Do not schedule a fundraising event without being certain that every board member can attend. If you expect to do much event-based fundraising, make sure that a stipulation of board membership is to bring a minimum number of guests to every event.

Board members should also be expected to send out a certain number of annual appeal letters to their friends, families, and colleagues. It may not be wise to require a minimum donation from these efforts — after all, people come from vastly different backgrounds, and some families can give handsomely while others cannot give at all — but it does make sense to ask the same amount of effort from everyone on the board. If you are not working with a fulfillment company, board members can also help you or your volunteer team with the physical assembly of the donor letters.

Soliciting for Funds

Solicitation — asking for money — is probably the single aspect of development that makes people squirm most. Some volunteers, even some employees and board members, will feel that it amounts to begging. Address these concerns immediately. Solicitation is a fact of life in the nonprofit world, and your organization cannot function without everyone's efforts. Remind reluctant volunteers, staff, and board members of what your mission is. Are they proud of helping people in this way? Are they passionate about the work they are doing and the changes they are creating in their communities? If they are not truly passionate, they should not be working for you. Explain that solicitation is not begging; in fact, the method works best if begging is the furthest thing from your mind. This is just one reason why many nonprofits eschew the word *fundraising* in favor of *development.* Solicitation involves, simply, describing the activities of the nonprofit and asking other people to get involved. In short, all you must do is speak passionately about something you love.

Solicitation Permits

Before you approach anyone for fundraising, make sure your solicitation permit is in order. See Chapter 3 for more details.

Technique

If you have a phone, a computer, or a mailbox, you have likely received a nonprofit solicitation in the past year. Stop and think for a moment about these requests. In the past year, which organizations succeeded in convincing you to support them? Make a list.

Now, look at that list. Star the organizations that you support regularly. Think about why you support them. You are perhaps familiar with their mission — maybe so familiar that you did not even stop to read that part of their direct-mail solicitation, or you interrupted their telephone spiel to ask how much money they needed. The bottom line is, they do something you believe in, and you trust them to accomplish it. This is the sort of relationship you want to build with your repeat donors.

Look at the organizations to which you donated for the first time. Why did you donate? Think about the messages you got from each organization. How did they get through to you? What caught your attention about the organization, its mission, and its communication materials? How do you feel about the donation now? Are you still proud of it? Do you wish you could take it back? Does it seem like a waste of money in retrospect, or would you give more if you could? Do you plan to give again? What sort of communication — if any — have you received from the organization since your donation? If you have received communications, how do you think they have affected your thoughts and feelings about the organization and your donation?

As you craft your solicitation approaches, start treating yourself as a research subject. Pay attention to the appeals that catch your eye — or ear — and how they work. And when you are tempted to toss a piece of direct mail in the trash without opening it, think about why you are not interested.

- Do you not agree with or support the mission — that is, are you just not a good potential donor?

- Is the message poorly crafted? Do you think you might support the mission if it came off more professionally?

- Do the message and the mission seem reasonable, but the organization is unfamiliar? Do you simply want to know more before you decide to trust them with your donation?

- Can you not give what they are asking at the moment — is it just a problem of timing?

Now, turn the situation around, and imagine that you are doing the asking. You face the same obstacles you have just raised. How do you solve them?

- The first problem is fundamentally a problem of research. No message can be 100 percent on target, but you can increase your success rate by paying close attention to your audience. Choose good prospective donors with the same care with which you evaluate your prospective clients. Look at Chapters 6 and 8 for more tips on marketing and interacting with your community.

- The second problem is a question of how you are handling your design, writing, and marketing. Amateurism can hurt you in development efforts: it can create the impression that the organization is not coordinated or legitimate enough to use donations responsibly. Fortunately, this solution is reasonably easy: Hire a professional, or find one willing to provide services pro bono.

- The third problem is not a terrible problem to have: it is simply one of time. If you reach a donor who is interested but not convinced, then your mission and message are both on target. The donor just needs to hear about you a few more times — on average, seven, according to the conventional wisdom of direct mail — before deciding to give.

7x

- Problems of timing do not usually have anything to do with your mission, but they do give you an opportunity to be more alert to the needs of your community. Are economic circumstances making people feel pinched? Did you just happen to call in the middle of dinner? You can fix problems of timing by providing multiple opportunities and ways in which people can donate, such as e-mail, Web site, telephone, direct mail, or events.

The Thank-You

Michael Bassoff and Steve Chandler, the authors of the groundbreaking development guide *Relationshift*, say solicitation does not even involve asking people at all — it is mostly about thanking them in the right way. The right way is personal, specific, and genuine. A few examples:

- The Christian Children's Fund has a successful TV ad campaign, showing destitute third-world children that need your help. But their real success comes from the followthrough. They do not just ask you to donate. Instead, you sponsor a child — a specific child — whose photograph you receive and with whom you may correspond. You know exactly whom you are helping and how. That is a well-structured appeal: the structure of the thank-you is implicit in the request.

- A Chicago theater company maintained a "wish wall" — a bulletin board listing different operational needs on pieces of paper so that would-be donors could pick up the piece of paper and sponsor the expense. The development director noticed that, for several seasons, the same couple had always sponsored the expense of toilet paper for the lobby bathrooms. Recognizing that they had a sense of humor, he wrote them a thank-you note on a clean square of TP.

In short, this means that you never ask for a donation without providing concrete evidence of how it is helping people. Almost everyone wants some proof that they are making the world a better place — perhaps that they are becoming better people — which is why they help nonprofits. Proof that their efforts are working is the most meaningful gift you can offer them.

Effective Solicitations

Numerous sources believe that the most effective request for donations is the face-to-face solicitation, which is also the hardest for many of us to carry out. Some organizations find it easier to have solicitors work in teams of two to provide each other with moral support and to allow solicitors to respond to the individual needs of different prospects.

There are several reasons that a personal request is so effective. It is harder to ignore someone on your doorstep than to ignore a piece of mail in the box. Additionally, saying no directly to a person conjures up feelings of guilt and regret in many of us. This is not to say that your solicitations should attempt to make your prospects feel too guilty not to donate — merely that personal interaction carries with it a number of nonverbal behavioral cues that cannot be duplicated in a card or a phone call.

Effective Requests

While the face-to-face request is the most effective method, a personal letter is a close second, with a personal telephone call to follow up. After that, it is a personal phone call, with a personal letter to follow up. Are you sensing a pattern here?

ADVERTISING

The least effective way to make a request happens to be the one on which it is easy to spend the most money: advertising. People know an advertising message is general, not personal, thus they often have no problem ignoring it.

What to Say

Good solicitation recognizes not only the interpersonal relationship, but also the specific circumstances of the conversation. You might not have time for a full development pitch; attempting to deliver it might only succeed in annoying a prospective donor. But if you are trying to convince someone to make a major gift — the sort that will put his or her last name on the new wing of the hospital — the person is likely to want to invest some time in that decision, asking you exactly what the terms of the gift will be, how the money will be used, what needs it will serve, and any other questions they may have. You will need to pay attention to your goals, the donor's goals, and the aptness of the moment.

First, listen. Ask the person how he or she is doing, and pay attention to his or her response. You do not need to have a development conversation right away. Never give the impression of being a busy executive who is only talking with them for the sake of their money. Learn more about the life of the donor. In this way, you can better understand his or her motivations for giving. They may be deeply personal — for example, a donor may wish to give to commemorate the life of a sibling who died too early — and you should recognize and honor the importance of these feelings. If the prospect does indeed make a gift to honor a dead relative, mention that person's name in your thank-you note. Understand that giving to your organization allows donors to achieve some sort of personal, spiritual, or emotional well-being, and help them reach it.

HELP DONR REACH FUFLUNM

When you sense that mentioning it will not destroy the conversation, you can mention some connection between what they are talking about and your mission — perhaps a recent incident with a client, something in your current show, or a conversation with another donor. Eventually, you can simply ask, "Would you ever consider supporting our organization?"

If the person says yes, that is fantastic. They may be ready to donate right away; they may want more information. Either way, give them what they need.

If the person says no, that is an interesting learning opportunity for you. Do not let the conversation end there. Ask, "Why not?" Then listen some more. They may have some sort of misconception about the organization. If you can correct the misconception, they may be ready to donate. They may raise a legitimate objection. Perhaps they disagree with your approach to rehabilitation, or perhaps they are already on the board of an organization they perceive as competing with yours. Thanking them for this information should come easily, as they really are doing you a favor.

ENJOYED TALKING

When the conversation ends, regardless of whether you have secured a donation, you must convey the impression that you have enjoyed talking with them, that you have learned something, and that it was a valuable personal experience for you — not just a professional exchange. Follow it up the next day with a quick thank-you note or e-mail. Even if this person has not donated, they have taught you something about the way your organization is perceived, or maybe they have shared a personal experience that reminded you of your commitment to serve others. One way or another, they *have* supported you. If they gather that impression as well, they may be more inclined to give financial support in the future.

Note that this conversation is about them; your attention is on the donor. You do far more listening than talking, and you respect what they have to say. You are not pushy, and you do not plead or beg — you suggest. No one wants to be forced into making a gift. Let your donors feel generous.

[handwritten margin note: MORE LISTENING]

Solicitations and State Tax

Depending on your state, you may need to report your solicitation efforts. In some cases, your Form 990 will suffice.

What Not to Say

If the ideal solicitation is donor-focused, a terrible solicitation is the opposite: You talk endlessly about yourself and your organization, you do not let the donor get a word in edgewise, and you are out of there as soon as you receive a check. Or you might refuse to take "No" as an answer, asking repeatedly, even when the donor has stated firm reasons for his or her refusal.

The following situations are all indicative of bad solicitation:

- Anything that sends a verbal or nonverbal message of disrespect
- Anything that makes the donor feel like a walking wallet

- Anything that ignores or belittles the personal element of your interaction

How to Handle Criticism

Thank anyone who offers you criticism, and learn from it. Not only will this approach disarm all but your most hostile critics, but it will also help you refine your approach to solicitation.

Donor Relations

The relationships you cultivate with your donors and prospects must be as genuine, straightforward, and friendly as your personal friendships. Following are some tips for accomplishing that:

- **Keep relations personal from day one.** As soon as someone donates, give that person a phone call or a handwritten thank-you note. Avoid form letters in this area, especially for first-time donors.

- **Stay in touch.** Talk to your regular donors — or the donors whom you hope to cultivate as regular donors — at least once every few months. Let them know what the organization is doing. If they have given in the past, thank them for that support, and make sure they understand that present efforts are tied to those donations. A quick phone call or e-mail suffices. If you are having an event for which a mass e-mail has just gone out, follow up that announcement with a personal note — "Hope we'll see you next Friday. How are Susan and the kids?"

- **Invite donors to talk to you.** Perhaps you could have a monthly meet-and-greet at the cafe around the corner, where you can exchange ideas with people who care about the future of the organization. Or, when you thank donors for their contributions, make sure it is clear that you care about their ideas and opinions.

- **Commemorate personal milestones** — birthdays, anniversaries, births, and graduations — with a note or a card. These little gestures make an impact.

- **Be open about bad news**. If the organization is in trouble, do not try to hide that from your supporters. Among other things, hiding it could create the appearance of financial impropriety, which people tend to take personally when it involves their donations. Your donors may want to help you out of a bad time, and they may have some good ideas. Be honest about the challenges you face.

Connectors

In *The Tipping Point*, Malcolm Gladwell identifies certain people as connectors. For connectors, social relationships are natural and effortless. Connectors thrive on interaction with others, on introductions and conversations. They automatically remember, for example, that a new acquaintance likes ballet, thus when a pair of free ballet tickets comes their way, they can easily pass that gift on to the person who will appreciate it most.

Not everyone is a natural-born connector. Plenty of people are hard-core introverts who prefer to cultivate just a handful of intimate friendships. There is nothing wrong with that, but in the area of donor relations, you will fare better if you tap into your inner connector and use those tendencies to their fullest.

Donor Contact Management

Following up effectively with hundreds of donors is difficult if you do not know what you said — or what they said — the last time around. Even if your donor base comprises a small group of your friends, it may not always. And if your board is doing its job, it will not be long until the donor base includes some people you do not know. You may need some form of contact management software.

Contact management software lets you track people's contact information, the different forms of contact you have made, the messages you have delivered, and important items you have learned from them. If they have an upcoming birthday, graduation, or other milestone, a card from you can be a touching gesture. There are numerous options for contact management software. Some, such as eTapestry or The Raisers Edge®, are tailored specifically to the needs of nonprofits.

Criteria for choosing donor contact management software include:

- Price
- Integration with other systems — for example, can you feed information from online donations or newsletter sign-ups directly into the contact management database?
- Accessibility to everyone within the organization

Since donors are not your only constituency, you may want to integrate your donor contact management software with other contact management systems, such as your volunteer database. This sort of solution can be expensive — but in terms of the time and effort it saves, it may be well-worth it. Remember to talk to an organization such as TechSoup about available discounts for nonprofits.

The Worth of Relationships

There is growing awareness in the nonprofit world that relationships are your real assets: They are the way you get things done, increase donations, and reach out to more people. As you evaluate relationship management systems, you might want to look at the results of Idealware's survey, "Creating the Relationship-Centric Organization: Nonprofit CRM." Their analysis is available at **www.idealware.org/articles/relationship_centric_org_ CRM.php**.

One other note: Even if you cannot afford the integrated software right now, this does not mean you should abandon the attempt to keep track of contact information. On the contrary, it is much harder to retrieve donor information retroactively than to maintain an ongoing record, even if that record is nothing more than a simple Word document or Excel spreadsheet. And you may be able to incorporate a multi-component software system in affordable increments.

Cultivating Long-term Donors

Annual funds and grants are all well and good, but your real support comes from the people who already believe in you and your mission — your long-term donors. They are the ones who make your development efforts cost-effective because, with long-term donors, it is possible to receive substantial income with little immediate effort per gift. Creating and maintaining a relationship with a long-term donor does take considerable effort, but it is the sort of effort that becomes easier with time. As you get to know your long-term donors, these efforts may even cease to feel like work.

If you have been following the preceding advice about donor relations, you are already well on your way to creating donors who are in it for the long haul. Share your long-term plans with your donors. Get them excited and involved.

Do not make the common mistake of dismissing someone who cannot afford to give a large gift now. A $10 gift from someone who is just out of school and passionate about your cause is still a $10 gift to your mission. Recognize the gift and the passion that underlies it. Ten or fifteen years from now, that person may be in a position to give several thousand dollars to charity, and he or she will remember the organizations that have treated him or her with courtesy and respect.

Saying Thanks

No two words are more important to nonprofit work than "Thank you." You must acknowledge every contribution, gift, and service. No one likes to see his or her work go unrecognized, and nothing is more certain to turn a long-term prospect into a one-time donor than absolute silence in the wake of a donation. Get in the habit of gratitude.

Event-Based Fundraising

Event-based fundraising can be a gamble, and few organizations rely exclusively on events for their donations. Two main reasons render event-based fundraising as so risky:

1. **Attendance is unpredictable.** Even if people have RSVPed, weather, traffic, mass-transit delays, work problems, illness, and other issues can keep them away. Revenue and attendance are directly tied. To some extent, you can remedy the problem by having people pay for

tickets in advance, but if someone pays for a ticket and does not show up, you still lose what that person would have spent on your auction, raffle, cash bar, or donation jar. You also miss an opportunity to speak to that person face-to-face — a chance to strengthen his or her ties to your organization.

2. **Events are rarely cheap.** If you have the event anywhere but your facility, you will likely need to pay rent for the night. Even at a nonprofit discount, rent for some event spaces can be in the thousands. You may be able to get food donated, but donations of alcohol are tougher and sometimes come with the stipulation that you may not actually sell the donated beverages to your guests. You can set out a tip jar, of course, but you forfeit the ability to set prices for what is potentially a large source of income. If you cannot get a donation of alcohol, you will likely have to purchase it wholesale. Between rent and alcohol, you are already starting at a loss. If the event is large enough, you may also need an event planner, as planning a large event can rapidly become a full-time job. You may also have to pay a live auctioneer — a good one is a worthwhile expense if you have the auction items to justify it — and other personnel. And you may need to rent specific equipment such as a PA system, tables, and chairs.

All these up-front costs mean that it is quite possible to lose money on a fundraising event.

That said, it is also possible to make a great deal of money from a single event. But you must be well-prepared. The following are several aspects of event planning to keep in mind.

Venue

Where will you have your event? The venue can have a great influence on the event. The right venue should:

- Fit the personality of your organization

- Suit the goal of the event

- Accommodate the expected audience size — remember to find out the venue's maximum capacity so you know where to cap attendance

- Be appropriate for the planned performances

- Fit your budget

- Be accessible to your constituents

It is no surprise many organizations opt for an open house, using the organization's own facility as the event venue. This has the advantage of allowing you to show prospective donors exactly how you help people, and letting them feel as though they know your organization and its people. But few business places are designed for parties, and you must be careful that guests do not damage office equipment and furniture — or compromise the confidentiality of information.

Once you have chosen a venue, do not forget to plan the decor. This may involve further rental costs, but talk to other nonprofits about decorations they may be able to lend you. And do not waste an opportunity to display posters, brochures, and other educational materials about your organization.

Invite Your Clients

As you plan an event, you may be so focused on the people who can help you that you forget about the people whom you have helped. In fact, your clients should be your guests of honor. No one can better attest to the life-altering impact of your organization. Your clients may be the best way for you to convert prospects to donors.

Timing

When is the best time to have your event? Is it tied to a holiday? Do you want it to precede another major event, such as the roll-out of a new program? You will need to think about a number of factors — and likely make a number of compromises and sacrifices — as you pick a date. Choose a date when all your board members and staff can attend, and do not forget to consider your donors' plans. If they are all on vacation in August, then that is not going to be the best month for your big-ticket gala.

Once you have chosen a date, start counting backward to create a planning schedule. You should give yourself at least three months' lead time — perhaps six, depending on the venue you hope to reserve. Three months is the minimum time you will need to ensure that your press releases go out in time to place your event in the calendar section of local monthly publications.

Ticket Price

Setting the price for your tickets can be difficult. You need to strike the delicate balance between raising adequate funds and not alienating your constituency. Your market research may be able to help you in this respect by giving you an idea of your supporters' demographics, what they can afford, and what they will be willing to pay.

However, an event may not necessarily be exclusively for your existing group of supporters — it is also an opportunity to expand that group. Your board members should each be expected to bring a minimum number of people. Business associates of the board may be willing to pay more for the event tickets than would your other supporters.

Keep in mind that attendance is not just about income, it is also about the atmosphere. If you run a theater company, some potential donors may arrive hoping to meet some of the people whose talents they have enjoyed onstage — so it may not be a good idea to price the starving actors out of attendance. If you are worried about alienating some parts of your constituency, you might consider offering tickets on a sliding scale, or offering a discount to early responders.

Touch the Art

One of the guiding mantras of arts development efforts is "touch the art" — that is, let donors and would-be donors see what is involved in making the art they enjoy. There are numerous ways to build "touch the art" into an event:

- Have multiple artists attend and circulate among the guests
- Kick off the event with a how-to workshop in painting, mask-making, improvisational comedy performing, hand instruments playing, singing, or dancing — you can charge less for people who do not want to attend the workshop portion of the evening

- Take people backstage for a behind-the-scenes tour of the scene shop, wardrobe shop, and dressing rooms
- Have a silent auction or raffle prize be a privileged seat at a dress rehearsal of the next performance
- Have an "on-call" artist of the night, who dashes off a quick painting based on a word or idea of your guests

Even if you are not running an arts organization, do not underestimate the power of the "touch the art" principle. All it really means is that the people who are interested in your organization want to get the inside scoop on how it works. They want to talk first-hand to the survivors of abuse — maybe even help run your hotline. They want to scratch between the ears of the rescued greyhound. They want to meet the people you help. An event is a wonderful way to bring your supporters into contact with your clients.

Other Forms of Event Income

Event income does not begin and end with the cover charge. You can often double your take at the door with a well-run auction, silent auction, or raffle — or all three.

The wonderful thing about auctions and raffles is that you almost never need to purchase the prizes: They can run entirely on donations. You may need to write a brief **donation request letter**, providing your organization's name, tax ID number, proof of tax-exempt status, and event name and purpose, to prospective donors. This is easy to do, and once you have written it, you can keep using it, updating only the addressee information and the specifics of the request and the event, as necessary. Donation request letters require far less effort than your annual appeal letters; they are essentially inter-business memos that provide the executive summary of what you are doing.

Here are some prizes to look for:

- Gift certificates, gift cards, or two-for-one meals at local restaurants
- Gift baskets from wine shops or other specialty food stores
- Tickets to upcoming productions of local theater companies and performance troupes — most companies will readily give these away, as box office is not usually a major source of income
- Massages, or other treatments at local spas and salons
- Tickets or special tours to zoos, museums, planetariums, and other "experience" destinations
- One-of-a-kind items, such as autographed memorabilia, pieces of art, and handcrafted clothing and jewelry
- Big-ticket experiences (for example, a board member might donate an afternoon for the winner and three friends on his or her sailboat; Steppenwolf Theater Company once auctioned off — for a five-figure price — dinner for 12 friends, cooked by John Malkovich on his French estate)
- Sports tickets
- Classes — cooking, dance, yoga, and music are popular
- Gym memberships
- Gift cards to online stores, such as Amazon® or iTunes®
- "It" gadgets, such as MP3 players or iPhone™s
- Items valuable to your particular demographic — for instance, if you have a fundraiser full of actors, you will sell plenty of raffle tickets if you are giving away a prize of a head shot session or head shot duplication

If you are acquiring such raffle and auction prizes, be sure to read the section on in-kind donations and accounting for them in Chapter 8.

Tax Implications for Major Raffle Prizes

Report raffle prizes on form 1099G. If someone at your event wins a prize worth more than $5,000, you will need to report it on Form W-2G, which requires tax withholding. See IRS Notice 1340, "Tax-Exempt Organizations and Raffle Prizes," for more information.

You should also be aware of state gambling laws. Some fund-raising activities can run afoul of gaming requirements or expose you to additional legal liabilities or restrictions.

Now, if you have been amassing many of these donations, you will need to determine which go in the auction and which go in the raffle. A prize with an obvious face value, such as an iPhone or a gift card, is a good raffle prize. A one-of-a-kind piece that could have sentimental meaning far beyond its actual worth is a good auction prize, as people may develop passionate attachments to it.

The decision of whether to have a silent auction or a live auction largely depends on the following:

- Your audience
- Your PA system
- The availability of a good auctioneer

A good live auctioneer makes the event entertaining. He or she gets friends involved in bidding wars, catches the interplay between husband and wife, and turns it into the big drama of the evening. When people are having more fun, they are more inclined to participate — and to bid more. If you have a strong auctioneer, you may see a substantial jump in the evening's revenue. Of course, you will have to decide whether you can afford the expense of hiring an auctioneer. However, if you are working with a volunteer auctioneer from within the organization, make sure he or she can genuinely handle the duties. A weak auctioneer — someone who just wants to get it over with, who suffers from stage fright, or who mumbles everything — is worse than a silent auction. Instead of bidding, people will just be biding their time until they can get back to the fun part of the evening.

The Rock for Kids Mix Tape Event

Rock for Kids is a rarity — an organization that earns the majority of its income from events. Rock for Kids, which supports music education for underprivileged kids, grew out of unique circumstances — it was the charitable arm of concert promoters Jam Productions. At first, it was nothing more than a collection box at concerts. Then, the original fundraisers recognized that they had something unique: connections to many major celebrities of music. They began collecting autographed rock 'n' roll memorabilia and auctioning everything off at a few annual events. Attendees could purchase such rarities as a piano bench signed by Elton John.

Of course, many music fans cannot afford signed piano benches — or even the tickets to such a pricey auction. Here is where Rock for Kids displayed its thorough knowledge of its audience: it created the annual Mix Tape event. This is a silent auction, held at a Chicago live music venue, where music fans can pay a $5 cover to hang out, drink beer, listen to good music, and bid on one-of-a-kind mix CDs assembled by luminaries of music, such as Wilco's Jeff Tweedy and critic Jim DeRogatis. It is an event structured to appeal to average Janes and Joes, and to get rabid music fans

— who understand the value of music education perhaps better than anyone else — involved with the charity.

This event would not work for every organization. It works for Rock for Kids because it reflects the organization and its mission, and because it evolved from an intimate knowledge of the organization's community.

Food and Drink

If you plan to serve food and drink, you have several additional responsibilities.

You must notify the venue of your plans. They may be subject to certain health code regulations, depending on how they are zoned. They may also have rules about how and where you handle food and drink.

You must make sure you are not in violation of local liquor licensing laws. If a volunteer will be serving alcohol, you may need to make sure he or she is over 21, and he or she will need to card attendees. Serving alcohol may impose additional restrictions on how you charge admission and advertise the event. Check your local laws.

Do not forget about all the other logistics of food and drink, such as silverware, plates, glasses, and napkins. Hiring a catering company can simplify this aspect of your planning — though, of course, that makes it more expensive.

Performance

You may want to have a performance or entertainment component to the evening, such as live music, improvisational comedy, standup comedy, magic, keynote speeches or lectures, theatrical performance, or circus acts. Many artists are no stranger to the nonprofit world and will donate their performances. However, few sound engineers are willing to do that, so if you have an act that requires sound checks, expect to pay something for the guy who runs that equipment. In addition, if you are working with union artists, you may have to complete certain contracts or forms to prove that they have willingly donated their services, and if you rehearse the event, you may be required to comply with performers' union rules for rehearsals. The performers themselves are the best source of information about what restrictions bind them, but you can also call the union office about the rules and regulations that apply.

Performance can be a great way to get your guests excited. For arts organizations, it can showcase recent or upcoming work and build an audience and funding. If the performance is structured right, it can involve the attendees. What you do not want, though, is a long performance that gives your guests no time to talk and mingle. Anything that might lead to social isolation goes against the purpose of the fundraiser.

Publicity

The challenge for any fundraising event is not merely to attract attention but to attract *new* attention — to build the donor base rather than just challenge it to give at new levels. Your current donors will have an easier time convincing their friends to come if the activities are not just beneficial to your cause, but also fun.

It is essential that you come up with a hook of some sort — an angle beyond "Our Annual Fundraiser" that you can use to get media attention and that will be memorable for the invitees and their friends.

Build adequate advertising time into your schedule. Use your full arsenal of marketing tools (see Chapter 7) and remember that people must hear about the event multiple times, in multiple ways, before they are convinced to attend.

When Donors Provide Publicity

If you are having an event that features many one-of-a-kind prizes, such as an art or memorabilia auction, the artists who create these pieces should be at the event, if at all possible. Not only will your audience want to meet these special people, but the artists are likely to tell others about the event — perhaps even to brag about being included. Make it easy for them to do so. As soon as you have fliers, stickers, bookmarks, or other publicity pieces, give a stack of them to each contributing artist.

Equipment

The right equipment depends on the activities for the night. If you are renting a venue that is routinely used for gatherings of this kind, you are in luck; the venue may already have appropriate equipment and furniture. Otherwise, you may want to consider acquiring:

- A PA system for announcements and live music performance
- Tables and chairs
- Chafing dishes and coffee urns for the buffet table
- A temporary stage

And wherever you are, remember that you will need:

- A cashbox for admissions
- A bowl for raffle tickets

- The raffle tickets themselves, available at office supply stores
- Depending on the venue, a stamp or wrist bracelet for attendees
- A way of noting which guests attend and how they have heard about the venue
- Your mailing list sign-up sheet with a writing utensil
- A large donation jar, in case people just feel like giving you cash in the course of the evening — it happens. But make sure you have someone keep an eye on the jar

Depending on the activities, you may also want

- Sign-up sheets and pens for all the silent auction items
- Bidding sheets to describe auction items
- Programs for the evening — offer advertising space to your event supporters and in-kind donors in exchange for their donations

Staffing

Having an event run smoothly depends in part on having enough people to run it. You will need to position staff, board members, clients, or volunteers at various points throughout the event. Positions to remember include:

- Greeter
- Roaming raffle salesperson
- Emcee
- Bartender
- Caterer
- Explainer of silent-auction items

Invitations and Responses

You will need to have a method of tracking attendance, so that you can get accurate estimates of the amount of food and drink to provide, as well as a way to send thank-you notes to all the attendees. E-mail is by far the easiest way to manage invitations and responses, because you can feed online responses automatically into a database. However, make sure you have another way to RSVP for your constituents who either do not like e-mail or do not have access.

Who's Who

The real meat of a fundraiser is in the interpersonal relationships it helps build. Help your guests approach each other and start talking. Early in the evening, either with a performance or with the MC's style, establish a culture of interactivity.

Everyone who works for your organization — staff, board, and volunteers — must be clearly identified. Beyond that, the guests should have name tags as well. Consider color-coding your name tags. You might also want to involve a brief ice-breaker game in the distribution of name tags. For example, rather than preprint the name tags from your RSVP list, have guests fill out their own tags, using a childhood nickname, the name of a personal hero, or a favorite literary character rather than their own first name. Anything works as long as it gets people talking, asking each other questions, and laughing.

Finally, do not forget about your own availability. Easy, informal access to you is one of the prime commodities of the night. Make a point of circulating among your guests and introducing yourself to people you do not know. Collect their business cards and take notes about who they are and why they are at your event.

This comes more easily to some EDs than it does to others, but it is an essential, unavoidable part of the job. You can work in a pair with a board member, if that makes you feel more at ease.

Annual Funds

An **annual fund** is, as its name suggests, a once-a-year appeal to all your constituents — donors, clients, volunteers, and prospects — for financial contributions. Most nonprofits time their annual appeal to go out in the last quarter of the calendar year, around the holidays, when people are a) feeling generous and b) looking for year-end tax write-offs; according to Smith, Bucklin & Associates, more than 90 percent of Americans make charitable contributions at holiday time.

Annual funds tend to have multiple components: direct mail, e-mail, and telephone. As discussed in Chapter 7, on marketing, these components reinforce your message by reminding recipients to give, and reach different subgroups within your audience.

The direct mail component, called an **appeal letter**, is typically the primary part of an annual fund. An appeal letter combines effective techniques of development, direct mail, and grant writing. It must be well designed, and in the flood of holiday mail, it must stand out as personal and important. Inside the envelope, it must present a compelling case for the organization, perhaps by describing plans for the coming year and showing how the recipient can get involved. Annual appeal letters typically include:

- The letter itself, which may take the form of a holiday greeting card
- A reply form

- A reply envelope, which may or may not include return postage, depending on your budget

- A promotional postcard, pamphlet, or sticker for an upcoming program

Appeal letters often include a **premium** as well — some small, inexpensive gift in return for prospective donors' consideration. Examples of premiums are the address labels you receive from nonprofits such as Amnesty International, U.S.A.® and Easter Seals; greeting cards; bookmarks; and flat, flexible magnets.

See the sample appeal letter in the appendix.

Keep It Personal

With a large annual appeal campaign, you may want to outsource the assembly and mailing of the letters to a fulfillment house. However, there is a large incentive for keeping this work in-house, perhaps in the hands of volunteers or board members. When people associated with the organization are doing the assembly, they recognize the names they know on the mailing labels. It takes more time, but if your volunteers can include a brief, handwritten note to these recipients, your response rate will soar. Similarly, having volunteers handwrite the address labels or include notes on the envelopes greatly increases the odds that your message will be read.

Capital Campaigns

A **capital campaign** is a concerted effort to raise donations for a specific cause, such as the building of a new facility. A capital campaign may last a few months or a few years. It likely involves special marketing and branding (see Chapter 7), special naming rights, dedicated solicitation efforts, and separate budget sheets.

The principles of good development strategy and personal thanks still apply.

Grants and Grant Writing

A **grant** is a gift of money — or, occasionally, another resource, such as a work space — from a funding body to your organization.

To receive a grant, you must apply, which typically involves making a written request that works something like a proposal in the for-profit world. Some grant requests are no more than detailed letters outlining what your organization has been doing lately and how you want to use the grant. Some require pages of supporting documentation, including finance sheets and board rosters. Almost all of them will require evidence of your 501(c)(3) status.

Between grants, thank-you notes, and donor appeals, the person in charge of your development efforts needs to be a strong writer. If you decide to work with a contract grant writer, you should know that it is not legal to have 100 percent of that person's compensation be dependent on the funds he or she raises. (And a good, experienced grant writer may not be willing to work on spec.)

Government Funding

Government funding is the lifeblood of some nonprofits. At the end of Chapter 6 is a case study with an executive director whose organization's budget is 85 percent state and federal funding.

Government funds can be an excellent source of income. The amounts are often large, the grants are often repeated annually, and governments have a vested interest in the welfare of their constituents.

The major hazard of government funding is that government budgets vary dramatically. If a state government is in financial trouble, nonprofit funding will be reduced. If you have come to rely on government funding as your main source of income, your organization's fortunes will rise and fall along with your state's.

Government funding is not the place for the disorganized amateur or the absolute beginner. Individual donors may be somewhat forgiving about the startup plans that take longer than you intended, the 501(c)(3) application that has yet to come through, or the programming that keeps changing, but government funding programs are not forgiving about this sort of thing. Taxpayers must be able to trust that the money is going to organizations that will use it well.

Some government funding programs, such as the National Endowment for the Arts, include a **site visit** as part of their evaluation process. In a site visit, representatives from the program come to tour your organization's facilities. They want to see how you conduct business day to day — the way you interact with your clients, the systems you have in place, and the plans you have for using the money you have asked for. If you are still running your organization out of your living room, you are not yet ready for a site visit. But do not be discouraged. Know what government programs are out there, and build eligibility for those programs into your long-term plans.

Accountability: Following Through on Grants and Bequests

When you receive a grant or major gift, it is not just free money. Many givers attach conditions to their bequests. Donors may stipulate, for example, that you offer a new scholarship to a specific subset of students in your educational program. They may ask for naming rights for a new program or construction. When someone gives you a grant or large donation, regular follow-up communication becomes even more critical. For one thing, it raises the likelihood that this may turn into a continuing source of funding.

Granting bodies have been established to fund quite specific types of activities. Giving you money supports their mission — as long as *your* mission does not change. It is not at all unusual for a granting body to have formal rules about how you handle the grant monies and how you report your activities.

Some granting bodies will not allow you to re-apply unless you can demonstrate exactly how you used their funds last time. But — more to the point — some grants come with the requirement that you collect receipts and keep separate accounting sheets for the grant monies. Failure to do so can lead to forfeiture of the grant. You do not want to have to forfeit a grant; you also do not want to have to tell your board that you have lost a major source of funding and consequently increased their fundraising responsibilities.

When you receive a grant, there are five things you should always do immediately:

1. **Review the grant application**, in detail. What did you say in your application? What reasons did you give for requesting the funding? Has anything changed about the plans that led you to request the funding? If it has, it is your duty to communicate those changes to the granting body.

2. **Go over the grant's record-keeping requirements** with your chief financial officer or board treasurer. Designate record-keeping responsibility and duties before you have spent — or deposited — one penny of the grant.

3. **Send a personal, signed thank-you note** to the granting body.

4. **Thank everyone** within the organization who worked on the grant application. Make sure their work is recognized.

5. **Celebrate**. This is a success for your organization and its community. Do not hesitate to share good news — with an update on the Web site or even with an e-mail news-letter. The success may inspire other people to support your efforts.

In-Kind Donations

An **in-kind donation** is a donation of space, food, services, or other non-monetary goods. The following are examples of in-kind donations:

- When a grocery store provides free deli platters for your event

- When a paper company gives you ten reams of discontinued letter stock

- When a theater company gives you tickets to its newest show for you to use as a raffle prize

- When a professional offers his or her services on a volunteer basis

In-kind donations, as these examples show, can be a fantastic resource for your organization. They often represent the easiest way for another organization to support yours. And if the donating organization is a nonprofit as well, you may be able to show your gratitude with an in-kind donation to them.

Planning to Request In-Kind Donations

Some companies, such as Whole Foods and Trader Joe's, are asked for donations so regularly that they have specific in-kind donation programs. You will probably need to fill out a donation request form, keeping in mind that your request is competing with others. Do not let the standardization of the form distract you from the need to create a compelling case for your organization. Because the process is standardized, it will probably take more time. Whole Foods, for example, usually needs at least six weeks between the time you make the request and the time you receive the donation. Work such delays into your event-planning schedules.

Be sure to acknowledge in-kind donors on your donor roll along with your other donors. You may want to include them, based on the value of their gifts, among other donors of the same tier. Or you may want to create a separate section for in-kind donations. And don't forget about the thank-you note and the personal thank-you call.

Accounting for In-kind Donations

Document in-kind donations based on what you would have to pay for the good or service if it were not donated. For example, if you receive a donation of an event venue that ordinarily rents for $3,000 a night, document this as a $3,000 donation of space.

For some organizations, the value of in-kind donations can exceed the total annual budget. In-kind donations can make you appear to have a surplus that has little to do with your actual bank account. Use the rules outlined in SFAS 117 to govern your documentation of in-kind donations. Form 990 has separate fields for documenting donated cash and donated spaces and services.

In some circumstances, you can take **depreciation** on donations of long-lived assets, such as cars. A CPA or nonprofit tax specialist can help you know when these conditions apply.

236 Nonprofit Management: Everything You Need to Know

Emergency Fundraising: What Happens When Development Efforts Fall Short of Needs?

Budget shortfalls happen to every business. If you are running on a shoestring start-up budget, though, a shortfall can mean that the entire effort grinds to a halt while you scramble to scrounge up cash. Following are some steps to take in such situations:

- Talk to your long-term donors. Explain the situation.

- Talk to your board members. If they have not made their required annual contributions, now is a good time for them to do so. If they have ideas for other sources of funding, they should act on those ideas.

- Send out an e-mail appeal letter. If you are active on social media, appeal to that community, too.

- Plan a low-cost fundraising event, such as a sponsored night at a bar.

- If you have an excellent relationship with your community — if your organization is beloved in the neighborhood and in the city at large — send out a press release. Make sure the whole community knows that you are struggling. If you do enjoy strong goodwill, people will rally to help you recover.

You should already have a good sense of your budgetary priorities — which expenses you can scale back and which ones are vital to your core mission. While you raise emergency funds, try to govern the organization based on these core priorities. Prospective donors will be less inclined to help you if they see you being irresponsible with the funds you do have.

CHAPTER 9

Working with the For-Profit World

Charitable giving as a percentage of GNP has remained relatively steady over the years, although the number of charities has increased. That means more organizations are competing for the same dollars. For a new source of income, many nonprofit organizations have turned to alliances with for-profit companies. This chapter covers the different kinds of for-profit alliances, the risks and benefits involved, and how to find the right corporate alliance for your organization.

Corporate Funding

Many corporations give philanthropically. Their reasons can vary:

- Their founders might simply consider giving as part of being a corporate good citizen — as is the case with Target and numerous other companies

- The corporation needs to improve its public image because of past controversy — as is the case with the tobacco companies

- The corporation has built a brand of social awareness and uses giving to reach out to consumers who also consider themselves socially aware — as is the case with Ben & Jerry's®

- The corporation is a large entity that uses philanthropic work as a way to connect with local communities — as is the case with Northern Trust

Before you approach a corporation for funding, it is important to have a sense of why they give and the typical programs they support. Your organization may not be a good fit.

Remember, too, that corporate funding accounts for only 4 percent of most nonprofit budgets. Big corporate gifts can be tempting, but there is a great deal of competition for them. Before you spend too much time and energy pursuing corporate gifts, remember that your most significant donations are likely to come from individuals. Corporate giving gets considerable publicity — in part because of the corporations' extensive PR dollars. The publicity may or may not help your organization.

Applying for corporate funding is much like applying for any other grant. You must learn exactly what sort of information the corporation needs from you and write an application that supplies that information. You will need to state your needs clearly.

Some people opine that corporate givers are more particular than other funding bodies when they evaluate your organization's financial statements. Whether this is true likely depends on the corporation, but your financial statements should be clean enough not to give anyone pause.

Sponsorships and Licensing

Sponsorships and licensing are arrangements between nonprofits and for-profit businesses that allow for the reciprocal use of names and identities.

In a **sponsorship,** the for-profit business provides money or other resources for an event or program for your nonprofit. In return, the corporation's name and logo are displayed in the publicity for the event or program. The sponsor's name may be prominent or understated. It is still, clearly, your nonprofit's event. Examples of such arrangements include corporate logos on the T-shirts for charity races and corporate naming rights on the pavilion or mezzanine of a concert hall, which may be in exchange for continuing annual gifts rather than sponsorship of a single event.

When you enter a **licensing** agreement with a for-profit corporation, you allow the corporation to use your organization's name and logo in exchange for a royalty payment to you. This may allow the corporation to sell goods or services that are closely tied to your mission or your audience, such as gift-shop shirts, books, and trinkets. Your logo expands the pool of interested consumers, and you make money from the royalties on each sale. You must take care not to create the impression that the logo signifies your endorsement of the product. For example, if a literacy association's logo appeared on a book for young children, the licensing agreement would have to make it clear that the literacy group encouraged young children to read the book — but not that it was specifically recommending the book as a teaching tool.

Mission and Corporate Partnership

Before entering any partnership with a for-profit company, make sure there is a logical overlap between your missions or communities. You do not want your association with the company to alienate any of your donors or clients. For example, a group that champions free speech would not want to enter a partnership with a video-rental company that had recently been censoring movies.

Cause-Related Marketing

In **cause-related marketing**, a for-profit business embarks on a specific marketing initiative that is tied to the nonprofit's mission. For example, a homebuilder might announce that for every new home purchased in January, it will give $1,000 to Habitat for Humanity. Carson's, a department store in Chicago, holds an annual Goodwill Sale, in which customers receive discounts on pricey goods if they bring clothing donations for Goodwill to the store.

As these examples show, there is usually some overlap between the cause — the nonprofit's mission — and the product or service the corporation is trying to sell, but not always. A corporation trying to gain ground with female consumers might start a cause-related marketing program that benefits a domestic violence shelter or a feminist organization, as is the case with Playboy®, which gives generously to the National Organization for Women and Emily's List. A savvy development director keeps an eye on local corporate issues — such as a prominent discrimination lawsuit or an executive with a possible ethical lapse — that might leave a business groping for ways to reconnect with a key demographic. If that demographic is at all tied to your organization's community, your development director can then approach the corporation and propose a cause-related marketing initiative. However, if the corporation is indeed attempting to rebound from a scandal, you must be careful that your organization does not become tainted by association.

Another consideration of cause-related marketing is that the marketing must clearly state what the benefits to the nonprofit will be. Consumers want to know exactly how their purchase is helping. "A portion of the proceeds from this sale" is not specific enough, according to the Better Business Bureau Wise Giving Alliance. Consumers who buy the product and later discover that only a small percentage of their money went to the nonprofit may end up feeling betrayed by both the corporation and the nonprofit.

Operational Relationships

In an **operational relationship**, the nonprofit actually provides goods and services to the for-profit company. Such arrangements are typical of training programs, rehabilitation programs with job training, and the like. They allow the for-profit business to satisfy a business need at the same time that it supports a philanthropic cause, and they allow the nonprofit to gain visibility and provide a tangible educational and financial benefit to the clients who work in the program.

In a **joint venture**, a nonprofit and a for-profit corporation embark together on a new initiative, which may or may not be treated as a new entity. The IRS requires the joint venture to be charitable. The joint venture can give you access to all the resources of a major corporation. At the same time, you must make sure that it allows you to continue carrying out your core mission.

Choosing a Corporate Partner

You must know what you hope to accomplish before you enter a corporate partnership. You will need to make sure your mission has clear, reasonable relevance to what the for-profit business does. The logic of the arrangement should probably be clear enough to explain in a brief marketing message, such as a subway poster or a 30-second ad. You will also need to conduct due diligence on the corporation to ensure that its past does not contain any controversies that would reflect poorly on you, and that its current behavior is consistent with the image you want to project.

Start small, with a single event sponsorship. Corporate alliances can involve considerable time, money, and effort, and you do not want to discover halfway through that your missions are not at all compatible.

Make sure you have an actual business plan for the corporate alliance, detailing the initiative, the people and resources involved, the products and services to be offered, a market analysis, the financial assumptions, the standards you will use to measure success, the possible risks, the things you do not know, and the way you will carry out the work.

Risks and Benefits of Corporate Alliances

We have already discussed some of the hazards of corporate alliances. The corporation's efforts may alienate your community, or the corporation may become embroiled in a scandal that reflects badly on all its associations. You will also need to adjust for the simple fact that you are working with a corporation, not another nonprofit. It exists to make money. You will be interacting with executives whose goals and assumptions are manifestly different from yours. There may be difficulties communicating about things that you think ought to be taken for granted. And because you are dealing with two different organizations with different agendas, you will need to be especially alert about mission creep.

The benefits of a corporate alliance can be wide-ranging. Corporations have larger marketing budgets than do many nonprofits, so an alliance can be a good way to raise your profile in the community without depleting your budget. Some corporations inspire immense customer loyalty, and customers may become loyal to your organization by default. If you work carefully, you may even be able to retain them as long-term donors. In the case of operational relationships and joint ventures, the alliance may allow you to serve clients in ways you simply would not be able to afford otherwise.

CASE STUDY: I.C. STARS
(INNER-CITY COMPUTER STARS)

Mission: i.c.stars provides opportunities for inner-city young adults to harness the strength of business for social and economic leadership. By integrating business training and leadership development, i.c.stars is shaping the next generation of community leaders.

Sandee Kastrul is president and cofounder of i.c.stars, which she has led for ten years. She has been in the nonprofit sector for 19 years. She works with a staff of ten people and a board of 30 people that meets quarterly. A volunteer base of 700 puts in 2,000 hours of labor annually. Kastrul says the board is neither a working board nor a giving board, but a "relationship board" — the board is responsible for bringing relationships to the table.

The i.c.stars organization is supported by foundation grants, corporate sponsorships, events, and individuals' contributions. The organization actively engages patrons as volunteers and members of the i.c.stars community of more than 11,000 stakeholders in Chicago. The organization's leadership mission and vision "attracts a very hands-on set of supporters who enjoy providing direction and seeing an organization respond to that direction very quickly," says Kastrul. "We are also fortunate to attract an entrepreneurial set of supporters who are helping us in the journey to identify and manage self-sustaining forms of income." The organization does not take government funding. This is an intentional strategy to position the organization as an opportunity, not a charity. It means that "investors" from the business and IT community help i.c.stars to train community members in relevant skills. The business and social communities both benefit when companies can hire the next generation of technology leaders from local talent.

Kastrul says: "[Our greatest challenges are] growth and scaling our current program and service offerings to reach our vision of 1,000 community leaders by 2020.

How do we scale the resources (trainers, recruits, funding, jobs) and the

CASE STUDY: I.C. STARS
(INNER-CITY COMPUTER STARS)

training model to support 120 enrollees per year within Chicago?

How do we create an organization capable of enrolling 120 participants per year?

How do we create a process to objectively measure the development of Community Leaders and the impact of the opportunities made?

What is the best operating structure to expand the model geographically?

Can i.c.stars expand beyond IT skills to other functional areas of skill development, and how does leadership curriculum adapt to localized cultural nuances and specific challenges?

What parts of the organizational design are replicated in each locality?

"[A personal challenge is] keeping up with the industry. I am an educator at the heart, and I live in a world of technology and innovation. While I enjoy the challenge of change and teach transformation, balancing the business side of 'overstanding' the technology industry to develop partnerships with businesses and IT leaders, the rate of change can be exhausting. The culture of our business is to add value to all of our constituents, our participants, our corporate partners, and our community clients. I cope with these challenges by teaching through transparency. Our participants know there is no place I would rather be than with them, so they help to own the perceptions of the organization and are responsible for building our network. In essence, it's their company, and I keep the lights on. To cope with the ambiguity of change, I teach change and transformation, and it grounds me.

"Make opportunities for your funders. Create win-win partnerships that truly add value to all involved. Figure out your niche in the community sector, as well as the sector you want to receive funding from. Always ask yourself what's in it for them. Finally, create a ritual that energizes you. Take good care of yourself, and then take good care of your organization."

CHAPTER 10
Budgeting and Accounting

This chapter covers the fundamentals of what is, for many nonprofit founders, the most daunting aspect of running a business: accounting and budgeting. Start-up nonprofits may need nothing more than a simple checking account, but this chapter can serve as a primer on what the future may have in store. Grant writers may also wish to look at this chapter to get an idea of the financial information that many funding bodies will request. Finally, your CFO or board treasurer can read this chapter to learn about ways to handle the organization's financial records.

Bookkeeping

Bookkeeping is the documentation of the organization's financial affairs, involving tracking income and expenses. It is a question of keeping records and verifying their accuracy. Many software tools can help you with bookkeeping.

Accounting

Accounting refers to the set of rules and systems that govern financial transactions.

Financial accounting is where strategy enters the picture, in which you are asked not merely to calculate, but also to set policies and choose directions that support the organization's plans. Financial accounting is often important to people outside the organization, as well as those inside. A prospective funder may be interested in your financial accounting sheets as an indicator of future plans, relevance of spending to the mission, and efficiency.

Managerial accounting, by contrast, is what goes on within the organization, sometimes within individual departments. The ED needs this information, as does the CFO. But it may not need to go beyond the organization's walls.

Cash Basis Versus Accrual Basis

The **cash basis** of accounting deals with money you currently have on hand. The **accrual basis** deals with money you can reasonably expect to receive, such as donations promised but not yet given, and grants awarded.

Each method has its pros and cons. Operating on a cash basis can keep you in the black, but it can also severely limit your activities. It may give you an unrealistically low idea of what your actual budget is. It may not provide any way to account for future obligatory expenses, such as programming you must implement as a condition of a grant. On the other hand, operating by accrual can be dangerous if you fall into a pattern of spending money you do not actually have.

For external financial reporting, you must use the accrual basis, which is widely considered to be more accurate.

Cash Flow

Cash flow is the movement of money into the organization from all sources, including donations, grants, and investments. You or your CFO should know exactly how this works. You will need to be able to document your cash flow for potential donors.

Accounts Payable and Receivable

Accounts payable are the funds that you owe.

Accounts receivable are the funds you are due to receive. Promised donations fall into this category and must be documented on financial statements as "grants and pledges receivable."

Assets and Liabilities

An **asset** is an entry in the positive column — a source of income or an object of value. Assets include donations, grants, equipment, real estate, and other possessions.

A **liability** is an entry in the negative column — a cost or a source of expense. Liabilities include employee payroll and benefits, programming costs, and rent and utilities.

Calculate **net assets** as the difference between assets and liabilities. In a for-profit company, this difference is called "equity." On your balance sheet, your assets should always be equal to the sum of your liabilities and your net assets. $A = L + NA$ (OE) $A L O E$

Liquid and Illiquid Assets

Liquid assets are in the form of cash or other monetary balances — that is, they may easily flow. **Illiquid assets** are material assets. To be converted to a liquid asset, a material asset must be sold. The money you receive for it is the liquid asset.

Depreciation

Depreciation is the gradual loss of value of a material asset, such as a car or a computer. You treat this as an expense on your financial statements, even though you are not paying out any money.

Expenses, Overhead, and Support Services

Expenses are the money that leaves the organization. Program expenses are what you spend to execute your mission. For example, program expenses could include the cost of your outreach program and the salaries of the employees who are working in that program.

Operational expenses refer to the inevitable costs of doing business. **Overhead** is the cost of administration and fundraising. These are often considered support services because they support the mission but do not directly affect it. The cost of a development campaign would go in this category, as would the development director's salary.

Operating Income

Fees

For membership organizations, member **fees** can be a steady, relatively predictable source of income.

Gifts

Private **gifts** — donations — are the major source of income for most nonprofits.

Operational Revenue

Operational revenue is the blanket term for all other sources of income. Among other things, it includes grants, income from fundraising events, and income from any sales of inventory.

"HYBRID VIGOR"

Diversifying Revenue Sources

In biology, hybrid vigor is the principle that hybrid plants and animals — the mutts — are often better equipped to survive than are their pure-bred counterparts. Because the hybrids have greater genetic diversity, they are less susceptible to genetic disease.

The principle of hybrid vigor applies to business income as well. The more sources you have, the less your income is susceptible to problems. Think of a nonprofit clinic that gets 50 percent of its funding from a state health agency. When that agency is shuttered by a budget-slashing governor, it is a calamity for the clinic. By contrast, a clinic that got 10 percent of its funding from that agency would certainly take a hit, but it would likely be able to make up the amount from other sources without unreasonable effort — possibly even without imposing austerity measures such as pay cuts or programming freezes. Likewise, if your organization has any sources of investment income, such as endowments or retirement funds, you must take care to ensure that they are invested in a wide variety of corporations in multiple industries, with different levels of risk.

A sound development strategy seeks not only to develop long-term relations with repeat donors, but also to increase the number of those donors. Make sure your financial strategy addresses growth — not merely in amounts, but in the number of sources.

Operating Reserves

An operating reserve can act something like a savings account or a "rainy-day fund." You can fall back on it in times of need, but it should not be a part of your day-to-day cash flow. Having a healthy operating reserve may be a part of your risk management strategy (see Chapter 11). You may have it invested in a conservative, secure vehicle, such as a certificate of deposit (CD).

If your operating reserves grow, your board may decide to convert some of the money into an endowment.)

Restricted and Unrestricted Funds

A **restricted fund** is income that carries some limitations as to how you may spend it. Examples of restricted funds include a major donation that the donor specified was intended to help a specific program or a grant that you must use on your operating budget.

An **unrestricted fund** can be spent as you see fit.

Endowments

An **endowment** is an investment designed to be a perpetual source of income for your nonprofit. The investment is structured so that annual investment growth always exceeds the amount of income the organization receives and spends. Universities use endowments, for example, to provide scholarships; if a donor endows a fellowship, the university creates such an investment structure to ensure that it will be able to award the fellowship repeatedly, rather than to a single student.

Endowments and Investment Risk

Because they are investments, endowments are not 100-percent-guaranteed sources of income. Many universities have lost catastrophic percentages of their endowments in the financial crisis of 2008–2009. Good investment planners will balance your investment to provide a stable combination of growth and security, but no one can prevent a major market collapse, or entirely avoid its consequences.

A **board-designated endowment**, as its name implies, is created by the board, usually from operating reserves. Once the money leaves the operating reserves and enters the endowment, it is a long-term investment. The board may no longer be willing to use this money to deal with short-term financial problems. The responsible creation of an endowment involves leaving adequate resources in the operational reserves.

A **permanent or pure endowment** is created by a donor. The previous example of a university fellowship is a good one here as well. Permanent endowments are restricted funds. The board has no ability to halt the investment, redirect its income, or rename the fellowship. Changing these aspects of the endowment may involve getting permission in a court of law, or working with the donor or his or her estate.

Financial Statements

Balance Sheet

The **balance sheet** shows your organization's finances at a given moment. Remember that the assets should always be equal to the sum of net assets and liabilities.

Statement of Activities

A **statement of activities** shows your organizational finances over a period of time; it is the equivalent of a for-profit profit and loss (P&L) statement. A statement of activities goes into some detail, explaining expenses and revenues by category and providing numbers for each category.

Charity Evaluations

Maintaining a good financial statement is not just a matter of legal compliance; it can actually help the organization get donations. Some watchdog organizations use nonprofits' statements of activities to judge whether the nonprofit is being reasonably well-run, and is therefore a good place for would-be donors to give their money. Watchdog groups look at ratios between what you receive from donors and what you spend on programs; between what you spend on programs and what you spend on development; between the amount you spend on overhead and the total budget; and between your reserves and your total budget. A vague or careless statement of activities will not make a good case for your organization.

Statement of Cash Flows

A **statement of cash flows** breaks down your operational income by source. It should include an entry for accounts receivable to document the cash you are due to receive as well as what you have actually received.

Statement of Functional Expenses

A **statement of functional expenses** examines the ways you spend your money. It breaks your expenses down by category — operational expenses and support services, as opposed to expenses directly related to your program — and then further divides them into subcategories, such as employee compensation, legal fees, postage, utilities, and professional dues.

Accounting for Donated Time

You must account differently for **mission-related volunteer work** — the standard activity of your volunteers, such as stocking the shelves at the soup kitchen — and **pro bono services** — donated services from a lawyer, designer, or other professional. Only pro bono services may be documented as revenue on your financial statement of activities. However, you may still wish to calculate the value of your volunteers' time. See Chapter 13 for more information on estimating the worth of this time and ways to use these estimates.

Measuring Your Organization's Financial Health

Ratios and Other Standards of Performance

Opinions differ on what exactly constitutes sound performance, and ratios will not remain perfectly consistent from year to year. Look at the standards of the *Nonprofit Good Practice Guide*, as well as of the Better Business Bureau® Wise Giving Alliance®, Charity Navigator, and other watchdog groups, to get a sense of what sound financial performance means.

Because nonprofits' operations can vary so dramatically by scale, many measures of financial soundness depend on ratios — measuring an organization's spending in certain areas in proportion to other elements of its budget. Among other measures, you need to calculate:

- The ratio between development expenses and development income. On average, what does it cost you to raise a dollar from a private donor? How efficient are your efforts?

- The ratio between development income and program spending. This can help gauge your donors' commitment to your mission.

- The ratio between development expenses and total budget. This can gauge whether your priorities are sound — that is, it ensures that you are not funneling all your income back to further development efforts.

- The ratio between overhead expenses and total budget. This measures your operational efficiency.

- The ratio between the operating reserves and other assets and the operating budget. This helps measure your ability to weather a crisis, but very large reserves may raise questions about whether you are truly operating as a nonprofit.

Profitability, Liquidity, Asset management, and Solvency

Profitability looks at the relationship between assets and liabilities. If the liabilities exceed the assets, you are operating at a loss.

Liquidity is, as its name suggests, tied to cash flow. It refers to how well the organization can deal with fluctuations in cash flow.

Asset management refers to how you handle your equipment, investments, inventory, buildings, and other assets. It involves not just maintenance — preventing unnecessary expenses and losses — but also optimizing use — for example, figuring out that a room could be rented out, in off hours, for an extra source of income.

Solvency is the organization's financial health. A solvent organization has the resources to continue operations. An insolvent organization does not.

FASB Standards

FASB stands for Financial Accounting Standards Board, an entity created by the professional association of CPAs to develop and promote responsible accounting practices. The FASB has developed specific recommendations for nonprofit accounting practices, including ways of documenting net assets, pledges receivable, and restricted funds. Adherence to these standards can be another measure of your organization's financial health and responsibility.

Audits

An audit may not be a sign that the IRS suspects malfeasance; sometimes an audit is a condition of receiving a large government grant. If your books are already up to FASB standards, you will fare better.

Transparency

Transparency refers to the accessibility and availability of an organization's financial records, and it is an important measure of an organization's health. It is common for people to assume that an organization with confusing or unavailable records has something to hide.

Form 990 and Annual Reports

A **Form 990** or Form 990-EZ is the federal form you use to report your finances to the IRS. As a nonprofit, you are not typically liable to pay income taxes, but because of this, the IRS is on the lookout for for-profit initiatives that masquerade as nonprofits in order to evade taxes. You will be subject to penalties and fees if you do not file, or if you file late. You must also keep your Form 990 on file; it is a public document, and members of the public

For-profit tax evasion

must be able to examine it if they want. This allows potential do-nors to make sure your organization is healthy, for example.

You will also need to file an **annual report**, a brief description of your activities with a listing of the names of the officers and the board members, with your state. Failing to file an annual report can cause you to be listed as in poor standing with the state's at-torney general, a status that may scare off potential donors and board members. Getting the organization out of poor standing may involve not only filing the delinquent report, but also pay-ing a fine.

Budgeting

Budgeting should take into consideration not just the amounts of money you expect to receive and spend, but also the way you want employees to behave with it. The terms you choose, and the way you discuss your budget, can help you create a culture of fiscal responsibility.

Operating Budgets, Capital Budgets, and Cash Budgets

An **operating budget** deals with organizational expenses and revenues. A **capital budget** tracks whether you are buying or sell-ing your physical assets. A **cash budget** tracks cash flow.

Cost Centers and Profit Centers

One approach to budgeting views different divisions of the non-profit as either **cost centers** or **profit centers** based on whether the division largely sends money out (programming) or brings money in (development). The reasoning behind this approach is that it gives division heads a reason to think independently with their division, working to reduce costs, raise profits, and try new initiatives. Naturally, this means that less control lies with the CFO.

Controllable and Uncontrollable Expenses

All budgets have some expenses that vary and some that remain fixed. Fixed expenses are easy to budget for because they do not change. They include costs such as rent and licensing.

Controllable expenses are expenses over which you have some discretion. For example, you can decide how much the organization spends on coffee. You can make payroll and benefits controllable expenses in the way you set compensation and benefits policies. However, beware of controllable expenses that masquerade as uncontrollable expenses, such as heavy employee overtime hours that make the payroll budget spiral out of control. You can control this expense by requiring a manager's written approval for all overtime past a certain threshold.

Uncontrollable expenses are the ones you truly cannot control, such as what it cost to pay the plumber on the day you discovered your bathroom was not adequate for 24 volunteers. For a department manager, some overhead costs — such as rent and utilities — also count as uncontrollable expenses because, even though they are tied to the function of the department, the department manager has no discretion over them.

Departmental Accountability

If you have multiple departments, each department should be responsible for its own budget. Among other things, this gives department heads an incentive to spend responsibly and look for savings opportunities. You should establish fiscal responsibility practices in writing.

Annual and Monthly Budgets

In most cases, departments should have both annual and monthly budgets. Annual budgets provide an important overall picture of financial health and strategy, while monthly budgets are more detailed and offer early warnings if you seem to be going off track. A monthly budget should show not just the amount spent that month but the year-to-date (YTD) expenditure in that category. It should also have a column showing the amount allocated to that category for the year.

Surplus and Deficit

A **surplus** occurs when you have more money than planned. A **deficit** occurs when you have less money than planned. You may want to put surpluses into your operating reserves so that you can use them to help you get through times of deficit.

Fiscal Years

The **fiscal year** is the 12-month period you treat as a year for your budget calculations. It may or may not coincide with the calendar year. Schools may want to have a fiscal year that corresponds with the school year, while arts organizations may want one that corresponds with the theater season.

If your fiscal year is the same as the calendar year, your Form 990 is due by May 15. If your fiscal year is different, you must turn in your Form 990 by the 15th day of the fifth month after your fiscal year ends.

CASE STUDY: BR. DAVID DARST CENTER FOR JUSTICE & PEACE, SPIRITUALITY & EDUCATION

Director Melinda J. Rueden says: "The Darst Center faces a number ofchallenges, with funding and visibility as the primary challenges. The Darst Center's mission is unique in that it is not one, specifically, of direct service, nor is it clearly social change. As a result, identifying the appropriate funding sources has been challenging. In addition, the Center's work primarily with non-local groups has limited the visibility generated in the local community.

"Day-to-day challenges most often relate to a limited staff capacity, relying on the capacity of only three staff people to fulfill the responsibilities of programs, administration, development, facility maintenance and housekeeping, public relations, IT ...

"I stepped into the position of Executive Director for the Darst Center because there was no other title available — there was only one staff person. Experienced in program development, I was able to enhance the Center's programs, but I was ill-equipped for all else that falls under the Executive Director's job description. In order to fulfill these responsibilities, I sought out every free, or nearly free, professional development opportunity I could find. In addition, I connected with another not-for-profit director so as to learn from her tutelage."

What advice would Rueden give to someone just starting out in the non-profit world? "I would encourage them to take advantage of the wealth of experience and resources available to them in fellow not-for-profit professionals. Ask the questions, admit the ignorance, and take notes!"

CHAPTER 11

Leadership and Management Strategies

Many people come to the not-for-profit world simply because they want to make a difference in the lives of others. Few of them realize at first that nonprofit work demands the same leadership and strategy expected of successful managers in the for-profit world. But the good news is that these skills can be learned. This chapter covers several different approaches to leadership, as well as the questions a nonprofit leader must constantly ask to stay in touch with his or her organization.

Being an Effective Leader

There are plenty of different leadership styles, so do not try to assume one that feels incongruous with your personality. It would be ridiculous for a quiet intellectual like Bill Gates to adopt the brash, boisterous style of Richard Branson, but both of them have built successful companies. Some leaders, like Gandhi, accomplish great things by setting a shining example and articulating a moral cause quietly and with dignity. Some, like the revolutionary theater director Peter Brook, succeed by visionary splashes of brilliance. Some, like Betty Friedan, so deeply understand the problems and motivations of their communities that they know how to tap into great groundswells of power. Think about the leaders you admire, but also think about the traits you like most in yourself — the qualities that have attracted friends, and the qualities you would be loath to sacrifice for the sake of your organization. Remember those qualities, and lead honestly.

To lead well, you must know what you want to accomplish. That means taking the time to make a plan. In some decisions, you will have no choice but to make the rules as you go, but if you want people to join you for the long haul, you must provide some greater sense of security and reliability. Work with your board to plan long-term goals. Ask questions about what you do not understand; if other people have questions later, you will probably be the person they ask, and it will be much easier for them to trust you if you know what you are talking about.

Leading people well means understanding their motivations. You should know the things that people enjoy about their work and the things that they do not like; then, work to increase the good and reduce the bad.

Several studies indicate, for example, that pay is not the main motivation for people who seek work at nonprofits. Nonprofit employees are more likely to want responsibility, work that feels socially and morally sound, a sense of personal growth, and the knowledge that they are making their community better. That does not mean you can get away with paying trained professionals minimum wage, but it does mean that, as a good nonprofit leader, you should look for ways to keep employees in touch with your mission. Make sure everyone feels involved, and make sure everyone hears about it when you receive proof that your organization has changed a life.

By the same token, think about the things that make a workplace unpleasant, such as office politics, annoying co-workers, inadequate equipment, arbitrary policies, poor or unreliable administration, or a disrespectful boss. You can probably come up with a few others if you think about the worst job you have ever had. Work to establish an **organizational culture** (see Chapter 12) that prevents most interpersonal problems before they start. Work to create fair policies and to enforce them fairly. If an employee seems dissatisfied or disengaged, it is your job to find out why and to correct the problem.

You should understand that what you need and want will influence the way you interact with others. Be careful not to assume too much. Your motivations may not be the same as those of your employees, and you must be fair-minded in dealing with someone whose motivations are different from yours. Do not decide that their motivations are inferior to yours. What they want is based on their life, just as what you want is based on yours. Try to match people's wants and needs to their duties.

A good leader clearly establishes what is expected of the organization and everyone in it. Work with employees and board members to set personal goals that support the mission and programs. Make sure people continue to enjoy their work and find new challenges and personal fulfillment. Help everyone see how their actions affect the organization. Give people a clear sense of their own importance, and acknowledge their contributions with appropriate rewards.

Working with Consultants

A consultant can provide information and help you with decisions that you may find difficult. Consultants can conduct research — including employee and constituent surveys — to answer your questions. They may also be able to assist with planning, as well as developing and meeting goals. They can help with communication materials, development, outreach programs, accounting, and PR. And for all that, they charge a great deal of money. Before you decide to work with a consultant, it is a good idea to do your homework:

- Know what you want from the relationship
- Get recommendations from other nonprofit EDs about consultants who have offered them valuable help
- Make sure you have exhausted the other resources at your disposal, including board members and volunteers who may have significant business management expertise; community information resources, such as the Donors Forum or the *Nonprofit Good Practice Guide*; and charitable nonprofit consultation services, such as the Executive Service Corps

Your ED Support Group

Having a good ED support group (see Chapter 1) can often take the place of having a consultant, or at least help you emerge into the consulting relationship armed with plenty of information. You and the consultant can both save time — and you can save money — if the consultant does not need to spend time educating you.

Choosing a consultant ought to involve many criteria, including:

- Your reasons for wanting one
- Price — know your budget and the consultant's rates
- The consultant's experience, particularly with nonprofits
- Referrals
- The consultant's background, credentials, and training

Sometimes — especially in new organizations — the expense of hiring a consultant means that you must postpone adding another employee. If that is the case, you must weigh which services you need more.

With a consultant, as in any professional relationship, do not be afraid to speak up if you are not receiving the services or seeing the results you expected.

SWOT Analysis

A **SWOT analysis** is an honest evaluation of the strengths, weaknesses, opportunities, and threats inherent in a given situation. You can use this acronym to make sure you have given adequate consideration to the pros and cons of a decision. SWOT analyses can help you perform spot-checks on the organization itself or judge the wisdom of embarking on a new program.

Of course, no tool will actually make the decision for you. Part of being a leader is choosing. Sometimes you will be wrong. Learn from these mistakes as much as you can. Talk to board members and to your mentor, and learn from their mistakes, too. You cannot hope never to make mistakes, but you can try to make only new ones.

Making and Revising the Five-Year Plan

Where do you want the organization to be in five years? Where do you think you *should* be? Where do you think you *will* be? At any given moment, you should be able to answer those three questions. Not only with the answers help you budget, prioritize programming, and hire strategically, but you will find that it is virtually impossible to ask for funding — especially grants — if you cannot articulate how you will be using that money in the long-term.

To make a five-year plan, involve the board and the other managers — everyone who has a major stake in the future of the organization. Together, ask plenty of questions, and try to come to consensus on the answers.

Start with the mission. What actions must you take to carry out the mission in the next year? Ask the same question about the next two, three, four, and five years. How would you like to see the mission expand? Are you doing anything right now that you think the organization might eventually outgrow? Talk about these plans and ideas. They will not overlap exactly, and that is important. Hash out the differences, and set priorities.

Next, look at your community. How are you serving them now? How do you want to serve them in the future? Can you assign numbers to these goals? Be as specific as possible, and make sure you include a way to measure the results. For example, a homeless shelter might currently have 40 beds. They might set the goal of opening a second 40-bed facility in 5 years, and adding a job-training program and soup kitchen by year 3. For the job program, they might set a goal of 100 trainees; for the soup kitchen, they might decide to serve 250 meals a week. An arts organization might know that it currently has 500 dedicated audience members; it might set the goal of having an audience of 1,000, as measured by repeat attendance.

Now that you have a specific idea of how you want to serve the community and how you are going to prioritize those goals, look at the resources you will need to achieve those goals. Do not just think about money — think about the number of volunteers you will need, whether you will want additional board members, and whether you will need additional equipment or facilities. You can set numeric goals for these resources too. (This part of the process should feed into your development strategy. See Chapter 8.)

Think about the risks and complications that could keep this plan from happening. Think about financial risks as well as obstacles, such as zoning and licensing. Think about possible staffing problems or technical difficulties, and think about ways around these problems.

Now, write your five-year plan as a **business plan.** In writing, set down the step-by-step process that will need to take place in order for you to reach your goals. Include the numbers and the measurements you will use to monitor your progress. Include a contingency plan you can put into place if things do not go as expected. Include all the financial assumptions you are using to guide these decisions. Finally, write an executive summary so you can easily present this plan to potential donors and partners.

Be prepared for your plans to change. Once a year, you and the board should sit down with the five-year plan. Compare the dream to the reality. Look at what worked and what did not, and think about what you can learn from the things that did not work. Project another year into the future.

Finding the Right Management Team

There is no one-size-fits-all solution to management. The people whom you need in charge will change depending on what you are trying to accomplish and the number of people involved in the efforts. The people who are right for those tasks will differ depending on your organization, mission, working style, and goals.

The **executive director (ED)**, or chief executive officer (CEO), is in charge of the organization as a whole. He or she works with the board to set strategies and make plans for carrying out the mission. The executive director is often the organization's first paid employee. Many nonprofits go for years with no one but the executive director, the board, and a team of committed volunteers. In those cases, the executive director does a bit of everything, including development, outreach, IT, and financial strategy.

A **development director (DD)** will probably be the first manager you hire after an executive director because without a development director, you likely will not have the budget to hire anyone else. The DD solicits donations, manages donor relations, researches and applies for grants, and helps the organization gain the funding to carry out its mission. Many organizations expect the development director to bring in an amount of money that is a multiple of his or her salary; three times salary is a fairly common rule of thumb, although it may change depending on the DD's tenure and the organization's growth. You may also want to consider extenuating circumstances. Many organizations are seeing their development income drop, through no fault of the DD.

A **human resources (HR) manager** handles issues of personnel, such as hiring, firing, training, employee grievances, workplace policies, and sometimes payroll and benefits administration.

An **information technology (IT) manager**, or chief information officer (CIO), helps you establish the technological infrastructure that you need to accomplish your mission. This can involve working with your marketing team to establish your online presence, managing the server that provides you with Internet service and data storage, making buying decisions about software and hardware based on your needs, and staying alert to new technological developments that can help you serve your clients better or reach them in new ways. If you have done careful recruiting, you may have a board member who can serve this function for a long time. When an organization reaches a certain number of employees, though, it probably needs a dedicated, full-time IT manager. You will have to be the judge of when that moment happens.

A **chief financial officer (CFO)** handles the organization's book-keeping and taxes and works with the ED and the DD to set a financial strategy that will support the mission and enable the organization to carry out its plans. The CFO ought to set and enforce the organization's fiscal policies, such as requiring board approval for expenditures over a certain amount, and may keep an eye on individual project budgets as well as the overall organizational budget. This is another function that can often be served by a board member, even the board treasurer.

Some organizations may need a **director of client services**. This should be someone with a strong understanding of the actual day-to-day interactions with your clients. In a health care organization, for example, this role should be filled with someone with clinical experience. This person helps you ensure you are continuing to meet the community's needs in the most effective way. He or she can report problems with programs and suggest new approaches. He or she may also be the person who helps you conduct market research.

Depending on your organization's size and scope, you may want to hire a **marketing director**. This person should work closely with the DD, the ED, the IT manager, and the director of client services to find the best way to deliver your messages and connect with your community. The marketing director creates a marketing strategy that is fully integrated with your development, finance, HR, and information strategies, as well as with your goals for the organization. You may be able to survive for quite a long time without a full-time marketing director — as long as you have a freelancer, consultant, or board member to handle strategic marketing.

In an arts organization, you may also have an **artistic director**, a **managing director**, a **producing director**, and a **technical director**. Sometimes these directors' functions are similar to what we have already discussed for the ED. Sometimes the jobs are quite different, with the ED handling the business side of things and the artistic director handling the art. The producing director may have responsibilities similar to a producer's — securing funding for specific projects — or may leave that work entirely to the DD and focus instead on managing productions. Again, you will need to strike the right balance for your organization — but you must ensure that every task is completed.

In selecting managers, look for people who are passionately committed to the mission but do not always agree with you. Do not seek out conflict, but do not hire "yes-men." It is important to include different points of view and to work with people who are not afraid to defend their beliefs.

Risk Management

In any business, some elements are left to chance. You cannot avoid risk entirely. You do not know exactly how the stock market will behave — you do not know how your endowment will fare this year, or whether your pension fund will be healthy in October. You do not know exactly how well the next development initiative will succeed or how many guests you will have at the annual fundraising event.

A sound risk-management policy involves understanding the risks of any enterprise before you embark on it, taking appropriate measures to minimize the risks within your control, and having a backup plan that can help you if the worst-case scenario comes true. Risk management will be an element of any sound five-year plan, and you should consider risk management for event planning, marketing initiatives, and new programs, as well as early hiring decisions. Work with your board and your CFO to develop some options. If you have a development director, involve him or her in your risk management planning as well: the development director will usually be the person who has to put in the most work of making up budget shortfalls, but he or she may also have some unusual ideas about where you can find extra income.

Many organizations — for-profit and nonprofit — are seeing their worst-case scenarios come true. Pay attention to these news stories; look in particular at the ways organizations succeed despite major setbacks. There are many risk-management lessons in the credit crisis — or in any major public crisis. You must understand how your investments work on a small scale and on a large scale. Due diligence has taken on a new meaning. You may also notice that where there seems to be an element of contradiction in official messages — for example, "Americans must spend more to help the economy" and "Americans' personal debt is higher than it's ever been" — a crisis may be brewing. Finally, you may find inspiration and a renewed commitment to your mission in the stories about individuals, families, and organizations that are abandoning the culture of easy credit and conspicuous consumption for a life style that places more emphasis on intangible values. These people are your future volunteers and donors — your best defense against risk.

Management Theories

Management theories evolve like any other social trends. Most management theories boil down to some belief about human motivation.

Cognitive psychology can play an important role in management theory. Many theorists draw on Abraham Maslow's hierarchy of needs — the Maslow Pyramid — which postulates that people must satisfy basic needs of survival before they can attend to social needs and personal happiness. This can mean, for example, that the employee who is worried about being laid off may not be able to have an effective development conversation with a potential donor. Other theories, such as Myers-Briggs, rest on beliefs about different personality types. (It is worth noting that some skeptics consider the Myers-Briggs personality test unreliable and unscientific, an example of confirmation bias. But it may at least help you assess different people's priorities.)

A cognitive theory that has recently gained credence is the theory of multiple intelligences supported by Howard Gardner and others. Gardner suggests that intelligence is much more multifaceted than previous models, such as IQ, would have us believe. For example, some people have intelligence in interpersonal communications, while some have extraordinary auditory intelligence — they learn best by hearing. This model is already in use in some schools, where teachers use it to reinforce lessons in different ways — some students will understand best when they read a passage, others when they hear it read, still others when they act it out. Clearly, this has implications for the workplace: You must deliver messages in a number of different formats and styles if you hope to make them stick, and you should be alert to people's preferred ways of interacting with the world. Work to accommodate these preferences.

At heart, management theory is no substitute for management practice. It is fine to learn about cognitive science, but you must put this research into action. Understand your own motivations and needs; be clear and honest about what you want for yourself, from yourself, and for the organization. Work to arrive at the same understanding of your employees' and board members' wants and needs. You must find ways that having people do what they want and need to do will serve your goals for the organization. Then you must remove the things that get in the way of their work.

Project Management

Project management means vastly different things for different organizations. In a health care organization, a "project" could be a medical case. In a theater company, it could be a set design. We will use the term **project** to mean any of the following types of tasks:

- One that has a beginning and an end
- One that someone in your organization is working on
- One whose outcome affects the success of the organization

At any given time, your organization probably has many projects going on. You might be planning a community meeting, drafting a grant, working on a donor initiative, recruiting volunteers, looking for spaces for the fundraising event, and scheduling meetings between volunteers and clients. Your marketing director might be working on publicity for the community meeting, creating a portfolio to support the grant application, coming up with themes for the fundraising event, and writing press releases about the volunteer efforts. Your development director might be researching ten different grants and a corporate alliance. Each of these things is a project. How do you keep projects from being lost in the shuffle?

- Prioritize. If you have a solid plan for the year, you should know the projects that are most important, and the consequences of neglecting them.

- Have weekly project meetings in which the person in charge of each project gives a brief update to the management team. Make sure these meetings are regular and frequent. Each meeting functions as a mini-deadline and lets people know they are expected to make incremental, measurable progress.

- Keep projects and their status visible to everyone in the organization. Use a white board or magnet board in a public location to post updates and celebrate small successes along the way. If people have problems with a certain part of the project, they can use the white board and the weekly meetings to ask for help. Remove obstacles to productivity — and remove people's excuses for not doing their work.

- Some organizations may want to maintain a project database, using project management software. This may or may not be the right decision for you. It makes sense for a health care organization or an educational institution to have an electronic database of patients or students whose numbers are going to grow rapidly and whose individual circumstances must be tracked. Other organizations might be fine with donor management software or a grant calendar, but no single project management system. If you will have many projects of a similar type, project management software can likely help; if your projects will vary widely, you might need to come up with a different system.

Lead Management

In the for-profit world, a lead is a potential sale. In the nonprofit world, the word is often used to refer to a funding possibility — such as a grant program or an individual donor — or an opportunity to participate in a program, festival, or other event that might help further your mission.

These opportunities will come your way casually — through friends' and family members' referrals — and because of dedicated research. Most of them will require multiple contacts and extensive follow-up — the process known as **lead management.** If you hear about a funding opportunity, for example, you might:

- Google the name of the foundation
- Download the application requirements to read later
- Read the requirements
- Call someone at the foundation to ask for clarification on a few points
- Decide that you are eligible
- Go back to the Web site to download the application form
- Assemble a grant proposal, drawing on information and ideas from board members
- Send the grant proposal
- Follow up with your foundation contact to thank them for their help
- Thank the person who originally told you about the opportunity

There are several steps, and you will have many leads. Some will work out, some will not, but *none* of them will succeed if you do not take the initiative of pursuing them and following up on them. That means you must have a system for tracking your efforts and staying on top of your to-do list for each lead. Your system could be as simple as a spreadsheet you create yourself. You may want to invest in lead management software, or incorporate lead management with another database requirement of your organization, such as donor contact management.

Performance Measurement: Evaluating Managerial Effectiveness

You should establish the criteria for success early, before you have reached the point where you are looking around and realizing you are surrounded by your own failure but have no idea how you got there. Work with your board to set some definitive criteria for measuring your success. Get these criteria in writing, and use them in your annual review.

You may or may not want to have formal written evaluations of yourself and other managers. For some people, this can smack too much of the corporate, for-profit world; it can seem like one more annoying, arbitrary policy to follow. But without a written record of performance, it may be harder to convince the board of the wisdom of a pay raise — or a termination.

Pay attention to day-to-day indicators of success, too. You should have a sense of how happy your employees are. If turnover is low and people are clearly committed to their work and the mission, you may have succeeded in creating a good working environment and communicating goals. In contrast, unhappy employees are hard to miss. They are late or absent, whine through meetings, shoot down ideas, and make cynical remarks. In a small organization, one employee's discontent can become an office-wide problem, so be alert to these signals and address them directly. Do what you can to remedy the problem as quickly as possible.

CASE STUDY: ALLIANCE TO END HOMELESSNESS IN SUBURBAN COOK COUNTY

Mission: The Alliance to End Homelessness in Suburban Cook County is a nonprofit organization responsible for planning and coordinating homeless services and housing options for all of Cook County outside of Chicago and Evanston. Jennifer Hill is the ED of the Alliance. She is the group's first executive director; the organization existed as a voluntary task force for ten years prior to hiring staff. There are now four full-time employees, plus an intern. The board of 30, a working board, meets every month. There are an additional dozen volunteer committee members. Including time spent on board and committee participation and leadership, volunteers contribute more than 200 hours per month.

The Alliance is supported by the U.S. Department of Housing and Urban Development's (HUD) Supportive Housing Program and by Community Development Block Grants, as well as foundation support and individual giving.

Hill has worked in the nonprofit sector for 14 years and in her present job for almost five years. She describes some major challenges:

"Three years into the job, I had to advise the board to cancel a large contract with a technology vendor. This began a turbulent year of board conflict, low staff morale, and funding sources questioning our ability to get the project back on track. We came through the conflict by employing an active communication plan, making sound hiring decisions, scrutinizing our financial policies and contract management procedures, and building a formal partnership with a similar group that already offered the technology services we needed. During the transition to the new system, I sent weekly e-mail updates to funders and board members on the project's accomplishments and progress. Constant communication was the linchpin to meeting all of the project's benchmarks as quickly as possible.

"The most challenging part of being an executive director for me has been the breadth of responsibilities. In addition to being the main 'project' person, I have also had to learn the roles of being a financial manager, supervisor, fundraiser, and communications guru. It's an art form to know how to ask for the help you need when you feel personally account

CASE STUDY: ALLIANCE TO END HOMELESSNESS IN SUBURBAN COOK COUNTY

able for so much of what goes on in the organization. Also, as a young director (I was 31 when I took the job), I have sometimes had to guard against older colleagues underestimating my knowledge and abilities. I try to stay ahead of these challenges by prioritizing my own professional development. The executive directors I look up to the most are people who regularly go outside their own comfort zones, recognizing they can be part of something far bigger than the limits of their own abilities by assembling the right board and staff.

"A generation ago, good intentions and on-the-job training may have been enough to get you far in the nonprofit sector, but not anymore. Get concrete skills with a professional or master's degree in your field, and take advantage of every opportunity to get a broad array of skills. Non-profit leaders wear a variety of hats; be sure to hone your skills in financial management, project management, and human resources."

CHAPTER 12
Human Resources

This chapter covers the details and legal responsibilities of acquiring, having, and losing employees, as well as making sure that employees do what you want them to.

Deciding to Become an Employer

It can be tough to know when it is time to take on employees. Having employees significantly raises the organization's financial obligations, and development efforts must go up correspondingly.

At the same time, you may hit a wall: The organization cannot accomplish more without some paid help. This limit is in different places for different organizations. Some organizations can glide along comfortably for years on volunteer labor and the efforts of the board; others need professional workers and the technology to help them do their jobs. Still others may worry that if they do not hire new employees, they will be at risk for **founder's syndrome** (see Chapter 14).

Before deciding to become an employer, discuss the decision with your board. Carefully evaluate what needs to be done, and review the available skills on the board and in your volunteer database. Look at all the potential costs you may be taking on. Make sure your financial officer is up to the task of handling payroll taxes, and make sure you are up to the task of expanding your development efforts.

You may also face a bit of an emotional struggle if you decide to hire someone. Those of us who started nonprofits in order to effect social change may discover that having employees makes us uncomfortably close to being "The Man." People who enjoyed the cachet that came along with saying they ran a theater company may feel themselves losing cool points when they must spend an evening poring over brochures from health insurance vendors. And as a founder or inaugural ED, you may be the first employee yourself; you may have to serve as the guinea pig for the board's personnel decisions, and you will need to write the policies you will be obeying later.

Volunteer or Employee?

Some volunteers, such as retirees, may come to you expecting to give as much time as a full-time employee would. Others may want to give a weekend every month.

Volunteer labor may be less predictable than employee labor. If you have reached the point where you must know, without a doubt, that someone will be addressing a task every day, it is probably time to have an employee in that position.

Still, hire conservatively. Managers in the for-profit world sometimes hire someone talented simply because of that person's talents, assuming that, sooner or later, the company will figure out how to use that person. Nonprofit managers cannot take this approach. *Always* weigh hiring decisions against volunteers' willingness and ability to serve. Do not forget about board efforts, either. A working board may serve as well as five or ten employees. Imagine justifying your hiring decision to your biggest funder. Is it easy to defend this choice? Or does it seem as though you might be using the organization's money irresponsibly? The more conservatively you hire, the lower your overhead, payroll, and benefits costs, and the less you risk future layoffs.

The Tax Implications of Having Employees

Acquiring employees requires you to pay certain taxes:

- Federal Insurance Contributions Act (**FICA**) tax, which funds Social Security and Medicare
- Federal unemployment tax (**FUTA**); depending on what you pay in state unemployment tax, you may be able to get a credit for what you pay in federal unemployment tax
- State unemployment tax (**SUTA**); this goes to fund your state's unemployment benefits
- **Worker's compensation**; this goes to your state's fund, which provides income to employees who are injured on the job

Employees are exempt from paying unemployment and worker's compensation taxes, but they are responsible for a portion of FICA taxes, in addition to what you pay.

All employees must pay state and federal income taxes. Employees pay these taxes incrementally, through **withholding taxes** throughout the year. These taxes are removed from each paycheck based on an estimate of how much the employee will earn in the course of his or her employment, and how much he or she will be able to deduct, based on number of dependents and filing status. When employees start working, they complete a form W-4, which tells the government how much income tax they want taken from each paycheck. Your payroll administrator is responsible for deducting this amount and paying it to the government.

An employee's **gross pay** is the amount of the paycheck before taxes are calculated. An employee's **net pay** is the amount he or she actually receives after all payroll taxes and benefit costs have been paid.

Every quarter, you must report taxes withheld on a federal Form 941. If you offer benefit plans, you will need to report those annually with a federal Form 5500. The IRS takes these reporting requirements quite seriously and may decide to hold your managers personally liable if they fail to file.

Depository Receipts

When you owe federal or state tax greater than $500, you may be required to pay it directly to a bank instead of mailing it to the IRS.

Every January, you will need to send tax forms to the people who work for you: **W-2s** for your employees and **1099s** for your independent contractors.

Some Help Estimating Payroll Tax Costs

The Web site **www.Payroll-Taxes.com** provides information and tools to help you answer your questions about payroll and tax obligations. They also offer a number of free calculating tools to help you estimate the tax load of having an employee and the costs that might come along with offering that person a savings plan. Visit **www.payroll-taxes.com/calculators.htm**.

The IRS maintains an extensive Web site as well. Among other things, they offer a calculator to help new employees estimate how much income tax should be withheld based on their personal situation. You can find out more at **www.irs.gov/individuals/article/0,,id=96196,00.html**.

Payroll

An organization's **payroll** can be the roster of paid employees, or the total cost of their paychecks. The term *payroll* often refers to the act of paying employees and calculating all relevant taxes as well. When organizations talk about *reducing* payroll, they usually mean they must impose layoffs or pay cuts. When organizations talk about *outsourcing* payroll, on the other hand, they typically mean they are hiring an outside company to handle the administration of employee paychecks and related taxes.

Overhead

Do not forget about the other costs of having employees — the office infrastructure and technology that go into providing a place for the employee to work. **Overhead** can include furniture, space rental, software fees and licensing, expanded server capacity, phone lines, copy paper, coffee filters, the cost of your own administrative time, and many other expenses. Remember to budget for these costs as you make your hiring plans and your development strategy.

Employee Benefits

Employee benefits — sometimes known as corporate welfare — are the programs and services you offer your employees in addition to their paychecks. Benefits packages traditionally include health care, retirement, and paid time-off, but there are numerous other options.

Strong benefits packages can be one of the ways a nonprofit compensates for offering pay that tends to be lower than its for-profit counterpart. Running a social welfare organization can make certain benefits and programs easier for you to offer, or give you a better sense of the programs that will actually improve your employees' lives and inspire loyalty.

The world of employee benefits is changing rapidly. The health care system is in crisis; the retirement system has been in crisis at least since the dot-com bust. There is an overarching trend — not just in health care and in retirement, but in society at large — of transferring financial risk from corporations to employees, from institutions to individual consumers. You may find this trend at odds with your mission of social change, but you also may discover that defying the trend can be costly. Flexibility is a must.

CEBS

If you are planning to enter the world of employee benefits, consider hiring a consultant with CEBS certification. CEBS stands for "Certified Employee Benefits Specialist," and CEBS is to benefits as CPA is to accounting.

Health care Benefits

Employers often choose to offer health care benefits because employees work better and more efficiently when they are healthy. Offering health care can reduce absenteeism and turnover, but it can also be a giant expense. Current workplace trends show a reduction in the number of employers who offer this benefit.

Medical Insurance

Medical insurance can take a variety of forms — such as the **health maintenance organization** (HMO), the **preferred provider organization** (PPO), the **point-of-service plan** (POS), and the **indemnity plan** (also known as catastrophic coverage) — that differ in terms of how much care patients may seek and how they may seek it. Typically, you will offer insurance through one or more insurance providers, who work with you as vendors.

What all forms of employer-sponsored health insurance have in common is that the employee must pay a **premium** — a monthly, weekly, or annual fee to the insurance provider — and the employer covers a percentage of this cost. When the employee receives health care, the insurance company pays for some of the cost, and the employee pays the rest; these costs differ widely by plan, as well as by the kind of care the employee receives and how much medical care the employee has sought that year.

In a new nonprofit, offering medical benefits can pose quite a financial challenge. You may not have enough employees to offer **group health insurance**, a form of insurance that keeps costs lower by creating a **risk pool**. A risk pool is essentially a group of people about whose health the insurance company can make statistical predictions. The insurer sets the premium based on these predictions, and thus protects itself against losses. Because it is much harder to make predictions about the health of individuals, **individual health insurance** costs more. If you have only one or two employees but want to offer a company plan, individual health insurance might be your only option. However, do not overlook the following alternatives:

- Offering a health care **voucher** to help employees pay for a plan of their choice

- Joining or creating a collective of area nonprofit employees that have their own group plan

- Offering a tax-favored health care savings account (be aware that some such accounts — **HSAs**, or health savings accounts — require participation in a high-deductible medical plan)

- Paying for employees' membership in a professional organization — such as Actors' Equity and many other labor unions — that offers its own group plan

Your medical plan may include **prescription coverage**. Not all medical insurance does, though. You may want to consider offering a separate prescription program, but be aware that these are frequently a major source of costs.

Wellness programs, such as smoking cessation, exercise and weight-loss incentives, and the monitoring of chronic conditions like asthma and diabetes are a relatively new addition to the health-insurance scene. In a nutshell, healthy people cost less to care for — and, therefore, to insure. Employers have begun offering such preventive programs as a way of avoiding the significantly larger expenses associated with health crises, such as kidney failure or heart attacks. You may be able to offer a wellness program as part of your health insurance. Your life insurance vendor may have similar offerings. Or you can create your own — for example, distribute pedometers and offer a bonus to employees who walk a certain number of miles each month.

Federal law imposes some restrictions on employers who offer health care benefits. For example, the **Health Insurance Portability and Accountability Act (HIPAA)** mandates privacy of employees' health records. Insurers are usually required to waive their **pre-existing condition exclusions** for employees who join the organization's plan. If an employee leaves the company, he or she is entitled to receive a **certificate of creditable coverage**, which proves to future employers and insurers that he or she received health insurance while employed with your organization; this is designed to allow employees to bypass waiting periods for pre-existing conditions. Employees who depart are also entitled to receive **COBRA coverage** (Consolidated Omnibus Budget Reconciliation Act), which allows them to remain in the organization's health plan for a certain number of months after departure. The number of months varies depending on employees' circumstances; it can extend for more than a year. During this time, employees must pay the entire amount of the premium in addition to an administrative fee.

You *must* become familiar with federal law before offering health benefits, which is just one reason to work with a consultant rather than doing it yourself.

Dental Insurance

Costs in the dental world have been relatively stable compared to costs in the medical world, thus you will probably find it easier to offer dental care than health care. The cost arrangement of dental plans is essentially the same as that of medical plans. You and the employee split the cost of the premium, and the employee pays additional costs when he or she receives dental care. Dental insurance plans even mimic the structures of medical plans: There are dental HMOs, sometimes called DHMOs; PPOs; and POS plans. The point of dental care is maintenance, so there tend not to be dental indemnity plans. The other plans usually contain indemnity clauses that help employees get emergency dental care when, say, they fall and knock out teeth.

Some vendors, such as AFLAC®, offer dental insurance and other benefits that employees may convert to individual coverage when they leave the organization. In the insurance world, this is known as **portability**. It can be a nice perk for your employees, as it also acknowledges the realities of the contemporary workplace; we no longer expect one person to work for the same company for decades.

Vision Care Insurance

This benefit often looks nice on paper but can actually cost employees more than they would pay for eye exams, glasses, and contact lenses without insurance. However, you may want to partner with an organization, such as Costco®, that offers corporate discounts on eye care.

Mental Health and Substance Abuse Care

Sometimes this is bundled into your health insurance plan, but sometimes it must be a separate offering.

Not every employer chooses to cover mental health problems. Consider your field before deciding not to offer this coverage, however. Nonprofit work can be stressful, emotional, and demanding, and offering mental health benefits can help employees deal with what you are asking them to do. Furthermore, untreated substance abuse can lead to high absenteeism, poor work, and higher health care costs — even when it does not actually pose a danger to the affected employee and his or her coworkers.

Employee Assistance Programs (EAPs)

An EAP may be part of your medical plan, part of your mental health plan, or a separate offering. It typically takes the form of a 24-hour hotline that employees can call in times of stress or emotional distress. The hotline is staffed with trained professionals who offer free counseling over the phone and, if necessary, provide referrals to area therapists and counselors. Often, the EAP offers a discount for employees' visits to these providers. EAPs can be particularly valuable in times of company-wide crisis — when there have been layoffs, when state budget cuts threaten your funding, or when you have lost a beloved colleague or client. They can also help employees resolve interpersonal disputes without getting managers involved.

Retirement Income Benefits

Retirement benefits help employees take care of themselves in the distant future after they have stopped working.

Generous retirement benefits used to be a given, but the employees who entered the workforce with Generation X — and, in their first years on the job, witnessed employer-sponsored pension plans collapsing dramatically — likely have a different set of expectations about retirement than do older employees. Older employees came of age in workplaces that offered extensive employer-paid pensions in return for company loyalty. Younger employees probably expect to have to save the bulk of their retirement income themselves. They do not expect to get pension plans — if a pension plan is offered, they may not rely on it — and they are often cynical about Social Security. Offering a variety of savings and investment vehicles can help you meet the different expectations and needs of a heterogeneous workforce.

Nearly all retirement income benefits have a **vesting** requirement, which is essentially a retention incentive. Vesting means that employees must work for your organization for a certain amount of time before they are legally entitled to retirement benefits. The amount of time can vary, and employees may vest all at once or by degrees: so that, for example, after three years, an employee is 60 percent vested — if the employee leaves the organization after three years of employment, his or her pension benefit will be 60 percent of the company's plan contributions on his or her behalf.

Pension Plans

A pension plan is a retirement fund to which only the employer contributes money. The money is paid out to employees in retirement. To be entitled to this money, employees must have worked for the company for a certain minimum amount of time — usually between three and five years.

Pension funds come in two basic models. A **defined-benefit plan** guarantees retirees a certain amount of income (the benefit) that is usually set based on what they earned during their highest-paid years as employees, or, if not their highest-paid years, their years immediately before retirement. Contributing enough money to meet this guarantee involves complicated actuarial calculations, predictions about how long employees will stay with the company and how much they will earn, and savings and investments designed to meet those predictions. You can see the risk: Investment income is not guaranteed, and the predictions may not be right, but you are still legally obligated to pay the amount you promised. Because of that risk, this kind of plan is now rarely used.

A **defined-contribution plan** does not guarantee a specific payout. Instead, the employer makes a certain contribution to the plan for every full year an employee stays with the company. In retirement, the employee can take the employer's contribution as a lump sum or as some form of annualized income.

Some defined-contribution plans are also **cash balance plans**, which allow employees to receive their pension benefits before retirement upon their departure from the company. This sort of benefit is controversial. It was designed as a response to increased employee mobility; employers did not want the costs associated with maintaining pension accounts for people who had not worked for the company in years. But critics argue that the allure of the lump sum of cash acts as an incentive for departing employees to behave irresponsibly with money that would best be saved for retirement. And because they receive the money before retirement age, employees must pay heavy tax penalties on it — sometimes close to half of the total amount.

The argument over cash balance plans may be moot, as fewer employers offer pension plans at all. One notable exception in the nonprofit world is universities — although, as university endowments crumble in the wake of recent financial turmoil, the university pension plan may not be long for the world.

Retirement Savings Plans

Tax-advantaged retirement savings plans allow employees to set aside their own money in long-term investment vehicles that will eventually become sources of retirement income. Typical offerings are **IRAs (individual retirement accounts)** and **403(b) plans**, the nonprofit equivalent of 401(k)s. Employees are not required to pay income taxes on the money they put into these plans. They pay taxes later, in retirement, when they are receiving plan money as income. If you offer such a savings plan, you must be alert to ways in which it affects other calculations of employee income.

To encourage such responsibility, employers often offer a **matching contribution**, sometimes called a company match. This usually means that when an employee puts a certain amount in his or her retirement account, the company does too. Common arrangements are the **dollar-for-dollar match**, in which the employer matches 100 percent of the employee's contributions (often up to a certain limit), and the **50% match,** in which the employer matches half of the employee's contributions.

Some employers also offer a **profit sharing match**, in which — if the company has fared well in a given year — employees receive an additional year-end plan contribution. This acts as a retention incentive, as well, as employees who leave the company mid-year typically do not receive the bonus, even if they have opted to leave their retirement savings in the company plan. Obviously, the concept of "profit sharing" is a bit different in the nonprofit world. You might use such a structure as a development incentive to reward employees who help bring major contributions to the organization.

Employees are always vested in their own contributions to retirement savings plans. If you are worried about turnover, you may wish to impose vesting requirements on the organization's matching contributions.

Life Insurance

Life insurance benefits are designed to help employees protect their families' income in the event of their own untimely death. The cost of such benefits is tied to employees' income. Plan structures include:

- **Basic life**, the insurance plan most of us are familiar with
- **Accidental death and dismemberment (AD&D)**, which pays a benefit in addition to the life benefit if the employee

has died in an accident, and also offers a benefit if the employee is injured in such a way that will impair his or her ability to work in the future, such as blindness, hearing loss, paraplegia, or amputation

- **Voluntary supplemental life insurance**, which allows employees to pay additional fees to increase the benefits that would be payable if they died

- **Spouse and child life insurance**, which allows employees to pay additional fees so as to receive benefits in the event of the deaths of their family members

Disability Insurance

Many HR professionals consider disability insurance more important than life insurance because employees are more likely to become disabled than to die during their employment. Disability insurance defines "disability" broadly: It can encompass pregnancy and surgery as well as the times when someone may be on crutches for months.

Disability insurance takes up where sick leave leaves off. It replaces a percentage of the employee's income for the time he or she is unable to work. This percentage tends to be inversely proportional to the amount of time away from work. The employee might receive 100 percent of pay for the first two weeks of disability, 80 percent for the next four weeks, and 60 percent for the next three months.

Most disabilities will be covered by **short-term disability insurance** (STD), which usually applies to conditions that last up to six months. Occasionally an employee develops a more serious problem; that is when **long-term disability insurance** (LTD) applies. LTD may last up to two years.

Long Times Away from Work

Remember that the federal **Family and Medical Leave Act (FMLA)** governs many aspects of how you handle employees' long leaves. Make sure all your programs and policies are compliant with it.

Other Benefits

Special Insurance

Your insurance vendor may be able to provide options such as **home, auto,** or **pet insurance**. They may offer discounted rates to your employees. You may or may not be required to contribute to such premiums.

Child Care

Most working parents struggle to balance child care responsibilities with work responsibilities, sometimes to the detriment both of family relations and of work. Employers often provide benefits such as **day-care vouchers, emergency baby-sitting,** or **onsite day care.**

Onsite Exercise Facilities

In many cases, an exercise facility can complement your wellness program. Employees who exercise are typically healthier and have fewer long-term health problems, which can reduce absenteeism and related costs. Another option is offering **gym membership** or discounted gym membership as a benefit. Consider partnering with a local gym to waive initiation fees for your employees, for example.

Time Off

Time away from work is important (although, as a rule, American employers seem to think it is less important than do their European counterparts). There are numerous ways to structure paid time off:

- **Vacation time** may be issued in a standard allotment — two or three weeks a year (or more, depending on your field). You can also tie it to seniority: Employees who have been with the organization more than five years could be entitled to an additional week, for example. Employees may or may not be entitled to carry over vacation time from year to year. The amount of time to which they are entitled is then often called a **vacation bank**. In some states, you may be able to pay out a portion of unused vacation time as a year-end bonus. In most states, you will need to pay out unused vacation time when an employee terminates employment.

- **Sick leave** acknowledges the inevitable: From time to time, people will become sick. Employees usually receive an allotment of three to five sick days per year. The allotment does not carry over from year to year. If you have an STD program, it typically starts after three consecutive days of sick leave.

- **Holidays** are also inevitable. Some holidays are federally mandated, and the government releases an annual list of the dates of official federal holidays. Of course, some organizations — such as those that maintain crisis hotlines — need people working around the clock; on federal holidays, they may offer bonus pay or time and a half.

- **Paid time off (PTO)** typically combines vacation and sick days. Employees draw from the same time bank whether they are ill or hitting the beach. The organization may adopt a no-questions-asked policy about this time. PTO can lead to problems in that it can act as an incentive for employees to hoard their time — never taking vacations because they want to make sure they have a bank of sick days — which can increase burnout.

- In some states, hourly employees have the option of taking **overtime** pay in the form of additional time off, an hour of vacation for each hour worked. This can be a nice way to give a break to people who have put in extra time.

Depending on your number of employees, you may face some scheduling challenges with vacation time, especially at the end of the year when employees scramble to use their allotted vacation days. If you have carefully prioritized your needs, you can work out a way to meet these challenges — whether by simply shutting down operations for a few weeks or by coordinating volunteer and board efforts to take place in the weeks when your employees are off.

Long-term Care Insurance

This benefit helps employees protect themselves against future costs of major medical care for themselves or for family members.

Flexible Savings Accounts (FSAs)

These are tax-free savings vehicles that allow employees to set aside part of their pre-tax income to pay for certain expenses. Using an FSA helps an employee lower his or her income tax bill and budget for some costs of working. Employees contribute to the account with pre-tax dollars and then withdraw tax-free reimbursements as they incur expenses. You may choose to offer a **health care savings account** —not to be confused with a health savings account — a **dependent care savings account,** or a **mass transit savings account**. Because FSAs involve pre-tax dollars, your payroll administration will be affected by this benefit.

Legal Assistance

Legal assistance programs can help employees navigate home purchases, lawsuits, and other issues. These plans may be structured much like EAPs, with a free initial hotline call followed by referrals or discounted consultation services.

Corporate Partnerships and Discount Programs

This can be another way to offset the lower salaries of nonprofit work: Offer employees discounts on everything from computers to cars. A discount benefit may be built into your corporate partnership (see Chapter 9).

Tuition Reimbursement

If you are serious about helping your employees better themselves and gain skills, you may wish to offer tuition reimbursement for classes or degree programs tied to their job duties. While some universities and other educational nonprofits offer tuition reimbursement regardless of the employee's job duties, this generosity may be beyond the reach of other organizations. Tuition reimbursement is often tied to retention, with employees required to pay back a percentage of the tuition if they leave the organization less than a year after completing the training. These programs are also often referred to as **professional development**.

Professional Memberships

Many fields have professional organizations — such as the American Medical Association or the International Reading Association (for literacy professionals) — that help their members stay up-to-date on new research and thinking. Paying for employees' memberships can demonstrate your commitment to their learning and can help your organization stay current within its field. It can also be a good option for pension and health care; many of these organizations offer group plans whose scope is beyond the reach of a two- or three-person nonprofit.

Bonuses

Bonuses tie financial rewards to exceptional performance — employee performance and organizational performance. Bonuses are common for grant writers and other development professionals. As we are seeing in some of the Wall Street institutions that have recently received federal bailouts, bonuses can become problematic when employees start to feel entitled to these payments, regardless of their own performance on the job or the performance of the organization as a whole. To make a bonus program work, you must communicate all the requirements clearly from the beginning, and it must be clear that the bonus is not part of the employee's salary. Although a bonus is taxable income, bonus payments should have no effect on salary calculations for pension plans and similar benefits.

Supplemental Withholding Tax

Bonuses, overtime, and other benefits that involve extra pay are subject to federal supplemental withholding tax. How you withhold this tax depends on whether you are providing the extra-pay benefit in conjunction with another paycheck or as a separate payment on its own, and how much you withhold depends on the employee's annual salary. If the employee makes more than $1,000,000 in a year — admittedly, not a likely scenario in a start-up nonprofit — the supplemental income must be taxed at 35 percent. Otherwise, it is taxed at the same rate as the employee's other pay.

Of course, you need not be conventional in your approach to rewarding employees. Many nonprofits exist to fix the problems that conventional thinking has caused.

Use-It-Or-Lose-It Policies, Incentives, and Financial Liabilities

The way you make policies and budgets will inevitably shape employee behavior. You will need to think carefully about what you are rewarding and what you are punishing, as well as unintended consequences your policies may be encouraging.

An **incentive** is a reason for someone to behave in a certain manner. For-profit managers often speak of the need to "incentivize" a policy or a goal; the word raises hives on any editor, but it simply means that the company needs to give employees a reason to behave in the desired way. An incentive may be an active choice or a passive circumstance. For example, your wellness initiative may be sidetracked because the vending machines full of sugary snacks and soda are closer to the employees' desks than is the kitchen, where the fresh fruit and the water cooler are hiding out. The unintended consequence of the passive incentive — the location of the vending machines — defeats the active incentives — the wellness program and the offering of fresh fruit.

Pay and benefits can create incentives, but so can budgets. For instance, a use-it-or-lose-it budget — in which the department cannot carry funding over from year to year — may give the department an incentive to spend irresponsibly. Over time, that becomes a liability for the organization.

Balancing Organizational Needs Against Employees' Needs

Karl Marx believed that laborers and employers were essentially opposed, and that conflict between the two was inevitable. In the nonprofit world, things may not be quite so adversarial — in theory, you are all working for the same cause — but there can still be some differences of opinion. Employees are people, after all, with their own lives. What they need will sometimes be at odds with what is best for the organization.

It should be clear that many benefit programs can be double-edged swords. Sometimes a benefit can have a completely unintended effect and may induce employees to behave in a way that damages the organization. You may have to adjust the program or abandon it altogether. Be frank in your discussions with employees about what is and is not desirable behavior. Acknowledge the program's responsibility in contributing to undesirable behavior. Work as a group to come up with alternatives that will help employees and the company.

In offering benefits, you must strike a continuing balance. It shifts as employees' lives change, as the employee population changes, as the organization evolves, and as society evolves around it. Remember to stay flexible, and always have a clear idea of the organization's priorities.

The section on benefits, earlier in this chapter, may give you some ideas about ways you can use benefits to encourage employees to behave in desirable ways. See the section on hiring later in this chapter for a discussion of different types of time and pay arrangements that can help you strike a balance.

Workplace Policies and Conduct

Workplace policies defining every aspect of expected employee behavior should be clearly stated in writing. Behavioral issues to consider including in your workplace policy include:

- Compensation, including bonuses and overtime
- Benefits and benefits administration
- Tardiness and absenteeism
- Substance abuse
- Interaction with clients and donors
- Personal use of office technology
- Parking in the facility lot
- Sexual harassment
- Respect of client and donor privacy, and personal information (See the section on data integrity in Chapter 3.)
- Confidentiality of organizational information
- Plagiarism
- Intellectual property, particularly if employees will be developing any writing, images, or software
- Use of common facility spaces, such as conference rooms, break rooms, and the kitchen
- Attendance at fundraising events and other special programming — for example, if you require employees to attend your annual event, it is common practice to waive their ticket cost
- Involvement in development efforts. This varies greatly from organization to organization, as it may breed ill will to mandate employee involvement and mandate financial contributions, but the door should be wide open to voluntary contributions
- Referrals of potential employees or board members

If a given form of misconduct is grounds for termination, be sure to state that clearly in writing. Employees should receive policy documents on their first day of work. On that day, both the employee and his or her supervisor should sign the policy to indicate an informed willingness to abide by these policies.

Hiring

Bringing other people into your organization is a big step — and an expensive one. Do it only when you are certain it is necessary. How you define "necessary" is up to you, of course, but your criteria might include these:

- It would be inappropriate or impossible to have a volunteer or board member do the work that needs to be done
- The work that needs to be done demands at least full-time attention
- The work that needs to be done demands specialized training or certification and familiarity with the organization
- You have a budget to cover the salary, equipment, and overhead associated with an additional employee
- The work that needs to be done will continue to need to be done for the foreseeable future; that is, it is not a short-term or one-time need

Even if you are certain it is time to bring in a new employee, you do not necessarily need to hire that person full-time. You have several options, many of which can cost you less.

Contract employees, also called **1099 employees** or **freelancers**, do work for you for money but are technically self-employed. You do not pay their social security tax, Medicare, worker's compensation, or unemployment tax. (Above a certain threshold, you do need to report how much you have paid them on a federal 1099 form.) You do not provide them with benefits. Depending on the job, they may work at your facility, on your equipment, or from a home office. Contract employees can be a good option when you need skilled assistance for a relatively short-term project — for example, writing a grant or creating a marketing brand.

Temporary employees, or temps, come from staffing services for a set period of time. Like contract employees, they do not receive benefits from your organization. In many cases, the staffing service is considered the temp's employer and pays all related employment taxes. Temps are often administrative employees. You may want to bring in a temp to cover an employee's maternity leave or to help get a massive mailing out the door.

Because staffing services often provide software training and background screening, many organizations use a **temp-to-perm** hiring process for administrative employees. This means that the temp works for you on a probationary basis for a certain amount of time, perhaps three months, during which you can decide whether you want to keep the temp as a permanent employee. During the probationary period, the temp is still the employee of his or her staffing service. If the temp seems not to be a good fit for your organization, you can ask the staffing service to send someone else. If you do decide to hire the temp as an employee, you will be required to pay the staffing service a referral fee.

As uncertain economic times make employers hesitant to add full-time employees, many workers find themselves in a situation known as **permalance**. This occurs when a contract or freelance worker is retained indefinitely — sometimes for years. He or she may even have a company e-mail address and an assigned cubicle. Because permalance workers are still technically not employees, they do not receive benefits, so they cost the organization less, and they can be let go at a moment's notice with no required severance or unemployment benefits. For these same reasons, permalancing is a controversial practice; some workers, and some labor unions, feel it allows employers to sidestep hard-won legal worker protections. Employers that rely heavily on permalancers or long-term contractors may also find themselves at risk of greater government scrutiny, as the practice can leave state unemployment pools underfunded and saddle employees with the full cost of FICA tax.

Part-time employees are typically paid by the hour. Having a part-time employee may be a good solution if your workload varies from week to week or if the organization is in transition, and you are not yet sure that you have the work or the budget to justify a full-time hire. Part-time employees can represent further cost savings because they tend not to receive benefits such as health insurance. This is up to you, however; at some organizations — most famously, at Starbuck's — employees who work more than 20 hours a week are eligible to participate in the company health insurance plan.

In some organizations, "part-time" and "hourly" are virtual synonyms, while in other organizations, it is possible to have a full-time hourly employee. **Full-time** employees are usually expected to work at least 40 hours a week. This amount varies; at some companies, 37.5 hours — representing five 7.5-hour days — is standard. Full-time employees are typically **salaried**; their pay is annualized, or stated as a yearly amount, then broken into equal increments by pay period. Clearly, having a salaried staff can make it far easier to budget for payroll; but a salaried payroll also means you are subject to a hefty financial obligation, and your development efforts had better be up to the task. Full-time employees are also eligible for any benefits you choose to offer.

Many for-profit and nonprofit companies now offer **full-time, reduced hours** options — allowing employees to work 60 or 80 percent of a full-time week. Salary and vacation time are reduced by the appropriate percentage, but the employee retains benefits eligibility. What's the appeal of this arrangement? In a word, retention. The full-time, reduced-hours employee may be a new parent — even an employee returning from maternity leave — or someone who needs to take time to help a chronically ill family member. In arts organizations, the reduced-hours employee may be an artist who wants time to devote to his or her own artistic pursuits. Offering this option can help you hang on to qualified, dedicated employees who are familiar with your organization. In the long run, that lets you save on training and recruitment.

Overtime

When an hourly employee works more than 40 hours in a single week, you are required to pay him or her **overtime**. How much overtime depends on state law; in some states, after the employee has reached a certain number of hours — say, 43 — you are required to pay **time and a half**, or one and one-half times the employee's normal hourly rate for the additional hours of work. In some states, there is a second threshold after which the employee's rate doubles. Obviously, this can mean that your payroll suddenly and rapidly exceeds its budget. Consider overtime an incentive to manage employees' time wisely, and never ask employees to work any hours you would not work yourself.

In many organizations, part-time work is associated with administrative tasks and labor, whereas salaried arrangements are for managers, executives, and professionals. This is a convention, not a rule, and you are allowed to define your own arrangements. Your job candidates, however, may expect these arrangements.

Similarly, although the Monday-through-Friday workweek is conventional, it is not mandatory. The nonprofit world may see more workweek variation than the for-profit world; many non-profit organizations exist to remedy social problems that do not confine themselves to traditional working hours, and others — such as performance companies — must time their work to other people's time off. Some organizations, such as medical institutions, crisis centers, and shelters, expect and need weekend work. An environmental organization might realize energy savings by having employees work four ten-hour days, leaving the office dark for three days a week. In the educational world, summer vacation is a given, but no one expect teachers to stop working when the school day ends. Be alert to the conventions and expectations of your field, and be reasonable and flexible about work hours. You probably cannot afford to pay employees as much as their for-profit colleagues are earning; one way to balance that is by offering greater flexibility in working hours.

Recruitment

To find the right employees, you must start by spreading the word about your job opening. A few ways to do that include:

- Job placement services and staffing agencies (These can be a great option if you do not want to deal with background checks and other administrative details, but they are not free; the money you spend on a placement service or staffing agency is often money that could be going toward the salary of a qualified employee, so think carefully about when is the right time to use such services)
- Job boards, such as **www.Careerbuilder.com**®
- Online bulletin boards, such as Craigslist®
- Online nonprofit communities, such as **www.Idealist.org**

- Your board members
- Your ED support network, if you have one
- Your past colleagues
- Employee referrals

A good job post can help you weed out inappropriate candidates, such as those who do not care about your mission, who expect astronomical salaries, or who lack the right qualifications. Be specific, or you may find yourself wasting time answering questions from unsuitable job seekers. The post ought to include:

- The name and contact information of the organization
- The duties, hours, and location of the job
- The qualifications you are looking for
- A rough estimate of the pay rate and benefits available
- The date you hope to have someone start working
- The information you need from the candidate, such as a résumé or work samples

The post should also reflect your organizational culture (which is discussed later in this chapter). If your office has a sense of humor, it is OK to include something funny in the post. If your organization is faith-based, mention the importance of faith in your day-to-day work life. If the organization is full of outspoken, politically minded employees, say something about the informal lunchtime debates. These intangibles can help you attract people who are not only qualified, but also appropriate for the work setting.

The Hiring Process

If you have ever had a job, you likely have some sense of how the hiring process works. Following your post, you will receive a tide of résumés and cover letters. You may be surprised at how easy it is to pick out the qualified and unqualified candidates, simply based on their cover letters. But there are many people out there who will apply for any job, regardless of their appropriateness for it. Look for the candidates who meet the following criteria:

- They mention your organization by name.

- They demonstrate familiarity with and commitment to your mission.

- They express themselves reasonably well . After all, they will need to communicate with you and your team, and perhaps with your donors or clients.

Depending on the job, you may be looking for specific skills or qualifications, such as software expertise or a teaching certificate.

Once you have winnowed the list of applicants down to a reasonable number of candidates, invite them to the office for an interview. For promising candidates, you may follow this with a second interview and an introduction to the people who may be the candidate's future colleagues.

Background Checks and Due Diligence

Depending on the position's duties, you may want to conduct a **background check** on job candidates. In some situations, such as positions that deal with children, you may be required by law to conduct such a check. If you do not perform these checks, and the candidate goes on to abuse his or her position, you can be held legally liable for failure to perform **due diligence**.

You will need to inform job candidates in writing that you are conducting background checks, and candidates should sign a **consent form**.

A background check may delve into the following areas:

- Arrest records
- Credit checks
- Driving records, for employees who will be required to drive as part of their official duties
- Drug tests
- Verification of work and education history
- Googling the candidate to see how he or she is represented online

How much weight you give this information depends on your judgment and the organization's mission. If part of what you do is rehabilitate ex-convicts through on-the-job training, then you are probably not going to see many squeaky-clean background checks. Furthermore, no standardized evaluation system is a full substitute for meeting someone face-to-face. (We can call this the online-dating principle of hiring.)

It can be fine to trust your gut on a hiring decision. This is a question of personal appropriateness, and sometimes instincts can be a better judge of that than logic. But you must understand your own reasons in order to explain them to other people in the organization. If you have any reservations about someone and decide to go ahead and hire that person, you may want to make a note of those reservations so that you can spot early warning signs of problems and act to prevent bigger problems.

Referrals

Referrals — Job candidates who come to you from somebody, such as an employee, board member, or volunteer who already knows your organization, can be some of your best candidates. A referral candidate has already gone through something of a screening process, albeit an informal one: Your employee, board member, or volunteer knows the organization well enough to have an idea of who is a good fit for it, and knows that a bad referral will reflect poorly on him or her. (If standardized evaluations are the recruitment equivalent of online dating, this is the equivalent of meeting through mutual friends, with the attendant higher success rate.)

Referrals can be so valuable that some companies institute referral bonus programs, in which employees are rewarded for bringing talented candidates to the organization. A referral bonus program might work like this:

- When the candidate is hired, the employee who referred him or her receives a $500 bonus.

- If the candidate stays with the organization for a year, on his or her anniversary of hire, the employee receives a second $500 bonus. This condition is designed to promote retention. You don't want to reward the recommendation of candidates who are bad fits, or who see the organization as no more than a stepping stone to short-term gain.

- Bonus amounts may be tied to the job the candidate receives; the bonus tends to be larger for executive positions and positions demanding considerable training or specialized skills.

- To prevent abuse, the bonus does not apply in a situation where the final hiring decision rests with the employee, or where the referral would be reporting directly to the employee.

Although referral candidates can be wonderful additions to your organization, they must still be subject to the same background checks and due diligence that apply to everyone else who applies with you. Give referrals high priority, but not trumping power.

Firing

Sometimes an employee turns out not to be a good fit for your organization. Instances of **gross misconduct**, such as fraud or violence, are fortunately rare. But that means that a firing is often a more subtle, complicated judgment call. The person may show under-commitment, irresponsibility, laziness, or disrespect for the mission. The person's lack of courtesy or respect to others — either fellow employees or donors and clients — may damage the mission in other ways.

You're Fired!

Most of us have seen Donald Trump, also known as "The Donald," and his brusque, abusive way of handling "apprentices" who do not measure up to his standards. But in the non-TV world, his inescapable catchphrase of "You're fired!" is a *terrible* way of dealing with an employee who is not working out. You must do all you can to demonstrate that a firing is not a snap judgment, an impulsive decision, or a product of heated emotions. A termination conversation is going to be difficult for both you and the employee. Be calm, reasoned, polite, firm—and kind. The problem may stem from your decision to hire this person in the first place, so resist the temptation to lay all the blame at his or her feet.

Warnings

Any termination that is not a response to gross misconduct should be preceded by at least one written **warning**. Let the employee know that one or more of his or her behaviors is damaging the organization and giving you cause for concern. State clearly that you expect immediate improvement. Also state the consequences should the behavior persist.

In these conversations, be stern but compassionate. If the behavior is the result of a personal problem — such as marital strife or substance abuse — work with the employee to help him or her deal with the problem. Would now be a good time for the employee to take a few vacation days? Will your schedule permit some flex-time work or work from home so that the employee can accommodate a family illness? Can you refer the employee to a counseling service? This is not just a nice thing to do; it is an investment in someone who is already a part of the organization, someone you expended time, money, and effort to find and train. If you can indeed help the employee, he or she may become one of your most loyal workers.

Documentation

If you need to give an employee a warning, make sure this warning is in writing. Both you and the employee should sign and date the warning to indicate that the conversation has taken place. Add a copy of the warning to the employee's personnel file.

If the employee's behavior persists and you do need to terminate him or her, you must have a written record of the problem. More than one fired employee seeks state unemployment benefits. If your former employee applies for unemployment benefits, the state unemployment department will contact you to confirm the cause of termination. Unemployment benefits are intended to help people who are jobless because of circumstances beyond their control. You will need to demonstrate that the employee was, in fact, terminated for cause.

Similarly, if you must terminate someone, include a written statement of what is happening. Be clear that it is not a layoff, but a termination for cause.

In a termination letter, be clear about the benefits that the terminated employee can and cannot expect, such as access to COBRA coverage or recovery of moneys in tax-free savings accounts, and include contact information for all benefit providers, such as retirement plan administrators. Because benefits access rarely varies by employee, you can have much of this information on-hand as a stock termination letter; you need not scramble to assemble it at the last minute. By federal law, some coverages must continue to the end of the month in which an employee is terminated. Other benefits cease on the last day of work. Your HR specialist should know the difference.

Severance

Severance is money paid to employees who are unexpectedly terminated. It is most common in layoffs, not termination for cause. Depending on the situation and the budget, severance can be calculated as a flat sum or as an amount based on seniority — for example, two weeks' pay for every year at the organization, up to a maximum. There are minimum severance amounts and conditions that vary by state.

Layoffs

Layoffs, or mass terminations for reasons of business rather than employee performance, occur when there is not enough work to justify maintaining a workforce of your size.

Layoffs almost always involve severance pay. Employers also frequently offer job placement and career counseling to the terminated employees. If you offer an employee assistance program benefit, with free therapy or counseling sessions, now is a good time to remind employees of its existence. Layoffs are frightening and depressing, and counseling can help.

Such situations are not typically easy for anyone. If you experience a layoff, it has likely been preceded by news of economic problems and weeks or months of inactivity or low productivity for your employees. This means that layoffs are rarely a complete surprise to the affected employees; the employee rumor mill has likely been swirling for weeks in advance. Deal with such rumors honestly and quickly. A room full of employees who expect to have to box up their possessions by the end of the week can create an extremely toxic work environment.

Layoff Alternatives

Do not forget about other cost-cutting measures, such as **early-retirement buyouts**, **unpaid vacations**, across-the-board **pay cuts**, and **reduced-hours work weeks.** Some employers make these options voluntary; some make them mandatory. You will need to base that decision on your employees, your corporate culture, and your budget. If you make these choices optional, present them to your employees in a frank, straightforward manner. Remember that some employees may genuinely see this as a positive development — a chance to pursue a lifelong dream or start a second career. Embrace their enthusiasm. Positivity may be in short supply for a while, and it is a good idea to celebrate it where you find it.

If you must lay off employees, deliver the bad news fairly and honestly. Make sure employees understand the reasoning that contributed to the decisions; an arbitrary-seeming decision brews fear and resentment. Give each employee a severance letter outlining the terms of the layoff. At least one HR consultant recommends conducting layoffs early in the week to prevent depression; that way, terminated employees will be able to spend the rest of the week's workdays searching for new employment. If a layoff happens on a Friday, terminated employees may spend the weekend feeling frustrated and powerless about their job situation.

At least as crucial as how you handle the layoff itself is how you handle the aftermath among the employees who remain. You may notice a phenomenon, often called **layoff survivor's sickness**, in which employees withdraw, stop suggesting new ideas, avoid drawing any attention to themselves, and focus only on expected duties. Other employees may start looking for other jobs, so much that productivity drops or turnover spikes so that you wind up losing more employees than planned. Obviously, this is not a healthy state for the employees or the organization. A few strategies can help you prevent it:

- Make the first cut deep. If you have to make layoffs, be strict about it. Cut costs wherever you can, including your paycheck. The CEOs of Apple® and Whole Foods have both reduced their paychecks to $1 in times of crisis. Few nonprofit EDs can afford that, but think of a similarly dramatic gesture. The objective — one you should share with your employees — is to prevent ever having to do this again. People should not expect further rounds of layoffs; nor should they work as though they do.

- Be as generous as possible with career counseling, tuition reimbursement for job training, and outplacement services. Laid-off employees should not feel as though they have been cast adrift, and remaining employees should not feel as though that is a possible fate.

- Hire conservatively. From the beginning, you should acquire new employees only when the work demands a specialist, cannot be done by a volunteer or board member, and needs full-time attention. If you run a lean organization, you are much less likely to have to make sweeping cuts.

- Redouble your development efforts. Employees know their jobs depend on your fundraising. This is not the time to let anyone see you slacking, to finish a grant application only at the last minute, or to fire the grant writer.

- Help the remaining employees deal with their feelings. Part of the problem is simple grief and fear — people miss their colleagues and friends and do not know what will happen to them in the future. Employees may also feel trivialized or marginalized, as though their personal needs and concerns are being shunted aside because of larger concerns about the future of the organization. Reverse this trend by treating employees as individuals who matter. Make sure every employee can talk to a manager — even to you — about his or her feelings and problems. Listen empathetically and non-judgmentally. Practically speaking, to maintain your own productivity, you may need to offer a designated time of day for these conversations, or a certain range of hours in which your door is open. Employees will likely understand and respect this necessity.

In nonprofits, there is an additional risk that employees may begin to resent volunteers, who can be perceived as people who are giving their labor away for free and thereby stealing paying jobs from honest employees. If you have already established a firm policy of employee-volunteer relations and you have hired carefully, this should be less of an issue.

Being a Supervisor

There are as many different leadership styles as there are leaders, and the same techniques that succeed brilliantly for one ED may fail abysmally for another. But there are a few truths that hold for all people who must supervise others:

- **Be respectful.** Your behavior will set the tone for all employee interactions; yours is the example to which your staff is looking. Even if you strongly disagree with an idea or think it is obviously wrong for the organization, explain your reasoning and do not make fun of the person who suggested it. Do not dismiss the idea too quickly; ask questions about it and try to learn more. The same aspects that make you so hesitant to accept it could make for a brilliant surprise when it becomes part of a marketing campaign.

- **You cannot always be friends.** Sometimes you will hire someone you really like, and you will develop a fantastic working relationship. That is great; you want to hire people with whom you enjoy working. But what happens if you realize that person is visiting an inappropriate Web site on company time? Or if he or she becomes involved in a conflict with another employee, and you must act as the impartial mediator? At these times, hard as it is, you must ask yourself what you value more: the friendship, or the health of the organization.

- **Have friends outside the organization.** Many professional decisions are difficult enough, but they get even worse when they affect your entire social life as well as your nonprofit.

- **Understand your authority.** There is a certain amount of authority that comes from starting a nonprofit or from being hired as its ED. Unless you do something to undermine your own authority, people will automatically grant some weight to your words and actions. You probably do not need to yell, and you probably do not need to demand respect. These aggressive power plays can backfire; they sow resentment, which eventually undermines your authority. Many people who choose to work in the nonprofit world have come there because of a finely tuned sense of empathy, and they will be acutely sensitive to unnecessary displays of power. Your own sense of empathy will probably serve you better than a raised voice.

- **Be the last person to leave.** Do not ask people to work long hours if you are not working the same hours alongside them. Teamwork comes from a sense that everyone is in this together. Your employees know it, and they must know that you know it. Your actions will speak far louder than your words on this one.

- **Be on time.** Do not waste others' time — or your own.

- **Be available.** Make sure employees know how to reach you with questions and concerns. You might want to establish an "office hours" policy to invite employees to come and share their thoughts with you.

- **Be unavailable sometimes.** You will need to establish certain boundaries — hours when you cannot be interrupted and times when you have to be in charge.

- **Allow yourself to be surprised.** Sometimes you will not be the person with the best idea. Sometimes you do not know your clients as well as you think. Sometimes the rules of the game change. In these moments, it is more im-

portant to learn the facts of the situation than to insist on
the correctness of your own ideas.

- **Admit when you are wrong.** Hypocrisy is as unbecoming
in a leader as it is in everyone else — and it is far more
visible when you are in charge. It also goes a long way
toward undermining your credibility.

- **Give credit where credit is due.** If you have hired well
and trained well, everyone on the team should have some
share of your successes. Acknowledge contributors publicly. Take the time to comment on a specific, personal aspect of each contribution. You may not be able to reward
contributions with large bonuses or commissions the way
you might in the for-profit world, but that does not mean
you should not acknowledge them.

- **Celebrate successes.** But also acknowledge and analyze
failures.

- **Keep learning.** Create a culture in which everyone is striv-
ing to increase their skills and knowledge.

Finally, remember that there are limits to what one person —
in any position — can do for an organization. When you think
about how much our friends and our social circles influence our
behavior, you will understand why it is important to create an
organizational culture.

Creating an Organizational Culture

An organizational **culture** is, in essence, the sum total of all human interactions in your nonprofit. It encompasses the mood of
the organization, the feeling people get when they volunteer, the
expectations employees have about their colleagues' behavior,
the tone you strike in your marketing pieces, and the experience
every client has when he or she shows up at the door.

Think carefully about the kind of culture you want — the kind of environment in which you want to work, and the way in which you want to change people's lives. This is closely tied to your mission. If you still have your notes from crafting your mission statement (see Chapter 1), go back to them now. What adjectives describe your ideal organization?

To get started planning your organizational culture, look at the worksheet on the following page. It may be a good idea to complete this exercise with the other founders of your nonprofit, as well as with the person in charge of HR. The early decisions you make about culture will inform everything — the wording of your policies, the policies themselves, the office layout, the style of events, the donor communications, and more.

A true culture cannot be imposed from above. You must set the example in every interaction with every employee, volunteer, donor, client, and board member. In particular, cultures of courtesy, enthusiasm, and respect must be led by example.

If you encounter an employee who is displaying the traits you want to encourage in your culture, recognize his or her actions or attitude somehow. If someone stays late to help someone else beat a deadline, both people should be commended at the next staff meeting. If an employee is so passionate about AIDS awareness efforts that he or she has set up a Google news alert, build on that passion; talk about ways he or she could share that information with the rest of the staff.

EXERCISE: Planning an Organizational Culture

Which words describe your ideal workplace? Use the following checklist to get started. If you have additional adjectives, add them in the blanks at the end.

__ friendly	__ high-adrenaline	__ tea-drinking
__ courteous	__ quiet	__ water-drinking
__ formal	__ exciting	__ soda-drinking
__ conservative	__ private	__ beer-drinking
__ liberal	__ open	__ wine-drinking
__ personal	__ respectful	__ irreverent
__ anonymous	__ helpful	__ liberal
__ casual	__ smart	__ corporate
__ idealistic	__ curious	__ anti-corporate
__ politically involved	__ intellectual	__ passionate
__ fun	__ artistic	__ understated
__ professional	__ creative	__ in your face
__ Mac	__ colorful	__ NPR
__ PC	__ full of music	__ Fox
__ hip	__ hushed	__ CNN
__ sedate	__ reverent	__ gossipy
__ relaxed	__ innovative	__ informed
__ meditative	__ wired	__
__ fast-paced	__ coffee-drinking	__

Now, look at the adjectives you chose. Circle the ones that are most important to you. How many of your choices overlap with the choices of your cofounders, board members, and HR manager? What adjectives are those?

For each adjective, think of a program you could create or an action that you could take to foster that sort of culture. Bonus points if your idea costs under $50.

Did you choose any contradictory adjectives? If so, what were they?

Do you think the contradictory adjectives are the result of a simple difference in personalities, or do they point at different visions for the company? Discuss ways you could reconcile these differences.

Working with Friends: The Pros and Cons

When you start a nonprofit, nothing seems more natural than involving your like-minded friends. Maybe it was your passion for the same cause that brought you together as friends in the first place. Or it may have been an exciting, impassioned conversation together that first gave you the idea of starting a nonprofit. Of *course* you would want to involve your friends.

However, there can be many reasons not to. None of them is a hard and fast "absolutely not," but they all bear thinking about. Virtually every argument in favor of working with friends has a less appealing counterargument.

Pro: You communicate well.

Con: Other people feel left out. When employees feel left out, the rumor mill starts up in a hurry. Employees may start to feel that they will never be taken seriously because they are not your best friend. They may also feel as though they cannot trust you with anything confidential, because you might tell your friend. If your employees feel they cannot trust you, you have a major problem with their morale and your credibility. If your organization is one (such as a performing arts troupe) that routinely needs to bring in new people, you may also wind up creating a public perception of being cliquish or standoffish. This can alienate future donors, board members, and collaborators.

Pro: You know each other so well.

Con: Formalities such as promptness and deadlines may fall by the wayside. And if you are in charge and your friend is missing meetings — or is consistently lax about his or her responsibilities — you have three big problems: how to pick up the slack so that operations do not suffer, how to address these issues without destroying your friendship, and how to deal with the double standard other employees perceive. If your friend keeps dropping the ball, this may be a sign that he or she has outgrown his or her commitment to the organization. At this point, if you hope to keep your friendship, it is probably best to part ways as colleagues.

Pro: You are both madly passionate about your mission.

Con: You both have strong ideas about how the organization should be run, and these ideas are not always in sync.

Pro: You are inseparable.

Con: At the end of the work day, even if it has been a pretty good day, you need a break. With whom do you usually spend your evenings?

Pro: You can complete each other's sentences.

Con: So who is in charge?

Pro: You know everything about each other.

Con: You know *everything* about each other.

You have been warned.

CHAPTER 13
Volunteers

Volunteers may form the bulk of your workforce. If you use their time and skills wisely, they will keep coming back; they may grow into long-term donors or board members. If you waste their time, you throw away their — and your — most precious commodity.

Recruiting Volunteers

How you recruit volunteers depends largely upon your industry. Volunteer performers and designers often form the majority of the personnel in a fledgling non-union theater company's show; they are likely to be recruited via the local theater trade publication and then brought to the organization through an audition or portfolio-submission process. A food bank, by contrast, may be better served by recruiting whole groups of volunteers at once from local churches or businesses. A small medical clinic might find volunteer staff for its crisis line by advertising on Craigslist or talking to medical students at the local university. All of these approaches are viable.

If you carry on with strategic marketing and public relations efforts, then chances are, the volunteers will start to find you. Do you know what to say when a would-be volunteer calls you or corners you at a party? Can you think of a way you might be able to use this person's time?

Creating a Volunteer Strategy

You need a volunteer strategy, just as you need a development strategy and a budget strategy. Tips to get you started with a volunteer strategy:

- Think critically about the different tasks that must be done in the organization. Have you been assuming that they must be done by paid staff or board members? Have you assumed that they will fall to you because everything else does? Have thought you will have to hire a consultant or other specialist? You may be correct about the skills required, but not about the price. For each task, list the requisite skills or training. Also note any confidentiality or privacy issues that may accompany that work.

- Look at the list of skills. Where are you likely to find people with these skills? Is there a nearby university with graduate programs in these areas? Have you already talked to someone with these skills, and do you have a way to get back in touch with that person?

- Look at the tasks in the context of your five-year plan. Which tasks benefit the organization directly, and which benefit your clients directly? Which will enable the organization to reach more clients, or to serve existing clients better? What tasks must be done before other tasks can be done — for example, will someone need to design the home page before the online support group can get going? What is a high priority for the organization? What is a long-term goal? Which tasks do you have the resources to accomplish now, in terms of technology or equipment?

Use the answers to these questions to create a rough schedule of volunteer days.

- Think about how many people, with what skills, you will need for each of these tasks.

You now have the rudiments of a volunteer strategy. The volunteer strategy will overlap with the development strategy in several important aspects:

1. People are giving to the organization, and you must treat them with respect, courtesy, and gratitude.

2. People volunteer because they feel a personal connection to the organization or its mission. You must cultivate and strengthen that personal connection.

3. People will volunteer again when they have had a good time volunteering and can see the results of their efforts. People will not volunteer again if they sense that their time or effort has been wasted.

Communicating your Strategy and Mission to Volunteers and Would-be Volunteers

Now that you have a sound plan for using your volunteers' time, recruitment should be considerably easier. You will be able to outline the specifics of the tasks and describe any required skills or training. Unsurprisingly, people work better when they know what is expected of them. Good venues for seeking volunteers include:

- Craigslist and other community forums
- **www.Idealist.org**
- Local universities
- Local service organizations, including fraternal organizations

- The chamber of commerce — many corporations encourage employee volunteerism or have official days of service

- Local churches

- The local trade publication

- Job boards, particularly if you need volunteers with a particular skill set

- The Donors Forum

- Other nonprofits; you may even develop a reciprocal arrangement with the volunteers of a nonprofit with a mission related to yours

Training Volunteers

Training volunteers is not just a question of making the best use of their time; it is also a question of making the best use of the trainer's time. Your trainer is probably a staffer, a more experienced volunteer, or a board member — or you.

If you have a large group of volunteers all doing more or less the same thing, it is easier to have a single, classroom-style training session than 30 individual training discussions. Also think about using an apprentice-volunteer arrangement, in which each new volunteer is paired with a more experienced volunteer. This approach requires that you know in advance who is volunteering, and in the age of electronic invitations, that is often possible.

Once you have put the effort into training a volunteer, you must put even more effort into retaining that volunteer. A skilled volunteer who knows and likes your organization is a precious commodity. Make sure you regularly and meaningfully communicate your appreciation. One effective way to reward loyalty is with more responsibility and trust. If a volunteer clearly enjoys what he or she does for you, put that volunteer in charge of teaching the task to other volunteers or giving them their organizational orientation. For volunteers, working for your organization should be a privilege and a pleasure.

The Project: Philanthropy Approach to Training Volunteers

Project: Philanthropy had high volunteer retention, in part because the charrette approach maximized the impact of volunteers' time, and in part because the organization channeled volunteers with different skills into different groups.

A P2 charrette typically involved a writing group, a logo/identity group, a Web site group, and several brochure-design groups. After the initial full-group brainstorming session, volunteers with writing or PR skills went to the writing group, those with Web design skills went to the Web site group, and those with graphic design skills were divided evenly among the other two. Each group was led by a board member with special experience in that area. Volunteers were assigned to their groups in advance, usually a few days before the volunteer day, to ensure that no group contained all new or inexperienced volunteers. The volunteer experience was therefore a professional development experience as well, in which writers and designers who were new to the field could learn by working side-by-side with more experienced professionals.

Using Volunteers' Time and Skills Wisely

Before the volunteers arrive, there are a few things you should have in place:

- A sign-in sheet, with a place for volunteers to sign out as well; you will want to track the total number of volunteer hours for your tax records

- A schedule for the day and a way of communicating it to everyone
- Enough copies of the volunteer policy for every volunteer to sign
- Enough copies of the liability waiver for every volunteer to sign
- A way of collecting contact information from new volunteers
- A way to communicate to the volunteers about their tasks for the day
- A place for volunteers to stow personal belongings while they work
- Self-adhesive name tags, including some blank ones in case a volunteer brings a surprise guest
- Highly visible signs pointing the way to the bathroom and other important places
- A way of tracking the work that will be done
- A digital camera to document the day's efforts; these images can become part of future brochures or blog posts, can show prospective donors the level of commitment you have from your community, and can serve to recruit or motivate future volunteers

Build breaks into the schedule, but keep them efficient; limit them to the posted times. Remember that volunteers are here because they want to work. They want to see a change in your organization or in your clients' lives that has come about directly because of their presence today. If they do not get a chance to see that, or if you leave them standing around with time on their hands, they are less likely to come back.

Maintaining a Volunteer Database

You can probably use your donor contact management software (see Chapter 8) to maintain a database of volunteers. Volunteer information to track includes:

- Name

- Contact information and preferred form of contact

- When they first volunteered — A good technique for keeping long-term volunteers is to send an anniversary card to commemorate this date and thank them again for their efforts

- When they last volunteered

- How they have volunteered

- Whether they have received special training for certain organizational tasks

- Their most recent contact with the organization — Did they get a thank-you note after the last event? Did they e-mail you about future volunteer opportunities?

- Why they volunteered — Do they have a personal connection to the mission, such as a friend or family member who was a victim of the disease you are fighting? Do you give them a way to commemorate this person's life?

- Their special skills, training, and daytime occupation

- Their birthday, anniversary, and other special days

- Whether they might be interested in or appropriate for future board membership

Knowing all these things can help you find the volunteers who can help you deal with problems as they come up. Rather than send a generic "help us!" e-mail to all 200 members of the database, you can make four personal phone calls to the volunteers who understand HTML. As always, the more personal the request is, the greater its chances of being fulfilled.

Keeping Volunteers

See Chapter 8 on development for tips on retaining donors. Many of the same strategies apply — meaningful, personal thanks and recognition — for volunteer retention.

Volunteer Recognition

If you have used the apprentice-training approach to your volunteer day, have your senior volunteers send personal messages of thanks to all the less-experienced volunteers who worked with them. Follow-up with a message from you or another senior officer of the organization stating just how much work was done on the volunteer day — for example, 3,000 pounds of food sorted into boxes for hungry families, the new daycare room completely painted and decorated, a massive art installation now ready for the public — and reiterating your thanks.

Many organizations have regular volunteer appreciation parties. These do not have to be big, expensive events. You might just have a monthly volunteer get-together at happy hour at a pub, or a spaghetti dinner every quarter. The point is to get together and enjoy each other's company, and build the personal connections that make your volunteers feel like part of a special, privileged group. If it is possible to involve a few clients — the people whose lives your volunteers have changed — so much the better.

If you do have an annual event, consider offering volunteers a special discount on tickets if they make reservations within a certain, early window of time. The early window gives the volunteers more time to tell their friends about what they are doing that night. If you make it easy for them, loyal volunteers can recruit other volunteers — and other donors.

Similarly, an "I Volunteered for [Your Organization Here]" sticker or button for volunteers is a low-cost investment that can work wonders for both volunteer recognition and community awareness. It is one thing for you to be proud of your volunteers, but for their friends to be proud of them, or impressed by what they do, is priceless — the best recognition possible. Such premiums can give your mission added visibility. Many people have likely seen an "I gave blood today" decal and vowed to be more involved with the Red Cross. And who would not take pride in wearing a sticker that said "I changed a life?" Remember to work such premiums into the volunteer strategy and budget.

Motivating Volunteers

The wonderful thing about volunteers is that many of them are already motivated. If you work to justify that motivation — by using their time appropriately and well, and by recognizing their efforts — you have also helped extend that motivation.

Additional motivational techniques include:

- Playing music in casual group working situations — invite repeat volunteers to make their own mix CDs or MP3 playlists
- Having a door prize for the volunteer who, say, stuffs the most envelopes in an hour
- Paying for the volunteers' lunch
- Kicking off the volunteer day with a speech from a client of the nonprofit about how the organization has helped him or her — ideally, this should be the sort of inspiring story that leaves people misty-eyed

- Providing positive reinforcement for good work through-out the day — in particular, have senior volunteers show off the work of new volunteers who have made strides

- Assembling volunteers in smaller groups that each have team names — if possible, put volunteers with people they do not know so that all social interactions start out on equal footing

- Maintaining a volunteer hall of fame on your Web site or in your facility

- Taking the time to speak personally with each volunteer about his or her experience and suggestions — among other things, you can probably learn something about re-cruitment, training, and skills

Think about the last time you volunteered. Why did you do it? Was it a satisfying experience? Why or why not? If you have not volunteered in a while, go help out another nonprofit organiza-tion for a day, and pay attention to the experience. Talk to that or-ganization's volunteer coordinator and see what you can learn.

Relations Between Staff and Volunteers

Employees can resent volunteers. They may feel that volunteers are a threat to their jobs — either because they do the work for free or because employees may assume the volunteers are using the opportunity as an "in" with the organization. They may also see volunteers as well-meaning oafs, hopelessly unskilled, who must be taught the same skills each time and always mess up internal systems because they do not know the way things work. There may be a kernel of truth in each of these situations, but work to keep it realistic:

- Volunteers may indeed need to spend more time reac-quainting themselves with equipment they last used six months ago. Any employee who is in charge of getting volunteers back up to speed must be patient and empathetic. The solution is partly one of staffing, partly one of your own attitude; if you are always respectful toward volunteers, employees are more likely to follow your example.

- Volunteers may actually hope to get hired by your organization. They may, as it turns out, be excellent candidates; they already know what you do, and it is clear they already agree with your mission. That does not mean they are going to replace current employees. Having a clearly articulated volunteer-job-application process in writing can help put such suspicions to rest.

- If your hiring policy has been appropriately conservative (see Chapter 12), employees should recognize that you only add staff positions when the work is so vital to the organization and the mission that it cannot be entrusted to less-predictable volunteer labor. However, make sure you address such suspicions, which can blind employees to volunteers' legitimate skills and cause the organization to miss out on a potential source of talent and assistance.

Tracking Volunteer Time

A sign-in/sign-out sheet can help you keep track of volunteer hours. You may opt to give each volunteer a card on which he or she monitors his daily hours, much like a time card; this approach can be more precise, but it raises the risk that volunteers will lose their cards. Track the following information:

- Volunteer
- Work group or senior volunteer — this way, you can identify and recognize the people who are doing a great job at training and motivating your volunteers

- Task
- Date
- Whether any hours were devoted to training rather than work

Accounting for Volunteer Time

The Bureau of Labor Statistics sets the official dollar value of a volunteer hour, both for the nation and for individual states. (As of this writing, this value is $19.51.) The Web site www.independentsector.org can give you the most recent figures available.

You cannot, by law, include that amount on your tax forms, as you may only count skilled pro bono services, which are calculated according to industry rates. But calculating the dollar value of the volunteer labor you have received is a fantastic way to demonstrate the following to your community and your donors:

- How much work goes into providing your services
- How efficient your organization is
- How much people care about your mission
- How valuable your work is

These figures can also demonstrate to volunteers the impact of their work. Think about it: A single, eight-hour volunteer day, with ten volunteers, has a value of nearly $1,600. With a few such days in one year, the value of volunteer labor could be larger than the organization's entire budget.

UMM... DO YOU REALLY WANT
TO SHOW THEM THEIR
OPPORTUNITY COST?

CHAPTER 14

Dealing with Common Obstacles

The test of any organization is how it responds to a challenge. This chapter addresses some of the most likely challenges in the life of a nonprofit organization, and some ways to overcome them.

Budget Shortfalls

To lead a nonprofit, you must be somewhat comfortable with the idea that your organizational income is going to fluctuate. Factors beyond your control influence your organizational income:

- Dips in the stock market
- Larger economic trends
- The personal fortunes of individual donors
- The appearance on the scene of a similar nonprofit
- The fact that the hometown team wound up playing in a pennant game on the night of your big fundraising event

And that does not even take into account the spending angle of things. One program might have ballooned over budget. Or you might have managed everything perfectly, but then an employee caused an accident while driving the organization's van, pushing up your insurance premiums and making you responsible for a few thousand dollars' worth of repairs. Or your state might have eliminated the property tax that funded the agency that was your main source of grants. Sometimes your plans just cannot account for everything, and your budget winds up short.

Emergency Funds

Many nonprofits have been scraping the bottom of the barrel for so long that everyone gets into a sort of starvation mentality of "when you have money, you had better spend it all." That pattern of thinking keeps the organization broke. Your financial strategy ought to include an operating reserve that acts as an emergency savings fund — with a clear, written definition of what constitutes an emergency to keep people from dipping into it to cover costs that do not actually threaten the future of the organization. Work with your CFO or board treasurer to implement a savings strategy. That is your second line of defense against budget shortfalls.

Your first line of defense, of course, is to spend responsibly — never taking on debt, never making impulsive financial decisions, and always shopping around — and to hire conservatively. Discipline can stave off many budget shortfalls.

Asking for Crisis Donations

Sometimes, you may hit a more serious shortfall, when disciplined spending and emergency funds will not be enough.

Your first course of action is to determine the size of the shortfall. What upcoming costs are in your plans? What will you not be able to afford? Does this look like a short-term crunch or a long-term problem? Be as specific and thorough as you can in these inquiries. You will need to revise your financial strategy and goals regularly, so be on an intimate footing with them anyway.

Next, look at costs you can cut or freeze. Are there any nonessential programs or projects? In this context, define "essential" strictly: It refers only to what directly supports your core mission. You do not necessarily need to cancel these projects, but you might want to freeze them for, say, three months, while you try to regain the funds to cover them. Try not to interrupt your essential work. Austerity measures may hurt you and your employees, but try not to make them hurt your clients.

Talk to your board. If you have a required annual donation that not everyone has given, now is a good time to ask for it. They should know as much as you know about the budget shortfall, and they should be talking to all their contacts, looking for contributions to remedy the situation.

At this point, you should know:

- What your financial priorities are
- How much money you need to restore client services, if any have been frozen
- How much money you need to resume normal function

Use these numbers as you get in touch with your donors. It is time to ask for crisis funding.

See Chapter 8 for a discussion of effective development technique. Some aspects of this technique still apply. You must say "thank you," and you must keep in personal touch with the donors to show them how their contributions are helping you out. You must give an honest statement of your need — and that includes being honest about the budget problem and the programs at risk. Other aspects of development technique will change. Now is not the time to hire a phone bank or send out an elaborate donor card. Those things cost money, and donors will notice that you seem to be spending on the non-essential things. Instead, use the cheapest methods at your disposal:

- Personal phone calls — not just from volunteers, but from you, the board members, and the other managers; let the rank of the caller show your donors the seriousness of the problem
- E-mail
- Social networking groups

Create an informal event — nothing that requires you to rent a space, just an evening at a local pub or restaurant — where a set percentage of the evening's ring goes to the organization, and you have the opportunity to circulate among your constituents and tell them personally what is going on. Then, stay in contact with people. Describe your struggle on your blog (see Chapter 4).

You might even want to send out a press release. A story about your struggling nonprofit can be a wonderful human interest story — an easy sell for a journalist — and can help you widen your public appeal. More than one consultant believes that marketing and PR efforts should be some of the last programs you cut because they can have such an important effect on the size of your constituency and, therefore, on the potential size of your donor pool.

The more repeat donors you have, the better cushioned you are against budget shortfalls. Not only is your donation income more likely to be steady, but you also probably have a few people who want to support the organization for the long haul and are willing to help out in times of crisis.

Cutting Programs and Services

It is possible that the donors will not be able to come through for you and that you will have no choice but to cut back on what you are offering.

You should already have a good sense of the organization's priorities and the community's needs. It can be hard — and heartbreaking — to pick between programs to decide whether the homeless kids need you more than the recovering addicts who need job training. Look closely at the points where your programs overlap to see whether there are any opportunities to share costs or equipment. Look at the skills you are currently paying for, and look at the skills of volunteers in your database.

Then, if you have no choice, cancel your offering. Inform the affected clients with a personal phone call and a conversation. Not only will this help you preserve goodwill in your community, but your clients may not have been aware of your financial problems; they may have ideas you had not considered.

Cutting programs and services may also involve laying off some employees. See the section on layoffs in Chapter 12.

This can be a painful and humbling time for a nonprofit and its leaders. Do not be too hard on yourself because income always ebbs and flows in business.

Poor Meeting Attendance

Low meeting attendance can be caused by a number of factors. Let us start with the less severe ones:

- Inconvenience of location
- Inconvenience of time
- Poor timing of notification and reminders

All of these can easily be corrected. Figure out how much advance notice people typically need. Some people's schedules are more rigid than others — for example, because they will be charged extra if they pick up the kids late from daycare — so you must be alert to the potential hardship you can cause them if you reschedule a meeting at the last minute. Figure out the best methods of notification — telephone, e-mail, a Google calendar, or some combination thereof — and stick to it. If no single location is convenient for everyone, either find a place that is convenient to most people or have meetings in rotating places, near the houses and apartments of different people. Also consider options such as conference calls and video conferencing.

Some people may be reluctant to come to meetings because they feel that meetings never accomplish anything. If you are running the meetings, it is your job to challenge this perception. Use an agenda and share it with everyone in advance. Try to keep off-topic comments to a minimum. Let everyone know that you expect them to be there on time so that no one wastes time waiting for other people to show up. Be there early yourself so that if people have issues to bring up with you, they can do so before the meeting without interfering with meeting time. See Chapter 2 for more suggestions on running efficient meetings.

Now, let us look at some of the more serious causes of poor meeting attendance:

- Low commitment to the organization
- Low commitment to the mission
- Shame — people do not want to meet, or to commit to a meeting time, because they have not completed their assigned tasks; or, even worse, they are embarrassed about being involved in the organization
- Personality conflicts with other board or staff members
- Personal problems that are demanding attention or energy
- Burnout

These are all big problems, and you will need to deal with them as quickly as possible.

It may be difficult to solve problems of low commitment without losing a staff or board member. But that is still preferable to letting the problems drag on forever. Quite simply, you do not want someone with low commitment in your organization. He or she will do more harm than good. Someone who is not working enough sends the unspoken message to others that inadequate work will be tolerated. You may see overall productivity drop. Low commitment can have a lasting, even toxic, effect on your organization. The problem will not get any easier to address later; deal with it now.

If an employee or board member has personal problems, take a compassionate approach. Do not bring up the problems in the middle of the meeting; in a private conversation, mention that you have noticed some faltering commitment or other signs of trouble, and explain that you want to make sure the person is OK. Allow some time off without penalty. If you think the person might need some sort of counseling, offer a referral — either to your employee assistance program, if you have one, or to another trusted practitioner. Make yourself available as a colleague and as a friend. People may keep showing up because, despite their problems, they still feel a commitment to the mission, to the organization, or to you. That is wonderful. But they can serve best when they are able to give their full attention. Make it clear that no one expects them to sacrifice their personal lives for the organization.

Personality conflicts within the organization can be nothing more than simple misunderstandings, or they can represent severe disagreements over the best way to serve the mission. They can easily grow so severe that they keep people away from your meetings and events — not just the people directly involved with the conflict, but also the people who have witnessed so many arguments that they do not want to be privy to any more. In some cases, you may have to work to ensure that the people involved are not working in direct contact with one another. In other cases, that may be impossible. Later in this chapter, we offer some suggestions for conflict resolution.

For suggestions on dealing with burnout, see Chapter 14.

Founder's Syndrome

Founder's syndrome is the name for a cluster of problems that can occur when an organization outgrows its origins. It typically happens because the leadership and management style that worked to get the organization off the ground when it was new no longer serves the organization now that it is larger and more successful. The organization has come to rely too heavily on one person — its founder — and cannot grow beyond the abilities of that single person. The following are some symptoms of founder's syndrome:

- Short-term, crisis-style management ("putting out fires") with an absence of long-term planning or strategy

- A leader who relies on charisma or compelling, forceful ideas rather than organizational strategy — this is particularly common in arts organizations that have been started by one or two brilliant visionaries who have always seen the organization as no more than a means (funding) to an end (production)

- High board, staff, or volunteer turnover — or, worse, not even turnover, just attrition

- An unspoken assumption that certain things will always be done the same way

- Burnout
- Reactive decision-making — letting circumstances, rather than strategy and priorities, force your hand
- Faith that all the organization's problems would be solved with more money, rather than with more careful, strategic use of the resources the organization does have
- Tasks and responsibilities assigned based on loyalty rather than personal merit
- A clique rather than a team at the core of the organization, with the attendant problems of a clique: petty personal status wars, exclusivity, bickering, backstabbing, inside jokes, low trust
- A clique-style approach to development, with an overreliance on the same core group of donors rather than donor outreach; messages are likely impassioned pleas to help the organization in its time of turmoil and need, rather than positive attempts to get new donors excited about the mission
- Board members who are there because of personal loyalty, not commitment to the mission — this may be a fine reason for someone to join a board initially, but if it is the reason someone *stays* on the board, that is a board member who is not helping the organization as much as he or she could
- Leadership that shows disregard for the organization's own policies (this may be part of a wartime mentality that sees policies as not applying during extenuating circumstances—which, incidentally, have been happening continuously for the past three years)
- Infrequent or irregular meetings

- Staff, volunteers, or board members who have no idea what is happening, but must wait for the leader to tell them what to do; they likely have no way of predicting how their own work will help the organization's constantly shifting plans, so they have stopped initiating tasks on their own

Founder's syndrome can be challenging — not least because it is often so closely tied to specific people. If you are a founding ED, recognizing founder's syndrome means acknowledging that many of your old patterns of leadership no longer help your cause in the optimal way. It means conceding leadership to other people — the board, a management team, or perhaps even a new ED — and that can be painful. If frequent crises have led to staff or board burnout, founder's syndrome may mean the loss of a few friends.

Similarly, the board that recognizes founder's syndrome in its ED has a potentially unpleasant confrontation on its hands. The ED may see the discussion of the syndrome as a personal betrayal. Avoid personal challenges and focus on positive, long-term changes in strategy and policy. Consider raising the frequency of board meetings to reinforce the message that everyone is in this together.

If you are a new ED coming into an organization that has founder's syndrome, you have the challenge of adjusting everyone's expectations. You must ensure you are not letting people's habits steer you into the departing ED's patterns of behavior. You will need to communicate your ideas without sending the tacit but hostile message that all the old ideas were bad. If there are employees, you will need to adjust their expectations of how they interact with their leader and how they trust their coworkers (See the section on organizational culture in Chapter 12 for a few ways to do this.). You may also need to deal with the founder, who might not have left the organization altogether; he or she might have joined the board or stayed on in a non-ED managerial role.

Recovering from founder's syndrome can take a year or more. It takes persistence and personal attention from everyone in the organization. Even if you have had a healthy strategy planning session, it may not be enough to remove some staff members' sense of crisis planning; you may discover that as soon as someone else perceives a short-term problem, the careful strategy is abandoned, the troops are rallied, and the budget is blown once again.

To recover, get back to the mission. The mission is likely not being well-served by the constant crisis mentality of the organization. The drama within the organization is keeping everyone from focusing on the people you are supposed to be helping — the ones outside the organization. Get back in touch with your community and your clients. Make them true priorities.

You can also set a few policies to combat the specific behavioral habits of founder's syndrome:

- No all-nighters, no late nights. At the end of the workday, the lights go out, and everyone goes home. Plan so that you do not have to stay up all night before a deadline.

- Introduce a new person to the organization every week. That goes for everyone in the organization. You can have a weekly happy hour or brown-bag lunch; it can be quite casual. The point is to get people looking outside the office walls and interacting with the community.

- Make plans and delegate responsibility. As noted, staffers may be in the habit of expecting plans to change, and therefore not doing work until it becomes mandated by an emergency. Give staff decision-making authority in relevant aspects of the new strategy. Set goals with them. Make sure you are approachable if they have questions so they do not have to wait until a meeting to get the information they need. Have regular, frequent meetings, and ask for progress reports. Recognize success.

- Establish a "drop-dead" schedule for grant applications and other projects, and permit no exceptions. For example, if you have learned about the grant or funding opportunity less than two weeks before its application deadline, you will put it on the calendar for next year, but you are not going to scramble to meet its requirements and adjust your programming next year. If you want to have a marketing piece tied to an upcoming program or event, you have to have the design and copywriting complete four weeks in advance, or the organization will not pay for printing expenses. (You can reinforce such policies by talking with your regular vendors and freelancers; encourage them to impose crisis rates and fees when people from your organization contact them about last-minute projects. Let the prices make your argument for you: last-minute planning destroys the budget.) Again, this policy works only as long as *no* exceptions are allowed. As soon as you abandon it because of a good chance to make a quick buck, you are all back in the middle of founder's syndrome. This aspect of recovery demands personal discipline from everyone in the organization.

- Emphasize the development of new skills. Have a day in which everyone in the organization gets to try someone else's job. The next time there are tasks to be assigned, use this experience to break through the loyalty-based, "Dave has always done that" pattern of giving responsibilities.

- Get the board involved. They are responsible for the organization. Have them develop and implement active financial strategies. Having an existing team in charge, rather than a single person, can help the organization lose its unnatural dependence on the founding leader.

- Play an annual game of "What If?" Management consultant Carter McNamara recommends that once a year, the board evaluate the organization in terms of what would happen if the ED suddenly vanished. If the entire group would collapse, then the organization is too dependent on that person, and the board must take action to spread responsibility around. The founder should actively participate in this discussion; there may be no better, or gentler, way to recognize the flaws in his or her leadership patterns.

- Do not automatically dismiss the founder's ideas. They cannot be all bad; after all, the organization has come this far and attracted a number of people who believe in it. Treat the founder with respect and dignity. That is how that person will know that his or her mission is in good hands and that you are behaving out of concern for the organization — not out of personal antipathy toward him or her.

Compassion

If you are dealing with a case of founder's syndrome, remember to use compassion and empathy as you interact with the founder. He or she likely loved the feeling of being vital to the organization and may have a sense that, now, he or she is "useless."

Make it clear that this is not true, that you still value the person's opinions and efforts. The founder is not unnecessary; the point is simply that, for the organization to thrive, many more people are also necessary. It is no longer a one-man show.

Interpersonal Conflicts

People are passionate about nonprofit work, and where there is passion, there is the potential for bitter disagreement. Sometimes conflicts can arise among employees, between board members, or between volunteers. Ideally, people will be mature enough to resolve these conflicts on their own. But sometimes, people will appeal to you for help. Sometimes, too, the conflict is the inadvertent result of an organizational policy or activity, and it is actually good that the problem is coming to your attention — though it can be hard to remember that in the moment when you are facing two glowering staffers who are incapable of speaking to each other in civil sentences.

Preemptive Conflict Resolution

Be alert to interpersonal relations in meetings, on task forces, and in the day-to-day interactions of your staff. Emotions do get involved. If you sense trouble brewing, you can address it before it erupts into a crisis. Be aware, too, that you will set the tone for interpersonal relations by the way you treat other people in the organization. If you are fair, respectful, and reasonable, others will strive to imitate that example. If you are easy-going and casual, that attitude will permeate the culture — which, it should be noted, is entirely appropriate for some organizations.

Avoid conflicts by ensuring staff, volunteers, and board members know that they are expected to handle disagreements maturely. If you have already worked on creating a culture of respect (see

Chapter 12), conflict management should be built into your organizational culture.

If a conflict does come to your attention, deal with it immediately. Sit down with the people involved. Take a deep breath. Offer them a cup of tea. Get them talking reasonably, honestly, and quietly about what has happened. At this stage, your job is simply to listen; try not to interrupt. Take notes, and if a conflict is truly severe, as in a harassment case or another situation involving gross misconduct, or if it is the result of organizational policies, you will want to have a record of this conversation.

Once you have heard all sides of the situation, think about it. Consider the following questions:

- Has there been a clear breach of organizational policy — one that would ordinarily result in disciplinary action? Are the people involved aware of this policy?

- What is the true source of the conflict? Can you address the conflict by removing its source, or by removing one or both of the people from that situation?

- On what points do the people agree?

- On what points do the people disagree?

- Will there be an organizational impact if you resolve the conflict in a certain way?

- What will it take to get the two people to agree on the most important point? You can ask them this. They may not name concessions the other person is willing to make — but then again, they may want nothing more than a simple apology.

If disciplinary action is called for, you will need to make the offending staffer aware of the breach of policy. Do not take disciplinary action immediately, and especially not reflexively, unless the employee poses a hazard to others. Call in your HR director and have a discussion with the staffer about what constitutes a fair penalty. Make sure the person knows exactly why he or she is being punished.

If organizational policy is to blame for the conflict, as in the case of disparate pay raises, it is time to reassess your policy to prevent such a conflict from happening again. If you imposed the policy and now realize it is a mistake, you will gain, not lose, employees' respect by admitting your error. Be clear about the new policy, and make sure it is clearly communicated to employees. Depending on your organizational culture, you may want to invite all employees to speak to you about other policies they find frustrating, contradictory, or troubling. If you decide to revise a major policy, such as one about employee sick leave, make sure you communicate the change in writing, and obtain every employee's signature on the new document.

Staff Turnover

It is a rule of thumb in the corporate world that it costs 1.5 times as much to hire someone new as it does to retain the employee you already have. It pays to engage in **retention** efforts — ways to keep your current employees happy and productive. Programs such as flex time, on-site daycare, the opportunity for full-time reduced-hours work, telecommuting, parking or mass transit vouchers, and carpools can all go a long way toward accommodating the personal demands that pull employees away from work. Some of these benefits cost a bit; some do not.

You will need to think about which retention programs are best suited to your employees and their needs, but also about the programs that are suited to your most engaged employees — the ones most committed to the organization, the ones you most want to retain. There is no sense in catering to a disgruntled employee. Of course, if you are practicing a lean hiring policy, you should not have too many of those.

Sometimes, it is just time for someone to leave the organization. An employee may be moving to another city, having a child, going back to school, or getting ready to embark upon a new challenge. Or, less positively, someone may be locked in a personality clash with another employee, overcommitted, burnt out, or irredeemably frustrated with certain conditions of your work.

If someone decides to leave your organization, do not miss the opportunity to have a frank **exit interview,** in which you can openly discuss the person's reasons for leaving. An exit interview shows you ways to improve the organization's effectiveness, the internal culture, and your own style of leadership. It can be a humbling experience; you may learn more than you want to about your own failings as a leader. But this knowledge is essential if you want to continue to lead the organization, and to do it well.

In general, keep your exit interview friendly and informal. Leave questions open-ended, and let the departing employee talk. It is your job to listen — perhaps to ask for clarification, perhaps occasionally to offer explanation, but mostly to listen. You may have to resist the impulse to begin a spirited defense of your business decisions or your personal leadership style. Bite your tongue, and learn what you can. Sample questions to ask in an exit interview:

- What made you feel that it was time to leave?
- Were there any surprises about working here, welcome or unwelcome?
- Were you frustrated by any day-to-day aspects of your work? The answers to this question can often point you in

the direction of major sources of inefficiency. Fixing these inefficiencies can not only improve your employees' lives, but also help the whole organization run better.

- What was one thing you enjoyed about working here? What was a high point of your work here?

- What was one thing you did not enjoy about working here?

- Do you have any questions for me? Is there anything you want to tell me?

- Is there anything you think we could be doing better?

- How do you feel now about our mission?

If you have worked hard to create an open organizational culture, in which employees feel comfortable coming forward with their ideas and problems, few of these answers should come as a complete surprise. If you are surprised by some of what your employee says, then you may not be in close enough touch with what is really happening in your organization. Think about ways to change that.

After each exit interview, sit down with your HR manager and talk about opportunities for improving the organization's employee relations and culture. Are exit interviews pointing at any persistent or recurring problems that need to be addressed? How can you address those problems? Let employees know that you are taking these actions and that you take employees' opinions and feelings seriously.

Continuing Involvement

Someone who has left your employment has not necessarily abandoned your mission or your organization. If an employee leaves on good terms, he or she may very well return as a donor

— or even a board member — some time in the future. Maintain these relationships.

Burnout

Nonprofit work inspires passion. But it also invites over-commitment and burnout. Are you working 60-hour weeks? Are you asking your employees to do that? Are they doing it without being asked? In these instances, you are all at risk for burnout.

Remember that exhaustion and sleep deprivation will not help you save the world. You have to do the work in increments, bit by bit. Over time, you will see progress.

If employee burnout seems to be a risk, think of ways to build relaxation back into the schedule. These can be relatively small — a 15-minute tea break added to the afternoon schedule, a time for relaxed conversation and deep breaths. Perhaps you can invite a yoga teacher or a masseuse into the office for a longer break.

Or, if it looks as though burnout is on its way to becoming a more chronic problem, you might need to create bigger remedies:

- Look at ways you could be involving volunteers in the small tasks that are eating up employees' time.

- Schedule an office-wide paid day off that does not come out of employees' vacation banks.

- Think about investing in a piece of technology that will make everyone's work go more smoothly. For example, if you are paying a well-qualified grant writer by the hour, do you really want her to have to collate the ten copies of the proposal by hand, just because the copier will not do it?

- Think about programs, such as on-site daycare or workout facilities or telecommuting, that can help employees balance other aspects of their lives with the work you are asking them to do.

Talk to board members about finding resources to make these things happen. Ask employees for their ideas too. Talk to your ED peer group about ways they have combated burnout in their organizations.

Take a moment to remember your life outside the organization — your family, your friends, your hobbies, that art museum you have been meaning to go to. Remember that your organization exists to help complete people — not just to treat a disease, to raise awareness, or to make art in a vacuum, but to help people live richer, fuller lives. Remind yourself what a rich, full life is like. Your nonprofit work is part of it — a big part. But the minute it goes from "part" to "all," you risk losing the empathy, understanding, and sense of shared experience that drove you to nonprofit work in the first place.

Remember, you are doing as much as you can to make the world a better place. This is considerably more than what most people ever do with their lives. Be grateful for the opportunity to serve, be proud of what you have accomplished, and be excited about what is to come.

Inspiration

Even while doing what matters most to them, EDs can get burned out sometimes. Some ideas for staying engaged in your work include:

- Keep your mission statement visible — on your wall, on your screen saver, on your desk, on your T-shirt — somehow. You remember the lesson: Go back to the mission!

- Take a picture of the first person you helped — the first person whose life you know you changed for the better. Have that picture framed, and put it somewhere you can always see it.

- Keep a collection of the thank-you notes you have received from your constituents. Have a weekly ritual of choosing a thank-you note to read at random. This can be a great way of keeping employees engaged as well.

- Call a constituent. Ask how he or she is doing now. Ask how your organization could help him or her. There is no quicker way to happiness than to help someone else.

- Take a break. Sometimes nonprofit work is emotionally draining and physically exhausting. Do not treat yourself as an inexhaustible resource.

CHAPTER 15

Evaluating
the Organization

Once a nonprofit is established, how do you know it is doing what it set out to do? How many lives has it changed? Is it organized with maximum efficiency? Where could it expand its efforts? And, finally, does it continue to fulfill the people who care about it most?

Accountability

You must, ultimately, ask yourself:

- Are we changing lives in the way we want to change them?
- Are we changing them in the ways our community needs us to change them?
- Are we helping as many people as we want to?
- If resources limit the number of people we can help, are we taking constructive action to expand our resources and our scope?

Ask yourself these questions at least once a year. Especially in a small, one- or two-person operation, it is easy to get caught up in "chasing the money" — pursuing development dollars for the sake of organizational expansion — and to lose sight of your real purpose.

Depending on the formality of your organization and your relationship with your board, you may want to assign some numbers to these questions. Is there a target number of people you want to serve? Put that number in your annual goals. Is there some other quantitative way of measuring your impact in the community? Set a quantitative goal. If you miss these goals, take the time to think about what happened, and talk it over with the board.

Standards of Effectiveness

As long as we are talking about numbers, how do you know what numbers make sense? It is all very well to set a numeric goal, but how do you know if you are being unrealistic — or too modest?

Talk to your ED peer group, if you have one. Look at the *Nonprofit Good Practice Guide* and other online references to find out how the nonprofit world evaluates different aspects of organizational and personal performance. For example, a development director often has fundraising goals tied to his or her salary — a minimum number of new donors added, development income equal to three times the salary, or some other measure that clearly ties his or her work to the success of the organization.

It can be hard to set such standards for yourself. After all, who knows better than you what counts as the most effective behavior? Remember that your board has hiring and firing power, and consult with them. Also, look at industry trends. Remember that you do not get to let yourself off the hook just because you are in charge.

Responding to Poor Evaluations

If you hear the same thing from two different people, the truism goes, it is probably time to take a hard look at yourself. One poor evaluation could be the product of an isolated conflict, an employee or board member who happened to complete the evaluation on a bad day, or any number of other factors. Two poor evaluations — especially two that mention the same thing — are cause for consideration.

Obviously, poor evaluations hurt. Judging by the high incidence of burnout, nonprofit EDs tend to work hard and judge themselves harshly, and it can feel unfair if someone else considers all that work a failure. Nonetheless, resist the urge to get defensive.

If you need more information, have a calm conversation with the person who gave you a poor evaluation and ask what specific behaviors of yours have contributed to that negative impression.

If you already know what you could be doing better, you will need to set those behaviors in writing as formal goals. You will need to communicate them to the board. It is also not a bad idea — though it is a humbling one — to communicate them to the person who gave you the poor evaluation. They should know that their message got through to you and that you are working to correct the problem.

Updating the Mission

We have discussed mission creep a bit thus far. What happens when the mission changes in a good way? Perhaps you added a program that has become so successful that it is now viewed as your core effort. Perhaps you have entered a coalition with another nonprofit that has worked so well that the two organizations should merge. Perhaps — best of all — you have done all you can do in your original target community, and it is time to move on to helping other people.

It is time to revise the mission. You will need to look at the mission statement and cross out the parts that just do not match up with reality any more. Then go through the process of drafting and re-drafting described in Chapter 1. Be alert, of course, to the way this process may change your brand and your marketing efforts. You will need to overhaul your five-year plan and your development strategy. Do not count on having a steady budget; major donors may be alienated by your decision. It is worth a personal call to these people, who rightly see themselves as having a stake in the organization, to explain the decision and the future plans.

You might have thought you were done with drafting mission statements for good, but the truth is, you are never done with it. Most nonprofits are intended to outlive their founders, and their missions must evolve as society evolves.

Be aware that if you change the mission, you may need to notify certain state authorities. Check with your state attorney general's office. In some cases, you will need to notify the IRS as well.

Knowing When — and How — to Leave

Maybe you are burnt out. Maybe you are tired. Maybe you are ready to spend a bit more time with your family, your boyfriend, or your cat. Maybe it is time to care for a child or a sick parent.

Maybe you are not tired at all. Maybe your nonprofit work has given you a fantastic idea for a new organization you want to start, and the old organization is strong enough that you feel comfortable handing the reins to someone else.

Maybe a horrifying new social problem has reared its head and you want to help the community you have come to love.

Maybe you would like to learn something totally different and are starting to think about grad school.

Maybe you can accomplish more social change by running for office.

Maybe you have your own reasons.

You will likely know when it is time to leave. You will start to feel frustrated by the work in front of you, constantly sensing that work elsewhere is more compelling. A motivation in your own life may be too immediate and compelling to ignore. In any case — perhaps wistfully, perhaps dramatically, perhaps joyously — you will realize that is time for you to leave. If you are not sure, by now, you should know the correct action to take: Look to the mission. Is it still interesting? Does it still make you brim over with ideas?

Leaving is a hard decision, even when it is motivated by happy reasons. Make sure you seek adequate emotional support as you leave.

Meet frequently with your board to discuss your plans. Look for opportunities to educate them and others within the organization about what you do and ways you think policies and procedures could work in the future. Help them understand everything you have done so that they can function without you and prevent the organization from coming down with founder's syndrome after your departure.

Before you leave, remember to thank everyone — personally — for what they have done, both for you as a leader and for the organization. Take a moment to think about what you have learned. There should be a lot.

APPENDIX
Resources

Sample Bylaws

Source: Project: Philanthropy

BYLAWS OF PROJECT: PHILANTHROPY

ARTICLE 1: NAME AND PURPOSES

1.01. Name

The corporate name of this organization is Project: Philanthropy Inc. (P2). Project: Philanthropy is an Illinois not-for-profit corporation.

1.02. Mission

The mission of P2 is to further the causes of charitable organizations by fulfilling their design and marketing needs.

Through a group of volunteer designers, writers, editors, programmers, and other professionals, we will create and produce such items as identity materials, logos, stationery, Web sites, brochures, fundraising materials, advertisements, and invitations for nonprofit clients. We will also solicit paper vendors and printers to donate their materials and/or services in order to produce these materials free-of-charge to nonprofits.

1.03. IRC Section 501(c)(3) Purposes

P2 is organized exclusively for one or more of the purposes as specified in Section 501(c)(3) of the Internal Revenue Code, including, for such purposes, the making of distributions to organizations that qualify as exempt organizations under Section 501(c) (3) of the Internal Revenue Code.

ARTICLE 2: MEMBERS

2.01. Number

The corporation shall have 5–10 directors, and collectively they shall be known as the Board of Directors.

2.02. Qualifications

Directors shall be of the age of majority in this state. Other qualifications for directors of P2 shall be:

- Commitment to capital campaigns for the continuation and preservation of the organization
- Commitment and ability to seek the appropriate avenues for establishing an endowment
- Ability and willingness to donate time and talents
- Dedication to the mission of P2.

2.03. Powers

Subject to the provisions of the laws of this state and any limitations in the Articles of Incorporation and these Bylaws relating to action required or permitted to be taken or approved by the members, if any, of this corporation, the activities and affairs of this corporation shall be conducted and all corporate powers shall be exercised by or under the direction of the Board of Directors.

2.04. Duties

It shall be the duty of the directors to:

(a) Perform any and all duties imposed on them collectively or individually by law, by the Articles of Incorporation, or by these Bylaws;

(b) Appoint and remove, employ and discharge, and, except as otherwise provided in these Bylaws, prescribe the duties, if any, of all officers, agents, volunteers and employees of the corporation;

(c) Supervise all officers, agents and volunteers of the corporation to ensure that their duties are performed properly;

(d) Meet at such times and places as required by these Bylaws;

(e) Register their addresses with the Secretary of the corporation. Notices of meetings mailed, telephoned, or e-mailed to them at such addresses shall be valid notices thereof.

2.05. Term of Office
Each director shall hold office for a period of one year and until his or her successor is elected and qualifies.

2.06. Compensation
Directors shall serve without compensation. They shall be allowed reasonable advancement or reimbursement of expenses incurred in the performance of their duties.

2.07. Regular Meetings
Regular meetings of Directors shall be held on alternating Tuesdays at 5:30 p.m. at the principal office of the corporation (560 W. Washington), unless such day falls on a legal holiday, in which event the regular meeting shall be held at an hour and day agreed to by a majority of the Directors.

2.08. Special Meetings
Special meetings of the Board of Directors may be called by the President, the Vice-President, the Secretary, the Treasurer, by any two board members, or, if different, by the persons specifically authorized under the laws of this state to call special meetings of the board. Such meetings shall be held at the principal office

of the corporation or, if different, at the place designated by the person or persons calling the special meeting.

2.09. Notice of Meetings

Unless otherwise provided by the Articles of Incorporation, these Bylaws, or provisions of law, the following provisions shall govern the giving of notice for meetings of the Board of Directors:

(a) Regular meetings. No notice need be given of any regular meeting of the Board of Directors, but a quarterly schedule will be provided by the Secretary.

(b) Special meetings. The Secretary shall give at least one week's prior notice of each special meeting of the board to each director. Such notice may be oral or written, may be given personally, by first class mail, by telephone, or by e-mail and shall state the place, date and time of the meeting, and the matters proposed to be acted upon at the meeting.

(c) Waiver of Notice. Whenever any notice of a meeting is required to be given to any director of this corporation under provision of the Articles of Incorporation, or the law of this state, a waiver of notice in writing signed by the Director, whether before or after the time of the meeting, shall be equivalent to the giving of such notice.

2.10. Quorum for Meetings

A quorum shall consist of four members of the Board of Directors attending in person or by teleconference.

Except as otherwise provided under the Articles of Incorporation, these Bylaws, or provisions of law, no business shall be considered by the Board at any meeting at which the required quorum is not present, and the only motion which shall be entertained at such meeting is a motion to adjourn.

2.11. Action Without a Meeting

Any action required or permitted to be taken at a meeting of the Board of Directors (including amendment of these Bylaws) or of any committee may be taken without a meeting if a majority of the members of the Board or committee consent in writing (including e-mail) to taking the action without a meeting and to approving the specific action. Such consents shall have the same force and effect as a unanimous vote of the Board or committee, as the case may be.

2.12. Majority Action as Board Action

Every act or decision done or made by a majority of Directors present at a meeting duly held at which a quorum is present is the act of the Board of Directors, unless the Articles of Incorporation, these Bylaws, or provisions of law require a greater percentage or different voting rules for approval of a matter by the board.

2.13. Conduct of Meetings

Meetings of the Board of Directors shall be presided over by the President of the corporation, or, in his or her absence, by the Vice-President of the corporation, or, in the absence of each of these persons, by a Chairperson chosen by a majority of the Directors present at the meeting. The Secretary of the corporation shall act as secretary of all meetings of the board, provided that, in his or her absence, the presiding officer shall appoint another person to act as secretary of the meeting.

Meetings shall be governed by the President, insofar as such rules are not inconsistent with or in conflict with the Articles of Incorporation, these Bylaws, or provisions of law.

2.14. Termination of Membership

The Board of Directors, by affirmative vote of two-thirds of all the members of the Board, may suspend or expel a member.

Any member may resign by filing a written resignation with the Secretary. No director may resign if the corporation would then be left without a duly elected director or directors in charge of its affairs, except upon notice to the Office of the Attorney General or other appropriate agency of this state.

2.15. Vacancies

Vacancies on the Board of Directors shall exist (1) on the death, resignation or removal of any director, and (2) whenever the number of authorized directors is increased.

Unless otherwise prohibited by the Articles of Incorporation, these Bylaws or provisions of law, vacancies on the Board may be filled by approval of the Board of Directors. If the number of directors then in office is less than a quorum, a vacancy on the Board may be filled by approval of a majority of the Directors then in office or by a sole remaining Director.

2.16. Nonliability of Directors

The directors shall not be personally liable for the debts, liabilities, or other obligations of the corporation.

2.17. Indemnification by Corporation of Directors and Officers

The directors and officers of the corporation shall be indemnified by the corporation to the fullest extent permissible under the laws of this state.

ARTICLE 3: OFFICERS

3.01. Designation of Officers

The officers of the corporation shall be a President, a Vice-President, a Secretary, and a Treasurer. The corporation may also have a Chairperson of the Board and other such officers with such titles as may be determined from time to time by the Board of Directors.

3.02. Election and Terms of Office

Officers shall be elected by the Board of Directors at regular meetings of the board, or, in the case of vacancies, as soon thereafter as convenient. New offices may be created and filled at any meeting of the Board of Directors.

Terms of office may be established by the Board of Directors, but shall not exceed three (3) years. Officers shall hold office until a successor is duly elected and qualified. Officers shall be eligible for reappointment.

3.03. Removal and Resignation

An officer may be removed by the Board of Directors at a meeting whenever in the Board's judgment the best interests of the corporation will be served thereby. Any such removal shall be without prejudice of the contract rights, if any, of the person so removed.

Resignations are effective upon receipt by the Secretary of the Board of a written notification or at any later date specified therein.

3.04. President

The President shall be a director of the corporation and will preside at all meetings of the Board of Directors. The President shall perform all duties attendant to that office, subject, however, to the control of the Board of Directors, and shall perform such other duties as on occasion shall be assigned by the board.

3.05. Vice-President

The Vice-President shall be a director of the corporation and will preside at meetings of the Board of Directors in the absence of or at the request of the President, or in the event of the President's inability to act. The Vice-President shall perform other duties as requested and assigned by the President, subject to the control of the Board of Directors.

3.06. Secretary

The Secretary shall be a director of the corporation and:

(a) Certify and keep at the principal office of the corporation the original, or a copy, of these Bylaws as amended or otherwise altered to date;

(b) Keep the minutes of all meetings of the Board of Directors in the books proper for that purpose;

(c) See that all notices are duly given in accordance with the provisions of these Bylaws or as required by law;

(d) Keep at the principal office of the corporation a membership file (written or electronic) containing the name and address of each member, and, in the case where any membership has been terminated, record such fact together with the date on which such membership ceased;

(e) Provide such documentation to any officer or director of the corporation as requested;

(f) Perform such other duties as may occasionally be assigned by the Board of Directors.

3.07. Treasurer

The Treasurer shall:

(a) Have charge and custody of, and be responsible for, all funds and securities of the corporation, and deposit all such funds in the name of the corporation in such banks, trust companies, or other depositories as shall be selected by the Board of Directors;

(b) Receive and give receipt for monies payable to the corporation from any source whatsoever;

(c) Disburse or cause to be disbursed the funds of the corporation as may be directed by the Board of Directors;

(d) Maintain adequate and correct accounts of the corporation's properties and business transactions;

(e) Report on the financial affairs of the corporation at regular meetings;

(f) Prepare and certify the financial statements to be included in any required reports;

(g) Perform such other duties as may be assigned by the Board of Directors.

3.08. Paid Staff
The Board of Directors may hire such paid staff as they deem proper and necessary for the operations of the corporation. The powers and duties of the paid staff shall be as assigned or as delegated to be assigned by the Board.

ARTICLE 4: INDEMNIFICATION

Every member of the Board of Directors, officer, or employee of the corporation may be indemnified by the corporation against all expenses and liabilities, including counsel fees, reasonably incurred or imposed upon such member of the Board, officer or employee in connection with any threatened, pending, or completed action, suit, or proceeding to which he or she may become involved by reason of his/her being or having been a member of the Board, officer, or employee of the corporation, or any settlement thereof, unless adjudged therein to be liable for negligence or misconduct in the performance of his/her duties, provided, however, that in the event of a settlement the indemnification herein shall apply only when the Board approves such settlement and reimbursement as being in the best interest of the corporation. The foregoing right of indemnification shall be in addition and not exclusive of other rights to which such member of the Board, officer, or employee is entitled.

ARTICLE 5: ADVISORY BOARDS AND COMMITTEES

5.01. Establishment

The Board of Directors may establish one or more advisory boards or committees.

5.02. Size, Duration, and Responsibilities

The size, duration, and responsibilities of such boards and committees shall be established by a majority vote of the Board of Directors.

ARTICLE 6: FINANCIAL ADMINISTRATION

6.01. Fiscal Year

The fiscal year of the corporation shall be Jan. 1–Dec. 31 but may be changed by resolution of the Board of Directors.

6.02. Checks, Drafts, Etc.

All checks, orders for the payment of money, bills of lading, warehouse receipts, obligations, bills of exchange, and insurance certificates shall be signed or endorsed by such officer or officers or agent or agents of the Corporation and in such manner as shall from time to time be determined by resolution of the Board of Directors or of any committee to which such authority has been delegated by the Board.

6.03. Deposits and Accounts

All funds of the corporation, not otherwise employed, shall be deposited from time to time in general or special accounts in such banks, trust companies, or other depositories as the Board of Directors or any committee to which such authority has been delegated by the Board may select, or as may be selected by the President or by any other officer or officers or agent or agents of the corporation, to whom such power may from time to time be delegated by the Board. For the purpose of deposit and for the purposes of collection for that account of the corporation, checks, drafts, and other orders of the corporation may be endorsed, assigned, and delivered on behalf of the corporation by any officer or agent of the corporation.

6.04. Investments

The funds of the corporation may be retained in whole or in part in cash or be invested and reinvested on occasion in such stock, bonds, or other securities, as the Board of Directors in its sole discretion may deem desirable, without regard to the limitations, if any, now imposed or which may hereafter be imposed by law regarding such investments, and which are permitted to organizations exempt from federal income taxation under Section 501(c)(3) of the Internal Revenue Code.

ARTICLE 7: BOOKS AND RECORDS

Correct books of account of the activities and transactions of the corporation shall be kept at the office of the corporation. These shall include a minute book, which shall contain a copy of the Certificate of Incorporation, a copy of these Bylaws, and all minutes of meetings of the Board of Directors.

ARTICLE 8: AMENDMENT OF BYLAWS

These Bylaws may be amended by a majority vote of the Board of Directors, provided prior notice is given of the proposed amendment in the notice of the meeting at which such action is taken, or provided all members of the Board waive such notice, or by unanimous consent in writing pursuant to Section 2.11.

ARTICLE 9: CONSTRUCTION AND TERMS

If there is any conflict between the provisions of these Bylaws and the Articles of Incorporation of this corporation, the provisions of the Articles of Incorporation shall govern.

Should any of the provisions or portions of these Bylaws be held unenforceable or invalid for any reason, the remaining provisions and portions of these Bylaws shall be unaffected by such holding.

Sample Volunteer Application

Please print

First Name_____ Last Name _____

Address _____ City/State/Zip._____

Telephone _____ Social Security # _____

Date of Birth _____ Spouse's Name _____

Personal Information (please circle correct response):

Gender: Male   Female

Physical Limitations: No   Yes (Please Explain)

Education (highest level completed)

Grades: 1-5   6-9   11-12   College   Business   Graduate School
    Technical/Vocational

Former work/occupation _____

Most recent employer (optional) _____

List previous volunteer experience _____

Skills (List your skills and indicate proficiency level)

Skilled   Can Teach   Amateur

1. _____

2. _____

3. _____

Languages   Fluent   Read   Write

1. _____

2. _____

Volunteer availability: (Circle all applicable)

Number of Days per week: 1 2 3 4 5

Monday   Tuesday   Wednesday   Thursday   Friday

No Preference

Transportation: (How you will get to your assignment)

Public Trans.   Walk   Bus/Van Taxi/Car Svc   Car

In an emergency, notify:

First Name_____ Last Name _____

Address _____

City/State/Zip _____ Telephone _____

Volunteers hereby agree to serve any client who is assigned regardless of race, sex, creed, or national origin.

_____   _____   _____

(Signature/Volunteer)   (Signature/Staff)   (Date)

Sample Donor Appeal Letter

Source: Sansculottes Theater Company

Tell me a story.

It is the smallest request, one we all remember from childhood.

Help me sleep. Help me wake up. Help me understand. Help me laugh. Help me make sense of the world, of other people, of you. Help me live. Tell me a story.

At first the stories are simple. As we grow up, they change—but perhaps less than we think. They all convey the same struggle, the same ache, the same joy, and—if we are lucky—the same magic.

At heart, **telling a story is a tiny act of faith:** faith that someone will hear it and understand; faith that we can find meaning in a microcosm of life; faith that we are not alone. And when someone does hear and understand? **Magic.**

If speaking the words is a tiny act of faith, putting them on stage is **the true believer's leap across the chasm.**

Sansculottes Theater Company is now in its fourth season of telling stories. We have presented audiences with a recently dead painter coming to terms with the afterlife, with singing serial killers, with a little boy dressed as a ninja, with a tearful one-sided conversation from behind a closed door, with a BB-gun sniper, with a literally endless airport layover, with factory workers sprouting extra arms, with a couch that swallowed its occupant. We have been made to take such risks, to hurl ourselves again and again into the void. But **our supporters have been right there:** laughing, clapping, sighing, thinking, offering suggestions, catching us—time and time again. We have been overwhelmed by their creativity and generosity.

This year our new artistic director, Tom Horan, kicked off a **summer reading series** for new work, a first for our company. We staged readings and workshops for five plays in three months. We also began **our most ambitious collective writing project** to date, a month-long collaboration with designers and actors that started with six images by artist Jose Posada and became *The Posada Project.* And we've begun writing the spring sketch show, the latest installment in our popular *Screw Love* series.

This year, Suzan Lori-Parks is premiering her **365 Project,** a national festival of 365 short plays in as many days. Sansculottes is thrilled to be one of the participating Chicago companies. In April we will produce seven of her short plays alongside seven shorts we have collectively written. It is a great step forward into **working with the theater community on a local and a national scale.**

Our season will culminate in May with yet another world premiere, literary manager Adam Simon's *Fear of a Hood.* We believe it is **groundbreaking:** a play about race that doesn't feel like a play about race. Funny, sad, and unsettling, it places several friendships under a microscope, examining what we say and what we don't, and why.

We do not expect to run out of stories any time soon. We hope you'll be around to join in the telling—because we can't, in fact, tell them without you. We make the stories; **you make the magic.**

Please support Sansculottes' fourth season with a donation. Help us keep telling stories. Help us keep bringing them to new audiences. Help a big, mysterious, spooky, awful, joyful, heartbreaking, funny world come to life.

Help us finish one of the most exciting sentences in the world: *Once upon a time . . .*

Tom Horan

Artistic Director

Sample Donation Request (to a Business)

Source: Sansculottes Theater Company

Date: [Month] [Date], [Year]
To: [Name]
         [Address]
         [Organization]
From: [Name], Development Director
Re: Request for Donations

Sansculottes Theater Company seeks donations for a raffle to be held as part of our Art for Art's Sake benefit night on March 21 at the Peter Jones Gallery. We expect 100–200 attendees, most of them professionals under age 35. Because this group corresponds so closely with the customers [Organization] courts, a promotion from [Organization] is a natural choice for a raffle prize. A suitable donation might be a gift certificate, or [other industry-specific examples].

Proceeds from the Art for Art's Sake benefit will go towards the world premiere production of a groundbreaking new play, *Fear of a Hood*, by company literary manager Adam Simon. Quick, funny, moving, and ultimately tragic, *Fear of a Hood* comments on our relationships with the past, our contemporary hyper-awareness of race, and the tangled connections between capitalism and identity. We're incredibly excited about the production, which opens [Date], on Live Bait Theater's Bucket stage. [Obviously, this paragraph changes depending on the purpose of the donation request. Much of the language can be borrowed from your event press release.]

[Name], thank you for your consideration. Whether or not [Organization] can donate at this time, we invite you to join us on the evening of [Date] at the Peter Jones Gallery.

Sample Thank-You Letter to Fundraiser Attendees

Source: Sansculottes Theater Company

Dear [name],

Your friends at Sansculottes have been hard at work on our newest world premiere, *Fear of a Hood*, by Literary Manager Adam Simon. We wanted to take a moment to thank you for supporting us by attending the *Art for Art's Sake* event. We were able to raise our goal of $3,000, almost half of our entire budget for the show. The success of the event was critical for the creation of this show and has helped us pay for everything from the technical necessities to the brilliant work our actors and artists have contributed. We are so grateful for your support.

The cast and crew are very excited after working overtime to put the finishing touches on *Fear of a Hood*. The sneak peek you saw at the fundraiser has piqued a lot of people's curiosity, so we're happy to say that the curtain call is finally here. This is Adam Simon's first full production of a two-act play, and I think it is the finest piece he has written, balancing styles he has been experimenting with for years: slice of life realism, surreal theatricality, specific tonality and Adam's idiosyncratic humor.

With much more on the horizon, including our second annual *No Pants, Just Shorts Ten Minute Play Festival* and a late summer reading series, Sansculottes will continue to be a beacon in the fight to create original and highly collaborative new work. And we couldn't do it without you.

Never-ending thanks,

Tom Horan, Artistic Director

P.S. We think you are awesome – bring this letter with you when you see *Fear of a Hood* and we'll reward you with a super-cool Sansculottes button! Come on, all the kids are wearing them!

Online Resources

The Donors Forum: **www.donorsforum.org**

The Executive Service Corps Affiliate Network: **www.escus.org**

The Free Management Library: **www.managementhelp.org**

www.Idealist.org

www.irs.gov

Minnesota Council of Nonprofits: **www.mncn.org** (your state may have its own such council)

NoLo: **www.nolo.com**

The *Nonprofit Good Practice Guide*: **www.npgoodpractice.org**

Print Resources

Michael Bassoff & Steve Chandler: *Relationshift: Revolutionary Fundraising.*

Jody Blazek: *Nonprofit Financial Planning Made Easy.*

Peter F. Drucker: *Managing the Nonprofit Organization: Principles and Practices.*

Jeffrey Gitomer: *The Sales Bible.*

Malcolm Gladwell: *The Tipping Point.*

Jay Conrad Levin: *Guerilla Marketing.*

Michael A. Sand: *How to Manage an Effective Nonprofit Organization.*

Michael Worth: *Nonprofit Management: Principles and Practice.*

The Complete Guide to Nonprofit Management. Smith, Buckin & Associates, Inc.

The Chronicle of Philanthropy

GLOSSARY

501(c)(3): Federal tax code governing nonprofit entities.

501(c)(4): Federal tax code governing certain kinds of nonprofit entities, such as civic leagues.

501(h): Federal tax code governing lobbying by nonprofit organizations.

Accessibility, Web: Design of a Web site to accommodate color blindness, blindness, and other disabilities.

Accounts payable: Amounts an organization must pay to others; amounts owed.

Accounts receivable: Amounts an organization expects to receive from grants, pledged gifts, membership fees, and other income.

Accrual: An accounting method that operates on the basis of expected assets, such as gifts that have been promised but not yet received, rather than actual assets.

Activism: Efforts to change legislation and public policy through actions, such as petitions, boycotts, marches, and letter-writing campaigns.

Ad hoc committee: A committee that meets only as needed, rather than regularly.

Advisory board: A board retained, often in addition to the board of directors, for professional consultation.

Advocacy: Efforts to change legislation or policy by raising awareness, conducting research, or providing community education.

Annual fund: The general budget into which gifts from annual donor appeals are directed.

Annual report: A mandatory yearly filing with your state regulatory agency that briefly describes your financial activities for the fiscal year and identifies the officers and board members.

Appeal letter: A written solicitation requesting a gift from a private donor.

Arm's length principle: The principle governing business relationships among people who have other personal ties, or among board members' companies and the nonprofit; designed to prevent conflicts of interest, it requires that both parties conduct these relations as if they were strangers.

Arm's length transaction: A transaction conducted according to the arm's length principle.

Articles of incorporation: The document creating a corporate entity.

Asset: A source of income or a material source of value to the organization.

Asset management: Stewardship of assets so as to preserve their value, but also as to generate additional income for the organization.

Banner ad: An advertisement that appears across the top of a Web site.

Blog: An informal Web page, frequently updated with brief, casual, personal articles or entries (posts) about a given topic.

Board (board of directors, board of trustees, governing board): The group of people who are legally responsible for the nonprofit organization.

Bookkeeping: The process of keeping financial records for an organization and ensuring that transactions are monitored for accuracy and compliance with policies.

Brand, branding: The set of impressions that a community has about an organization or product.

Brand equity: The worth of an organization's brand, particularly as it allows products or services to draw a higher price.

Brand identity: The graphics, media, and messages that an organization uses to create a brand.

Brand management: The stewardship of a brand to maintain its equity.

Brand manual, brand standards: A written guide to brand management.

Brand recognition: The ability of a community to recognize a brand.

Burnout: The feeling of exhaustion or low commitment that comes from overwork.

Business incubator: A program that helps new businesses or nonprofits get started, sometimes by offering seed money or covering certain startup costs.

Business plan: A detailed, written outline of a business venture, covering personnel, assets, liabilities, known risks, market research, marketing plans, and criteria for success or failure, as well as a short synopsis called an executive summary.

Bylaws: The document that governs the boards' actions.

Call to action: The portion of a marketing or PR message that prompts the recipient or audience to behave in a certain way.

Capital campaign: An intense, high-priority development effort soliciting donations for a particular cause, often urging donors to help the organization meet a certain budget threshold.

Captcha: A graphic on some automatic e-mail signups designed to prevent their being exploited by spambots.

Care, loyalty, and obedience: The legally recognized principles of sound board decisions.

Cash: An accounting system that considers only the actual monies on hand.

Cash flow: A detailed statement of different types of income and when they enter an organization's budget.

Cause-related marketing: A type of alliance between a nonprofit and a for-profit business, in which the for-profit business pledges to donate to the nonprofit in proportion to sales of a specific product or service.

Chair: The person in charge of a committee.

Charity: An organization that may receive charitable donations.

Charrette: An intensive, collaborative, deadline-driven working session that ends only when the set task is finished.

Charter: A founding document of an organization. Sometimes used interchangeably with **articles of incorporation.**

Chunks, chunking: Small sections of text, or the practice of breaking large amounts of text into these sections, designed for improved readability.

Click-through rate (CTR): A measure of the effectiveness of e-mail marketing.

Client: Any person who receives services from a nonprofit organization.

Color palette: The range of colors allowed in a graphic identity, with ranks assigned (primary, secondary, tertiary) based on how and when they are to be used.

Competitive bidding: A process designed to ensure fiscal responsibility in vendor selection; prospective vendors are invited to submit their cost estimates for a given project.

Community coalition: An alliance of nonprofits that unite to support a certain cause, frequently tied to effecting change in legislation or public policy.

Compassion fatigue: A situation in which a prospective donor feels too overwhelmed by the scope of a tragedy or by the number of requests for help to give.

Conflict of interest: An ethical problem in which an executive or board member's personal financial interest is at odds with the financial health of the nonprofit.

Consent form: A legal contract that obtains a person's consent for their image, name, or personal information to be used in some way that supports the purpose of an organization.

Contact page: A section of a Web site that tells visitors how to get in touch with the organization.

Content management: The continuous process of keeping a Web site up to date.

Contract employee: A short-term worker who is not a W-4 employee of the organization and whose pay is not subject to state or federal withholding tax or unemployment.

Copyright: The official, legally defensible right of ownership to written material; may be obtained from the U.S. Copyright Bureau. Differs from authorship in that, under work-for-hire arrangements and certain other contracts, copyright transfers from the creator of the content to the purchaser of the content.

Coupon: A slip of paper offering a discount as an incentive to prospective clients. Usually tagged with a promotional code.

CPM: Cost per thousand (viewers), a measure of the effectiveness of advertising initiatives.

Credit card: A card that allows an individual or organization to make a purchase by receiving an instant, unsecured loan, often at a relatively high rate of interest.

Crisis communications: PR and marketing messages that an organization sends in tough times.

Data integrity: The safety of the information an organization collects.

Debit card: A card that allows an individual or organization to make a purchase by instantly deducting the amount of the purchase from a checking account.

Debt: An amount owed.

Deficit: A budget situation in which expenses are greater than income.

Depreciation: The gradual loss of value of a material asset, calculated as an expense.

Development: The process of bringing income into a nonprofit organization by cultivating long-term relationships with private donors and funding bodies.

Direct lobbying: Lobbying that directly attempts to influence legislators' decisions.

Direct mail: A marketing method that relies on mass mailings to a specific mailing list to deliver its message and encourage recipients to take a desired action.

Dissolve: To officially end a nonprofit organization and dispose of its assets.

Diversity: As a personnel strategy, the inclusion of people regardless of their age, nationality, gender, religious preferences, sexuality, or ethnic background. As an investment or development strategy, the pursuit of income from a variety of sources not all tied to the same industries or donors.

Domain, Web: The registered, official name of a Web site.

Domain registry: A company that allows others to pay a fee and reserve a specific Web domain for a given period of time.

Donation, charitable donation: A private monetary gift to a nonprofit.

Donor: A private individual who makes a monetary gift to a nonprofit.

Due diligence: The process of conducting a thorough investigation into a planned business deal, whether the deal is an organizational partnership, the selection of a vendor, or a hiring decision. Failure to conduct due diligence may expose an organization to claims of negligence.

Early-retirement buyout: A cost-cutting measure, usually reserved for times when an organization faces a serious budget shortfall. Employees who are close to retirement age are given a financial incentive to retire early. The incentive is less than the projected cost of retaining and paying the employees until they reach standard retirement age.

Elected board: A board whose directors are elected by members of the organization. Compare **self-perpetuating board**.

Endowment: An investment fund designed to function as a self-perpetuating gift to a nonprofit organization.

Event: A planned one-time program, usually conducted with purposes of fundraising, developing, or recognizing contributions or achievements.

Executive director (ED): The chief executive officer of a nonprofit.

Exit interview: A conversation between a manager, usually an ED or HR manager, and a departing employee in which the manager solicits the employee's frank opinions about what works and does not work within the organization.

Ex officio: Applies to a board member whose board membership is tied to his or her occupying another office, such as a certain faculty chair.

Fees: Membership dues that some nonprofits collect annually from their members. Not every nonprofit has a membership or fee-based constituency.

Fiduciary: A person or organization that has legal financial responsibility for another organization.

Fiscal year: The 12-month period that is the basis for an organization's annual financial statements and reports.

Font: A complete set of characters; a typical consideration in branding and graphic identity. Often used interchangeably, though inaccurately, with **typeface.**

Forwarding address (in e-mail): An address not connected to its own e-mail account, established to direct messages into another e-mail account.

Founder's syndrome: A collection of problems that result when an organization relies too heavily on a single, usually founding, leader and therefore fails to develop long-range plans or true organizational strength.

Freelance, freelancer: A common synonym for contract employment; usually describes a worker who is committed to being self-employed and has not joined an organization as an employee.

Fulfillment service: A company that prints, assembles, and mails mass mailings, such as direct-mail marketing and appeal letters.

Full-time: An employment arrangement in which an employee works roughly 40 hours a week for an organization and is entitled to whatever benefits the organization offers.

Fundraising: Efforts to bring cash into the organization. **Development** is now preferred, both as a term and as a strategy. Fundraising is more accurately applied to short-term efforts, such as bake sales, that do not attempt to cultivate longer donor relationships.

Gift: A donation.

Give-or-get policy: A policy that requires board members to be responsible for bringing a certain amount of donation income into the organization in a given year. The amount that a board member cannot solicit from donors must be made up out of his or her own pocket.

Giving board: A board whose main function is to provide or solicit financial support for the organization.

Grant: Money given from an organization (a granting or funding body, a foundation, or a corporation's philanthropic arm) to a nonprofit organization. A grant tends to be earmarked for a specific initiative and awarded in response to a request from the nonprofit.

Graphic identity: The images, typeface, colors, and overall feeling of an organization's visual communication, particularly when these elements are carefully chosen to communicate a nonverbal message.

Grassroots lobbying, grassroots efforts: An initiative that involves the community in efforts to change legislation. Rather than addressing lobby legislators directly, an organization incites the community to, for example, circulate petitions, call legislators' offices, or stage protests.

Guerilla marketing: Nimble, low-budget, situation-specific efforts to raise awareness and connect with a target audience or community. Often a response to low marketing funds; an attempt to out-think rather than out-spend the competition.

Home page: The central page of a Web site, typically the first one a visitor sees upon typing the domain name into a browser.

Host, Web: A company that provides server space and bandwidth to other companies, which pay an annual or monthly fee to store the data required for their Web sites with the host.

Human resources (HR): The corporate function responsible for employee policy, pay and benefits, hiring and firing, and resolution of grievances and conflicts within the organization. Also sometimes used (along with **human capital**) to refer to the actual people and abilities within an organization, although many employees find the term impersonal or demeaning.

Hybrid board: A board that combines the often separate qualities of a giving board and a working board.

Incentive: A motivation for a given behavior. Incentives may be active (deliberate, the result of planned strategy) or passive (unintentional).

Incorporate: To create a formal business entity recognized as separate from the individuals who create it.

Information architecture: The arrangement of information within a Web site, usually with an eye to helping readers easily find what they are looking for.

Intellectual property: Any idea, invention, writing, or other creative output to which an individual or organization claims the right of ownership.

Interest: Income earned on certain savings vehicles.

Intermediate sanctions: A federal penalty against people who abuse their relationship with the nonprofit for personal gain.

Intuitiveness: A quality of Web design that refers to design elements that behave as expected, links and menus that are clearly labeled, and information that readers can easily find.

ISP: An Internet service provider; a utility, much like a telephone company.

Layoff: A mass termination of employees in response to a major predicted or actual budget shortfall.

Layoff survivor's sickness: A typical pattern of behavior, including low engagement, withdrawal, and defensiveness, common to the employees who remain with an organization after a layoff.

Liability: A source of expenses.

Licensing: An arrangement between a nonprofit and a for-profit entity in which the for-profit uses the nonprofit's name and graphic identity to generate profits, some of which are paid to the nonprofit as royalties.

Line of credit: A borrowing arrangement, usually unsecured, in which a bank makes a certain amount of credit available to an organization and does not charge interest on the unused amount.

Link exchange: A reciprocal online marketing agreement among businesses in which they promote each other on their Web sites.

Liquid: Monetary, as opposed to material. **Liquidity** is one measure of financial health.

List churn: Turnover of names on a mailing list, especially an e-mail list; important for

marketing and development efforts. People who receive an organization's mass messages for more than two years are far more likely to give to the organization.

Loan: An amount of money borrowed from a bank, to be repaid with interest. A **secured loan** is one backed by collateral — the borrower's demonstration of ability to repay, usually in the form of a material asset that can be sold to generate funds if necessary. An **unsecured loan**, one not backed by collateral, is a greater risk for the bank and usually therefore carries higher interest penalties for the borrower.

Lobbying: Organizational efforts to influence legislation.

Logo: A graphic symbol of an organization.

Marketing: The business process of evaluating a given community (a **market**) to discover its needs and preferences, creating a product or service to meet those needs, and communicating with the market to raise awareness of the offering. Often used interchangeably, though inaccurately, with **advertising.**

Matching contribution: A way to encourage contributions to a fund by promising to donate the same amount. Some major donors offer matching contributions to encourage donations from smaller donors; some employers offer matching contributions to encourage employees to save for retirement. Either way, the thinking is the same.

Membership: In some nonprofit organizations, a fee-based method of supporting the organization and its mission. Membership sometimes, but not always, confers rights and powers, such as the right to participate in board elections, on members.

Net assets: The difference between assets and liabilities.

Nonprofit, nonprofit organization: A corporation that exists for the sake of effecting social change rather than creating wealth; the term tends to apply only to organizations that have federal 501(c)(3) or 501(c)(4) tax-exempt status, but it is sometimes used to describe organizations that have not yet applied for such status but are operating on a nonprofit business model. Many nonprofits operate much like for-profit businesses in that they are corporations with many of the same needs as for-profit businesses, such as administration, marketing, and technology,. However, they are forbidden from generating wealth for stockholders or owners.

Not-for-profit organization: Used interchangeably with **nonprofit organization.** Some people, notably fundraisers, believe **not-for-profit** is a better description because it highlights the charitable nature of the organization. Others use **not-for-profit** to characterize the activities of a **nonprofit** organization.

Open rate: A measure of marketing effectiveness: the number of recipients who open a mass e-mail message.

Operational relationship: An arrangement between a non-profit and a for-profit business in which the for-profit business relies on labor or goods from the nonprofit to offer its product, and the provision of labor or goods allows the nonprofit to fulfill its mission.

Operational revenue: Income from sources other than gifts and fees.

Operating reserve: An organization's savings fund; may function as a safety net.

Opt-in mailing list: A kind of e-mail list whose structure is designed to prevent spam. To ensure that all recipients have actually chosen to receive the messages, rather than having been signed up without their consent by a spambot or an unscrupulous marketer, the list structure requires new recipients to indicate their wish to join the list, such as by clicking on a link in an e-mail before they can actually receive messages.

Organizational culture: The emotional and intellectual climate — comprising work ethic, interpersonal relations, dedication to the mission, and other expected standards of behavior — within a business.

Outreach: Efforts to expand an organization's scope or message by expanding the number of people or communities it serves or involves.

Overhead: The costs of administration and fundraising.

Overtime: Mandatory pay to employees (usually hourly, not salaried) who work more than their allotted hours in a given week. Overtime rates may be higher than normal hourly rates. State law varies regarding mandatory overtime rates.

Part-time: Describes an employment relationship in which an employee regularly works less than 40 hours per week and may not be eligible for certain benefits. Often also refers to an employee who works for hourly wages rather than an annualized salary.

Permalance: Describes a long-term employment relationship in which a worker has most of the responsibilities and expectations of a W-2 employee, but remains a 1099 independent contractor.

Portability: In HR, the ability of a departing employee to continue receiving a benefit after termination, often as a result of converting it to an individual plan.

PR: Public relations; specifically, an organization's strategic interaction with the public.

Premium: In insurance, the amount the insured pays to the insurance plan for the privilege of being insured. In marketing, a free giveaway that accompanies a message and draws attention to it.

Press page: A section of an organization's Web site devoted to providing information, press releases, and downloadable photos to members of the press who might want to write a story about the organization.

Press release: A mass mailing to newspapers, radio and TV stations, and other press outlets about an event or program for which an organization is trying to gain media attention.

Privacy: In business, refers to the security of employees' and clients' personal data; a privacy pledge means an organization must take reasonable steps to prevent identity theft and other abuses of personal information. In the case of employer-sponsored health insurance, privacy is strictly regulated by the federal law HIPAA.

Pro bono: Describes professional services that are donated to a nonprofit.

Promotional code: A small code on a coupon that allows an organization to track which clients are receiving and heeding its messages, as measured by the number of clients who redeem the coupon.

Purchase order: A document authorizing a purchase; one way for an organization to prevent indiscriminate employee use of organizational funds is to require a purchase order for every purchase.

Readability: The ease with which a piece of text may be read and comprehended; an issue in marketing materials (where the focus is often on the interaction of layout, format, and message) as well as in educational materials (where the focus is on vocabulary and complexity of syntax).

Release agreement: A contract that permits an organization to use an individual's name and likeness, usually for promotional purposes.

Restricted fund: Income that comes to a nonprofit, often from an endowment or major donor, that carries the condition that it only be spent for certain purposes.

Retention, retention rate: The number of employees, board members, or donors who remain with an organization. Compare to **turnover.**

Retention bonus: Money paid to an employee who stays with an organization past a certain minimum amount of time.

Seed money: Money donated to a new nonprofit to help it cover the early expenses of incorporating, recruiting, and other costs. May or may not be a tax-deductible gift, depending on whether the organization is tax-exempt yet.

Self-perpetuating board: Also called permanent board. A board of directors whose officers are nominated and elected by the board itself, not by organizational membership.

SEO: Search Engine Optimization. Efforts to word and structure a Web site in such a way that it will be among the top sites returned when someone Googles certain keywords.

Signage: An organization's outdoor signs, banners, and

posters, taken as a collective and often discussed in terms of visibility or effectiveness.

Site map: A page-by-page diagram of the arrangement of information within a Web site.

Social media, social networking site: A usually free online service that allows for social interaction and the construction of extensive online networks of friends, associates, acquaintances, and colleagues.

Social organization: A nonprofit devoted to the social interaction of its members.

Solicitation permit: A state or municipal document allowing a nonprofit to ask for donations in certain areas, using certain methods.

Spam: Unwanted, unsolicited mass e-mail.

Spider, crawler, spambot: Programs designed to harvest e-mail addresses from the Web for the benefit of spammers.

Sponsored link: A paid ad that appears above relevant search results on a search engine such as Google.

Sponsorship: An arrangement between a nonprofit and a for-profit business in which the for-profit business provides cash or other resources for the nonprofit's programming in return for promotional consideration, such as prominent logo placement.

Startup cost: An early cost of creating a nonprofit organization; tends to refer to overhead rather than programming expenses.

Succession, succession planning: The strategy of choosing a successor for someone departing from an organization; also, attempts to make the transition between the departing person and his or her successor smooth and productive.

Surplus: A budget situation in which income is greater than expenses.

Swag, tchotchkes: Branded items — such as T-shirts, mouse pads, mugs, hats, tote bags, buttons, magnets, desk toys — that an organization gives away in order to reinforce its marketing message.

Take-one: A postcard, flier, brochure, or other promotional piece displayed in such a way as to encourage potential clients to take a copy for themselves.

Tax-deductible: Not subject to income tax; applies to certain expenditures, such as private contributions to nonprofits.

Tax-exempt: Not subject to income tax; applies to 501(c) nonprofit organizations and their income.

Telemarketing: Mass telephone calls, often through a phone bank or automatic dialer, in support of a marketing or development cause.

Term limit: A restriction on how long a board member may serve an organization.

Trustee: A person or organization that holds property on behalf of someone else. An endowment has trustees who are charged with managing the investment responsibly.

Turnover: Loss of employees, donors, or clients; sometimes with the attendant concept of their being replaced by new people.

Unrestricted funds: Income from gifts, grants, or endowments that comes to a nonprofit without stipulations as to how it is used.

Usability, Web: Consideration of Web design involving a site's ease of navigation, download time, predictability, and functionality.

Vendor: A person or organization who sells a good or service to a nonprofit.

Vesting: A retention incentive that places restrictions based on organizational tenure on an employee's right to a benefit.

Virtual office: A way of using the Web and employees' home computers to set up an office without renting a physical office space. A virtual office may rent server space for data storage and file sharing.

Volunteer: Someone who works without pay to help a nonprofit carry out its mission. Volunteer labor is distinct from pro bono labor in that *pro bono* applies to professionals who donate their professional skills in service of the organization. Volunteer labor may not be included on a federal Form 990, but pro bono service must be listed.

Voucher: An amount of money provided to someone for a specific purpose.

Web 2.0: A format of Web site that uses a blogging interface for content management, often allowing for multiple contributors rather than a single Webmaster.

Webmaster: The person responsible for Web site upkeep, content management, and, in some cases, design and programming.

Web presence: How an organization is represented on the Web.

Wiki: A Web site whose content management is the collective responsibility of its audience.

Work for hire, work done for hire: An arrangement in which the work product of a contractor or employee becomes the property of the organization that purchases it; applies particularly to creative services, such as graphic design or marketing writing, but also sometimes to scientific research or inquiry and technological inventions, such as software development.

BIBLIOGRAPHY

"Advocacy Tactics." Center for Lobbying in the Public Interest. Accessed Feb. 14, 2009. **www.clpi.org/nuts-a-bolts/advocacy-tactics**

"The CAN-SPAM Act: Requirements for Commercial E-mailers." Federal Trade Commission. Accessed Feb. 15, 2009. **www.ftc.gov/bcp/edu/pubs/business/ecommerce/bus61.shtm**

Jody Blazek: *Nonprofit Financial Planning Made Easy*. Wiley. 2008.

The Complete Guide to Nonprofit Management. Smith, Bucklin & Associates Inc. 2000.

Drucker, Peter F. *Managing the Nonprofit Organization: Principles and Practices*. Collins Business. 1990.

"Financial Statement Template." The Rasmuson Foundation. Accessed March 8, 2009. **www.rasmuson.org/index.php?switch=viewpage&pageid=192**

Kawamoto, Dawn. "ComScore posts: Google posts strong paid click rate for month of April." Accessed Feb. 15, 2009. **http://news.cnet.com/newsblog/?keyword=ComScore**

Kilian, Crawford. *Writing for the Web*. Self-Counsel Writing Series, Self-Counsel Press. 2000.

Lee, Ed. "Effectiveness of Email and Direct-Mail Marketing: The Importance of Integrated Marketing Campaigns." Accessed Feb. 15, 2009. **http://bloggingmebloggingyou.wordpress. com/2008/05/07/effectiveness-of-email-and-direct-marketing-the-importance-of-integrated-marketing-campaigns/**

McNamara, Carter. "Founder's Syndrome: How Corporations Suffer — and Can Recover." The Free Management Library. Copyright 1997-2008. **http://managementhelp.org/misc/founders.htm**

McNamara, Carter. "Starting a Nonprofit Organization." The Free Management Library. Copyright 1997-2008. Accessed Jan. 25, 2009. **www.managementhelp.org/strt_org/strt_np/strt_np.htm**

Miller, Steven. Remarks on Nonprofit Good Governance. November 2008. Accessed Jan. 22, 2009. **www.irs.gov/pub/irs-tege/stm_loyolagovernance_112008.pdf**

"The Nonprofit FAQ." Idealist.org. Accessed Jan. 25, 2009. **www.idealist.org/en/faqcat/5-5**

"Public Policy Planning Checklist." Center for Lobbying in the Public Interest. Accessed Feb. 14, 2009. **www.clpi.org/images/pdf/Public%20Policy%20Planning%20Checklist.pdf**

"Research: Value of Volunteer Time." Independent Sector. 2009. Accessed March 7, 2009, through About.com. **http://nonprofit. about.com/gi/dynamic/offsite.htm?zi=1/XJ&sdn=nonprofit&cdn =money&tm=53&gps=136_906_1276_577&f=10&tt=12&bt=0&bts =0&zu=http%3A//www.independentsector.org/**

Richardson, Tim. "Measuring Online Advertising Effectiveness: Banner Ads." Witiger. Accessed Feb. 15, 2009. **www.witiger.com/ ecommerce/banneradsMeasuringEffectiveness.htm**

Sand, Michael. *How to Manage an Effective Nonprofit Organization.* Career Press. 2005.

Wells, Susan J. "Layoff Aftermath." *HRMagazine.* Dec. 22, 2008. Accessed March 7, 2009. **www.dop.wa.gov/NR/rdonlyres/ A47F1788-A45B-48F7-8C87-C10454F215FF/0/LayoffAftermath. pdf**

Wing, Kennard; Gordon, Teresa; Hager, Mark; Pollak, Tom; Rooney, Patrick. "Help Your Nonprofit Clients Improve Their Accounting for Capital and In-Kind Donations." Indiana University at Purdue. **www.philanthropy.iupui.edu/Research/ WorkingPapers/JofA%20Accounting%20v2.pdf**

"Working in Coalitions." Center for Lobbying in the Public Interest. Accessed February 14, 2009. **www.clpi.org/images/ pdf/07_coalitions.pdf**

Worth, Michael J. *Nonprofit Management: Principles and Practice.* Sage. 2009.

INDEX